BlackBerry Town

How high tech success has played out for Canada's Kitchener-Waterloo

CHUCK HOWITT

James Lorimer & Company Ltd., Publishers
Toronto

James Lorimer & Company Ltd., Publishers acknowledges funding support from the Ontario Arts Council (OAC), an agency of the Government of Ontario. We acknowledge the support of the Canada Council for the Arts, which last year invested $153 million to bring the arts to Canadians throughout the country. This project has been made possible in part by the Government of Canada and with the support of Ontario Creates.

Cover design: Tyler Cleroux
Cover image: Erb Street West in uptown Waterloo with the Centre for International Governance Innovation on the right. Photo by Andre Renard on Flickr
Back cover images: *Waterloo Region Record*

Library and Archives Canada Cataloguing in Publication

Title: BlackBerry town : how high tech success has played out for Canada's
    Kitchener-Waterloo / Chuck Howitt.
Names: Howitt, Chuck, author.
Description: Includes bibliographical references and index.
Identifiers: Canadiana (print) 20190156929 | Canadiana (ebook) 20190156945 |
    ISBN 9781459414389 (softcover) | ISBN 9781459414396 (epub)
Subjects: LCSH: BlackBerry Limited—History. | LCSH: High technology
    industries—Ontario—Kitchener—History. | LCSH: High technology
    industries—Ontario—Waterloo—History. | LCSH: Kitchener (Ont.)—
    Economic conditions. | LCSH: Waterloo (Ont.)—Economic conditions.
Classification: LCC HD9696.2.C34 B53 2019 | DDC 338.7/6100416750971—dc23

James Lorimer & Company Ltd., Publishers
117 Peter Street, Suite 304
Toronto, ON, Canada
M5V 0M3
www.lorimer.ca

Printed and bound in Canada.

To Matt Walcoff, whose memory kept this project alive.

CONTENTS

Chapter 1

WHO WANTS TO BE CONNECTED ALL THE TIME?

Professor Mohamed Elmasry was puzzled by the quiet, serious-looking student who approached him after microelectronics class one day. Normally, students seeking one-on-one chats after his classes at the University of Waterloo (UW) wanted to talk about the lecture he had just finished or an upcoming assignment. But not this undergrad. He began peppering Elmasry with questions about wireless communications. The topic was not part of the course curriculum, which covered such wired hardware as transistors, capacitors, resistors and diodes. Nonetheless, the student's passion intrigued the professor, so he answered the questions as best he could.

The student, an earnest-looking chap named Mike Lazaridis, could not help himself. He was bursting with desire to learn more about the possibilities of mobile communications.

Lazaridis was something of a child prodigy. His parents had emigrated from Turkey and settled in Windsor, Ontario, where his father found work in a Chrysler auto assembly plant and his mother worked as part-time waitress and seamstress. At the age of four, Lazaridis made a toy record player out of Lego pieces and other spare parts lying about the house. At age twelve, with neighbourhood pal Doug Fregin, he built a solar panel out of wood, tinfoil and a small motor and entered it in the school science fair. When an electrical fire destroyed the main power source in his high school shop class, Lazaridis fixed the machine. He joined the school team preparing to compete in a provincial academic quiz show and discovered the practice buzzer didn't work. So he built a better one and sold it to other schools, earning enough to pay for his first year of university tuition.

But the lesson that really hit home, that would stay with him for years to come, came from high school shop teacher John Micsinszki, president of the local ham radio club that Lazaridis and Fregin had joined. Don't get too caught up with the computers and other electrical gadgets you enjoy tinkering with in your basement, he warned. Someday, someone is going to put wireless devices and computers together and that's really going to set the world on fire, the teacher told the wide-eyed students.[1]

In fall 1979, Lazaridis enrolled in Waterloo's five-year electrical engineering program, with an option in computer science. At the time, there were no specific courses on wireless communications.[2] He figured Elmasry, a world-renowned expert on integrated circuits, a key component of computer hardware, would be the next best thing. Will this work? What do you think of that? Where can I get more information on this? The curious student, eager to know more about the world of radio waves and electromagnetism, interrogated the professor. Elmasry was amused by Lazaridis and couldn't help but tease him a bit: "I told him, Mike, you should pay more attention to the topic of the lecture. If you don't listen to my advice, you will fail."

The visits continued all term, and Elmasry was so impressed by his protégé that, when the course was completed, he hired Lazaridis as his paid research assistant for one term. UW had implemented a trailblazing co-operative education program when it opened in the late 1950s. Students alternated study terms of three months with work terms of the same duration, and Elmasry's offer fulfilled the requirement for one of Lazaridis's co-op terms. The pair had even more time to talk about mobile communications.

They formed a close bond, and when Lazaridis left UW in the spring of 1984, they met occasionally for lunch at an Egyptian restaurant near the campus. Over shawarma, hummus, tabbouleh salad and the like, they would discuss Lazaridis's new company, Research In Motion. Elmasry soon joined the firm as a part-time consultant. Over the years, the lunches would become less frequent as Lazaridis poured more energy into his new enterprise. But once in a while, they would get together, particularly when Lazaridis was eager to celebrate a milestone or show off a breakthrough in his company's product line. He would bring along prototypes of RIM's new wireless gadgets and get Elmasry to try them out.

"No one is going to buy these devices," the professor told him, laughing about it now. "Who wants to be connected all the time?"[3]

* * *

Lazaridis soaked up much of the rich technological atmosphere he encountered at UW. He was clearly in his element. Friend and classmate Savio Wong remembers one of the professors scheduling an optional lecture one evening on the mathematics behind Einstein's theory of relativity. Wong was tired after a long day of classes, but dragged himself to the lecture anyway. He arrived to find Lazaridis sitting in the front row, looking as if he was about to enjoy a Beatles reunion concert. Afterwards, students were invited by the professor to the faculty club for more discussion. Lazaridis went eagerly and dived into the conversation. "He was so excited, he was almost giddy," said Wong.

The Einstein lecture was not a one-time event in the electrical engineering program at UW. Some professors in the faculty, especially Lynn Watt, made a habit of scheduling evening lectures on cutting-edge theory for the keenest students. Lazaridis was particularly drawn to Watt, a Winnipeg native who had joined the UW faculty in 1966 after earning his PhD at the University of Minnesota and teaching for seven years at the University of Washington in Seattle. While working toward his master's of science at the University of Chicago in the early 1950s,

Watt had studied under the legendary Italian physicist Enrico Fermi, creator of the world's first nuclear reactor and known as the architect of the nuclear bomb. In Lazaridis's second year, Watt taught a course on relativity and quantum mechanics. In the course, the students learned about the research of theoretical physicists such as Alain Aspect of France and Richard Feynman of the US and their groundbreaking work on energy at the tiniest level, the atomic realm, in a field known as quantum mechanics. A new dream began to take hold in Lazaridis's mind, one that would rival his obsession with wireless communications. "That was the beginning of my own deep fascination with physics and quantum physics," he would say later.[4]

In the second year, Wong and Lazaridis worked together on a final project for one of their courses. Wong thought they would be designing a simple program to illustrate how a seven-segment display worked. Instead, Lazaridis came up with a program that performed hexadecimal addition, a procedure used by computer system designers and programmers. Wong was amazed. It was far beyond anything he could dream of. Lazaridis was in another league but was happy to share his knowledge with a friend in need. In a later course on electronics, Wong was struggling to keep up. The final exam loomed, worth 100 per cent of his mark. Before the exam, Lazaridis came over and taught the essential components of the course late into the night. "Until this day, I am convinced that without Mike's tutoring, I could not have passed the course," said Wong, who went on to a career as a high school librarian.

Lazaridis always sat near the front during lectures. He was "very energetic and passionate" about his school work, said Wong. He was also not afraid to speak up if he thought the professor was wrong. Wong recalls a time when his friend got into an animated discussion with a professor because he was teaching a physics theory that had been refuted by new research. "Mike, we haven't come to that part of the course yet," the professor replied.

There were a number of bright students in their classes. Some had big egos and could get obnoxious, but not Lazaridis. "He would never put people down," said Wong.

They studied hard. They had no choice; electrical engineering was a tough program, Wong said. Even so, they still had time for a little fun. They weren't partiers or jocks. In their spare time, they played video games, went to the occasional movie or went out for meals. "We liked to eat," Wong said with a laugh. And "we weren't discriminatory." Their avoidance of the mainstream social scene in engineering is apparent in the 1984 UW Engineering Yearbook. There isn't much evidence of them in any of the pictures, apart from the graduate mug shots. The caption beside Lazaridis's picture says, "'Lizards' likes to tell the profs how to teach. His degree of keenness is 10, though he's often heard to say 'I'm gonna fail, I'm gonna fail!' Mike's life ambition is to build a time machine, probably so he can repeat his engineering degree."

In their fourth year, Wong remembers sharing a meal with Lazaridis at Fastbreaks restaurant near campus. Lazaridis was eager to share information about a company he had just started that was going to transform telecommunications. "When Mike talked, he would go at such a pace and in such depth that I would be playing mental gymnastics just to keep up."[5]

The University of Waterloo had another asset besides academics that Lazaridis came to appreciate after he started attending classes: It was not a jock school. While the men's basketball team won a national title in the 1970s, football was usually the barometer of a campus's interest in athletics. Football drew the largest crowds and attracted the biggest headlines in the local media. And for years, UW fielded one of the worst football teams in Canada. At W.F. Herman Secondary School in Windsor, Lazaridis had no interest in sports. Hunkered down in the school's shops lab, he couldn't help but hear the cheers for the more popular football and basketball heroes and the girls they usually attracted. It stung for the young electronics aficionado.

"In high school, it's all about football, track and field and social events, so I was kind of cloistered in the shops program. I had a few really good friends and we pretty well stuck to ourselves. All the popular people lived on a different stratum," he said.

At UW, much to his surprise, engineering, math and computer science students were held in high esteem. They were the big stars on campus.

"Everybody was like those people that I spent time with in high school."[6]

In addition to spending a co-op term with Professor Elmasry, Lazaridis spent several eye-opening work terms at Control Data Corp. in Mississauga, Ontario, a suburb just west of Toronto. Going to Control Data was what it would have been like for a co-op student to work at RIM in the 2000s. The Minneapolis-based company had achieved great heights and was one of nine supercomputer manufacturers of the 1960s and '70s. Even so, the glory days were starting to fade when Lazaridis arrived at its Mississauga research and manufacturing office in the early 1980s. And he was to get a taste of what was going wrong while there.

Early on, he wrote a diagnostic computer code that combed through circuit boards to identify any failures while office workers were at home in the evening. Previously, if one malfunctioned, a technician would have to laboriously check all the boards to pinpoint the problem area. The time-saving process earned the talented co-op student a desk beside the office's chief software architect.[7]

During another work term, he was assigned to an innovative team that was able to build a faster and cheaper computer than one of Control Data's flagship models, the Cyber 205. It was a once-in-a-lifetime experience for Lazaridis, who was working with some of the brightest minds in the computer business.

"The stuff that was happening at Control Data, that was a singular experience," he recalled. "What we were working on was brand-new integrated technology, new packaging, a new physics."

But the breakthrough discovery was not to be. Senior executives at head office worried that profit margins were too narrow. They ordered modifications to the new machine to cut costs. Angered by their interference, technicians who had worked sixteen- and seventeen-hour days to make it happen resigned en mass and relocated to Silicon Valley.

The debacle was a valuable learning experience for Lazaridis. He resolved to start his own business and to champion visionaries and groundbreakers rather than drag them down.

What happened at Control Data in Mississauga was "the kind of thing you see in a bad movie," he said. [8]

Despite his reluctance to be at the centre of the social scene at UW, Lazaridis was already demonstrating leadership qualities and a charisma that drew other students to him. How else to explain his persuading nine other students to pile into a van and drive all the way to Ottawa one weekend to attend not a rock concert or a football game, as most students would do, but a conference on physics. The keynote speaker was David Bohm, a legend among physicists, who had worked with Albert Einstein at Princeton University and was considered one of the most significant theorists in the field during the twentieth century. Here was Lazaridis's Jimi Hendrix or Keith Richards, a grey-haired sexagenarian who wielded a pencil and paper rather than guitar and amplifier.

Lazaridis was blown away by Bohm's address and the New Age vibe of the conference. "We came back and talked about this stuff a lot, what was happening in physics and how these problems had not been solved," he said. For him, the unanswered questions of matter and energy were like a drug. He would stay up all night thinking about them.

"You didn't need alcohol, you didn't need anything, you could get high on just these ideas, what they meant and what the implications were, where things were going and then start to apply them."[9]

While he did well enough in school, his mind was often on other things. Epiphanies about new inventions consumed much of his thinking.

"He was always coming up with neat little ideas on the back of an envelope, little things that might make some money," said Greg Anglin, a math student from Alberta who lived in the same pod and accompanied Lazaridis to the physics conference in Ottawa.[10]

Chapter 2
LICENCE TO BE RADICAL

Mike Lazaridis could have gone to almost any university in Canada. His marks were good enough to open virtually any academic door. And he did his due diligence, touring university campuses across Ontario as high school graduation neared in the spring of 1979. In the end, he chose a university that had been nothing more than a farmer's field two decades earlier. In the pantheon of Ontario universities, Waterloo was a raw teenager compared to the more seasoned and experienced adults that dominated the post-secondary realm in eastern Canada at the time, century-old and ivy-clad institutions with storied names such as Toronto, Queen's and Western.

But the old guard was starting to feel some pressure. Post-secondary education after the Second World War was a world in transition. Fuelled by the post-war baby boom and the gradual realization among high school grads of the 1950s and '60s that career success was more assured with a college degree, Ontario's cohort of universities would more than double as new campuses started popping up across the province in Windsor, Waterloo, Guelph, St. Catharines, Ottawa, Sudbury, Thunder Bay and in the north of Toronto. It became known as the era of the "instant university." While experience, tradition and history should have dictated continued dominance by the older institutions, longevity can sometimes prove to be a disadvantage. Older schools become conservative and set in their ways. Occasionally, it's better to work with a clean slate. Some of the rookie universities took advantage of this situation, none more so than the University of Waterloo and its founding president Gerald Hagey.

Inside the brown-brick building that bears Hagey's name hangs a painting of a serious, stoic-looking man with receding grey hair and black-rimmed glasses. Beside it is an inscription, written in 1975, six years after he retired as the university's founding president. It reads, in part, "to look at President Emeritus Hagey you would never guess that beneath that formal attire there beats the heart of a rebel." A more apt metaphor would be hard to find. In the early years of his presidency and the years leading up to it, few people did more to blow the university system wide open than Joseph Gerald Hagey. To borrow an expression from the high-tech world, Hagey was a disrupter *par excellence*, someone who hacked the post-secondary model. Kitchener-Waterloo is often referred to as the Twin Cities. How ironic that the metropolis should also have twin universities, and probably no one is more responsible for this reality than Hagey.

In the beginning, two universities were never his intention. Born in 1904 and raised in Hamilton, Hagey came to Waterloo in the mid-1920s to attend Waterloo College, an institution launched by the Evangelical Lutheran Church in Canada to complement the seminary it had opened on the same site in 1911. Hagey was eager to earn a degree at the college run by the church he had grown up attending. Paving the way were the arts degrees that it had recently started handing out through an affiliation with the University of Western Ontario in nearby London, a partnership made necessary because degrees in the humanities could not be awarded by a religious-based college. After graduation in 1928, he accepted a sales job at the B.F. Goodrich tire company, which had purchased a large rubber plant near downtown Kitchener several years earlier. Not for nothing was Kitchener known as the "Akron of Canada," after the US tire capital in Ohio.

A large influx of German-born immigrants to Waterloo County in the early nineteenth century had launched leather and tanning industries for shoes and saddles, and tires were a natural offshoot as automobiles took off in the early twentieth century. Hagey rose through the ranks at B.F. Goodrich to become advertising and public relations manager, but, according to Ken McLaughlin's 1997 book on the history of the University of Waterloo, Hagey's Lutheran roots and the college he attended were never far from his thoughts. Appointed to the Waterloo College board in the late 1940s, he led a movement to keep the college in Waterloo when local industrialist C.N. Weber tried to move it to Kitchener.[1] Board members took notice of the charismatic tire salesman. In a scene straight out of a Frank Capra movie, they urged their new hero to become college president in 1953. Despite fears of leaving a secure job to lead a small institution starved for funds, Hagey accepted the job. The appointment was unusual in another respect. He came from an industrial rather than an academic background, but that would later prove to be an asset.

In the early years of his presidency, Hagey took steps to boost enrolment and raise the profile of Waterloo College. But change was in the wind. A booming post-war economy stoked demand across the country for a new crop of engineers, scientists and technologists. A Kitchener-Waterloo economy built on tires, footwear, sausages and whiskey would need to raise its game. To Hagey, it was becoming obvious that Waterloo College needed to offer more than just arts degrees. Other colleges were moving in this direction. In his native Hamilton, McMaster University emerged from plans by a Baptist college to add a non-denominational science program to qualify for provincial funding. The same scenario played out in Windsor, where the Roman Catholic Assumption College morphed into Windsor University.[2] There was even competition locally. St. Jerome's College, a Roman Catholic institution affiliated with the University of Ottawa, had opened a new campus in Kitchener a few years earlier, and some thought it was just a matter of time before it created a secular science faculty. Knowing he had to act soon, Hagey began lobbying the Waterloo College board of governors and the Lutheran Synod. His aim was to create a separate, non-denominational college, still affiliated with Waterloo College and the University of Western Ontario, to offer science and engineering programs. It didn't take long for the synod and the Waterloo board to agree. The first step was to create a board of governors for the Associate Faculties, as the new college was to be called. Enlisting the help of B.F. Goodrich Canada president Ira Needles, Hagey stocked the board with a cross-section of local industry captains including Carl Pollock, president of Electrohome Industries, makers of TVs, radios, furniture and appliances; Carl Dare, president of Dare Biscuits; A.R. Kaufman, head of the Kaufman rubber and foot-wear empire; and Henry Krug, owner of Krug Furniture.

But Hagey had something far more radical in mind than just science and engineering. Around this time, he met Les Emery, head of the Provincial Institute of Trades[3] in Toronto, a school created by the province to provide academic training to apprentices in various trades. The Institute was experimenting with a program alternating semesters of study with work terms in industry known as co-operative education. To Emery, it was more than an experiment. He had seen the future, and it was co-op education. A visionary engineer and architect named Herman Schneider had started co-op education at the University of Cincinnati in 1906, and by the 1950s, it had spread to forty-two other universities across the US, including such prestigious schools as the Massachusetts Institute of Technology, Michigan, Cornell and Northeastern.[4] But Canada was still virgin territory and Emery aimed to change that.

Hagey invited Emery to speak to the Associate Faculties in 1956. It didn't take much to convince a body stacked with industry leaders that co-op could be a game-changer. Co-op students could earn money and gain practical experience while attending school, and better yet, Waterloo could enrol twice as many students. The Associate Faculties board liked the "sandwich model" of education, as co-op was informally known. So eager were they to dine on this scholastic lunch that they offered Emery a job to run the program. Seeing an opportunity to expand his co-op dream, he accepted.[5] Plans for a tour of American co-op schools and the recruitment of faculty began to take shape under his leadership. Among his first recruits was a young engineering professor from Queen's University named Doug Wright. At thirty-two, Wright would be the youngest dean of engineering in Ontario. Under his leadership, Waterloo would soon go on to attract the largest engineering enrolment in Ontario, propelling Wright into the UW president's chair for a twelve-year stint starting in 1981.

A hundred kilometres to the west in London, Edward Hall, president of the University of Western Ontario, viewed what was going on in Waterloo with growing alarm.[6] The idea of Waterloo College creating an Associate Faculties didn't thrill him. Nor did he like co-op education. To him, it was bad on all sides: Educational standards would be undermined, the work experience truncated, students might not want to return to the classroom and finding qualified teaching staff would be difficult. Making matters worse, Waterloo planned an enrolment of 700 engineering students by 1959, much higher than Western's total of just over 100. In Hall's view, the lead in such endeavours should be taken by established schools like Western, not this upstart from Waterloo. Western had spent two years studying the launch of an engineering program before deciding to proceed. Now Waterloo was going to upstage it. Hagey's roots in the industrial field, rather than academia, also rankled him. And Hall was prepared to play hardball to back his concerns. He began lobbying the province to oppose Waterloo's plan and went so far as to urge the Waterloo College board to remove Hagey from office.[7]

Rumblings of discontent were also surfacing from other universities across the province. At Queen's Park, politicians and bureaucrats were skeptical about the aggressive Waterloo co-op plan. But Ontario Treasurer and former Minister of Education Dana Porter[8] was not among them. He liked the daring Waterloo gang, whose audacity even extended to the design of the buildings on campus. In contrast to the Gothic and carved-stone architecture of older universities in the province, early buildings at Waterloo featured a clean, futuristic look. When Emery organized a visit to Northeastern University in Boston with Hagey for a firsthand look at its co-op program in early 1957, Porter assigned a senior official from the provincial education ministry to go with them. When the aide returned with a positive report, voices of discontent in Toronto were quieted and funding eventually approved for Waterloo's new engineering program and its radical co-op component.[9]

While that crisis was averted, another erupted. Hagey's dream was to build a shiny new campus around Waterloo College. Yet all the land around the college was occupied by housing or industry and would have to be expropriated at significant cost. When a group led by Emery recommended the purchase of farmland about a kilometre to the west at a much lower price, Hagey was torn. He was still president of Waterloo College and the Lutheran ethos it symbolized. At a board meeting in 1957, he and Needles opposed the purchase, but a faction led by Pollock and Kaufman voted them down. The two campuses would be split up.

Though the Associate Faculties board disagreed with Hagey on the land purchase, they weren't prepared to accede to Hall's demands to fire their new president. But the Western president's persistent warnings about the Waterloo plan had done their damage. Factions within Waterloo College and the Lutheran Synod began to have serious doubts about Hagey's dream. They worried that the co-op plan, the first in Canada, was too risky and would erode the Lutheran Church's control of their institution. It took a dispute over the arts program to drive the final stake into the heart of college unity. Waterloo College felt it should run the arts program at the new university as it had prior to the creation of the Associate Faculties. But professors hired by the Associate Faculties worried the Lutheran culture would weaken attempts to hire qualified teachers and attract students. A separate arts faculty was essential, they argued.[10]

In 1959, the province gave final approval to an act creating the University of Waterloo, with Waterloo College becoming a federated college of the new institution under the name Waterloo Lutheran University. But just a month later the WLU board voted to appoint its own president and administration. And a year later, the Lutheran Synod opted to rescind the federation agreement with UW.[11] The two schools would go their separate ways. In 1973, Waterloo Lutheran University would move to full non-denominational status and change its name to Wilfrid Laurier University.

Ironically, co-operative education's most vocal champion and the man who first put a bug in Hagey's ear about the game-changing plan would not be around to see its fruition. Les Emery wanted the co-op program to train technicians as well as university-level engineers. To not include a technical component was a deal-breaker to him. But Hagey strongly believed the engineering program should be blended with literature, history, politics and other courses in the humanities to offer a well-rounded education and to clearly separate itself from any technical school program. Something had to go, and it was the technical component, he decided. Stung by this rejection, Emery left to pursue a Master's in engineering at Queen's. But UW did not forget him. In 1986, Emery returned to receive an honorary doctor of laws degree for his contribution to co-op education.[12]

For the rebel with a cause from B.F. Goodrich, the successful launch of UW was bittersweet. On the one hand, Hagey's dream of bringing Waterloo College and the University of Waterloo together under one umbrella had failed. On the other, he had accomplished something remarkable, the creation of what would prove to be one of Canada's most disruptive universities, an institution that would lay the foundation for a dynamic tech sector and the birth of such companies as Research In Motion. His faith in co-operative education would prove to be well placed. Co-op enrolment would triple within the first five years, to 2,100 students by 1963. Close to 250 companies were employing students by 1960.[13] Today, according to its website, UW operates the largest post-secondary co-op program of its kind in the world, with an enrolment of 19,800 students and 6,700 employers. For his efforts, Hagey was invested as a member of the Order of Canada in 1986, two years before his death at age eighty-four. The main street running through UW's David Johnston Research and Technology Park bears his name.

* * *

The co-op program was a big draw for Mike Lazaridis. In addition to the work experience he would gain, it helped pay some of his tuition costs and living expenses. He was also attracted to UW by its engineering program. Within five years of opening its doors, Waterloo boasted an engineering enrolment of 846 undergraduates, the second-largest contingent in that subject in Ontario and the third-largest in Canada.[14] Courses were offered in all the main engineering disciplines, including chemical, civil, mechanical and electrical engineering, the program that attracted Lazaridis.

But the course that really sealed the deal for the Windsor high school grad was computer science. By 1980, only twenty-three years after accepting its first students, Waterloo had become a computer science juggernaut in Canada and the world. And there was no more tangible evidence of its success in the new subject than the Red Room. Standing two storeys tall, its walls and floors decorated in red tiles to cover the cables running underneath and to contrast with the big, blue IBM 360/75 machine it housed, the Red Room was home to the largest computer installation in Canada when it opened in 1967. Adding to its mystique was the way it was configured in the new math and computer building, which had opened at the same time. The spacious room was equipped with windows on the upper floor so students and faculty could look down on the long series of blue cabinets housing the mammoth computer and the network of terminals and printers in the middle. Rather than hide the 360/75 away, the arrangement made a statement: "We have the biggest and the best and we're proud of it." The installation soon became a tourist attraction, and Lazaridis was stunned when he saw it. His search was over. UW would be his home for the next five years.[15]

By this time, the university was turning out 1,350 computer science grads a year, one-quarter of the total in Canada, and garnering world press and industry attention. As early as 1968, the *Sunday Times* of London, England, had proclaimed, "In many ways, Waterloo leads the world in developing the methods of mass education for the computer age."[16] In the early 1980s, the *Wall Street Journal* was moved to report that "Waterloo chases high school math students the way Madison Avenue stalks soap consumers."[17] In 1981, the American computer-maker Honeywell rated Waterloo as the top high-tech school in all of North America, ahead of such heavyweights as Stanford and the Massachusetts Institute of Technology.[18]

Unlike older universities that were more set in their ways, Waterloo had the aforementioned advantage of working without any baggage or immutable agendas when it opened in the late 1950s. Throw in the fact that computers and computer science were still in their infancy in business and education and the stage was set for someone to execute a bold vision. To be sure, many students and faculty had a hand in building Waterloo's reputation in computer science, but no one played a bigger role than James Wesley "Wes" Graham. Eventually he would come to be known as the father of computing at UW.

"Wes was a great enabler. He put the environment and resources in place for students to excel," said Ian McPhee, a UW grad who would join Graham in launching Watcom, the university's first software spinoff company.[19]

A native of Copper Cliff, Ontario, near Sudbury, Graham earned his degree in math at the University of Toronto, then went to work in the Toronto office of IBM.[20] He was lured to UW in 1960 by Ray Stanton, who taught Graham at U of T and headed the new math department at Waterloo. Graham was like Gerald Hagey in two respects. Rebelliousness coursed through his veins and industry, not academia, guided his thinking. At UW, his philosophy was simple. Procure the best and latest computer equipment on the market, put the brightest students possible in front of that equipment and watch the magic happen. And it did. Told he would have to wait fourteen months for the IBM model he wanted after arriving at UW, Graham ordered another one instead. There was no time to waste. Just three years later, he ordered two new IBM computers, one to do calculations and the other for input, output and printing. An integrated installation had never been done before in Canada nor had it been tried much in North America.

But Graham's crowning achievement was still to come. In 1966, IBM brought out its most sophisticated computer yet, the 360 series. As usual, Graham had his ear to the ground. He wanted model 75, but the price tag was $3 million ($24 million in 2019 dollars), well beyond the university's budget. It looked as though UW would have to pass on the 360/75. But Graham wasn't happy. There had to be a way to get his hands on the powerful new machine. Then came an epiphany. The university was planning to erect a new building for the math and computer science departments. Why not make the computer part of the furnishings? That way it would qualify for provincial funding as a capital budget item. It was an audacious idea, but the province fell for his ruse and the financing was approved. It didn't hurt that Graham had known education minister and future Ontario premier Bill Davis at the University of Toronto. When other universities heard about this, they were flabbergasted, then livid. But Graham got to keep the 360/75. Special arrangements had to be made to fit the mechanical leviathan into the basement of the new building. The machine was so large it took up as much space as a gymnasium. The legend of the Red Room was born.[21]

UW could have the best computing equipment in the business but if it didn't have a steady source of smart students to work on it, all would be wasted. Graham had a strategy for this too: computer science days for high school kids to play with the equipment at UW on Saturdays, an idea that soon spread across the province; the first computer studies courses in Ontario high schools were designed by Graham; nationwide high school math contests run by UW that attracted 25,000 students at their zenith, with UW recruiting many of the winners. All these tools were used by the father of computing to lure the best and the brightest to Waterloo. "Everything at Waterloo in those days was done bold," said Wayne Bradley, a student at Eastwood Collegiate in Kitchener who attended the computer science days in the 1960s.[22]

So what did these brainy students do with the best hardware in the business? Plenty, as it turns out. They started designing some of the best compilers in the business. A compiler is a piece of software that translates computer language into simpler code. Several students at Waterloo designed a compiler for one of the first IBM machines on campus. It made the computer run 100 times faster. It became known as the WATFOR compiler, named after the Fortran computer language it translated. Compilers on subsequent models sped them up too and spotted tiny errors such as a missing comma or misplaced bracket. Previously, such errors would cause the computer to spit out a massive stack of paper. Pinpointing the error was like finding a needle in a haystack. The compilers and a textbook on how to use them were eventually licensed and sold to thousands of universities and businesses around the world.[23]

In 1965, several students used one of the IBM computers to tackle an ancient Greek puzzle that had never been solved before. Their solution to the Archimedes cattle problem ran to more than 200,000 digits. It was written up in scholarly math journals and garnered headlines across Canada.[24]

More innovations were to follow. In the mid-1970s, students began inputting jobs to a mainframe computer using smaller computer terminals instead of punch cards, and a portable computer on wheels was built to take around to high schools across the province so students could input jobs on the spot.[25] By this time, word had spread throughout the industry about what was going on at Waterloo. Computing giants such as IBM, Digital Equipment Corp. and Hewlett-Packard began donating equipment to the university so students could play around with it and write new software for later commercial use. Using this equipment, UW created its own personal computer network and one of the first local area networks, featuring an early version of email so users could communicate with each other. [26]

In many ways, Randall Howard was the prototypical Waterloo student. Growing up in the small town of Listowel, just northwest of Waterloo, he was among the winners of a UW high school math contest in Grade 9, a title that earned him an invitation to play on Waterloo's best computers in 1968. Enrolling at UW in 1972, he recalls joining a group of computer hackers in 1974 to write a rudimentary email program for about 1,000 users on a Honeywell computer acquired by the math department. Email wasn't used for assignments or anything to do with courses, he recalls. "We mostly used it either socially or to gather information and learn from others. It was still highly novel and highly experimental." Students even used it to pass around jokes and notes about who was single and who wasn't. "So I suppose the 1970s were the beta test for some people of Match.com and Lavalife," he jokes. The group was partly inspired to write the email program by Steve Johnson, a researcher from the famous Bell Labs in New Jersey, who spent a sabbatical at UW around that time.[27] Howard would go on to co-found one of Waterloo's largest software firms, MKS, in the 1980s, then move into a second career as an investor in tech startups.

Graham, whose titles over the years would include professor, director of the UW Computing Centre and dean of computing and communications, was an avid supporter of Waterloo's co-op program. Not only did it give students practical experience, it gave him a window into what was going on in the industry. Students returning from co-op placements could expect a grilling on what their employers were up to. "Wes was always looking at what came next," said McPhee.[28] The program worked both ways. Instructors whose lessons or equipment weren't up to date would be called on it by students returning from co-op placements. Graham also believed that students and professors who developed new software and technology might want to start their own spinoff businesses. He decreed that they should retain the intellectual property rights to it instead of having it stay with the university. Under this policy, fifty-nine high-tech firms were spun out of university research from 1973 to 2001.[29] The policy did much to set the stage for Waterloo to become, arguably, the Silicon Valley of Canada.

In 1973, Graham created the Computer Systems Group to distribute UW's line of compilers and to serve as an incubator for spinoff companies. Common in the tech communities of today, incubators were almost unheard of in the early 1970s. This led to the creation of Watcom, Waterloo's first major software spinoff company. With Graham serving as chair, the company developed software so students could program in five computer languages on personal computers. It was eventually adopted by the entire Ontario university system and sold well internationally. Later, Watcom moved into the software industry itself, developing a line of optimizing compilers that made computers run faster using less space.

One of its compilers helped Microsoft fend off a major challenge from IBM for operating-system supremacy, earning praise from Microsoft CEO Bill Gates at a computer trade show in Las Vegas.[30] Gates would later make UW his only Canadian stop on tours of half-a-dozen of the best tech universities in North America in 2005 and 2008. Why didn't more American universities copy Waterloo's successful co-op model, he wondered in a speech during the 2005 visit, noting that for many years UW had more students working at Microsoft than any other university in the world.[31]

Graham also came up with an innovative way to finance the launch of Watcom. The system of angel and venture-capital financing that is common today was virtually unknown at that time. So were software companies. Microsoft was still in its infancy. But Graham rounded up a bunch of angel investors from the university faculty to finance the creation of Watcom and enabled employees to buy shares on favourable terms.[32] At its peak, Watcom employed 100 people and might have grown into a much larger enterprise had it possessed the marketing and research capital of larger players in the industry. As it was, the company was eventually acquired in the mid-1990s by California-based Sybase,[33] which kept much of its workforce in Waterloo and built the first major office building in the university's new research park in the early 2000s.[34]

Another high point came in the early 1980s, when UW landed a contract to computerize the *Oxford English Dictionary* over twelve other competitors, all from the business world. As it happened, the estates manager at Oxford University in England was Mike Brookes, who had been Waterloo's first superintendent of buildings and grounds before returning to his native England in 1964. When he heard about the dictionary project, he immediately got in touch with UW President Doug Wright, with whom he had remained friends. Wright travelled to Oxford to sell the merits of hiring Waterloo and brought Graham with him. Waterloo was the only university to bid on the project, with the ubiquitous Graham playing a key role in explaining the advantages of working with UW and developing a licensing agreement that benefited both parties.[35] The string search software developed for the Oxford project has been called one of the world's first search engines and led to the creation of another spinoff company. Called Open Text and based in Waterloo, it has grown into one of Canada's largest software companies, specializing in the digital filing of records and documents for business.

In 1999, UW closed Graham's beloved Red Room to create additional space for offices and other equipment. Seriously ill with colon cancer, the father of computing at UW, the great enabler, still found the energy to attend a ceremony marking the demise of the famous computer installation that had attracted so many students and so much international acclaim. Later that year, while Graham was in the last throes of cancer, the federal government rushed to invest him as an Officer of the Order of Canada, an honour that many felt should have gone to him at least a decade earlier. In a scene straight out of a Hollywood weeper, Ontario's Lieutenant-Governor Hilary Weston went to Graham's home to present him with the award. Graham died three days later at the age of sixty-seven. Wes Graham Way was named after him, the same road on which the Sybase building is now located. And the university continues to bestow an annual medal in his honour to grads who demonstrate the entrepreneurial and innovative qualities he championed. In 2017, it named a new supercomputer installed at the university, one of the most powerful machines in the country, after Graham.[36]

* * *

The high school math contests went a long way towards attracting some of the top students in the province to UW. It turns out the math faculty also boasted another secret weapon, though no one knew it at the time. In 1962, a quiet, unassuming professor from Britain joined the faculty of Waterloo. William Tutte had earned his PhD at Cambridge University then immigrated to Canada in 1948 to accept a teaching position at the University of Toronto. He was recruited to Waterloo by Ralph Stanton, head of math and the same unsung hero who brought Graham to the university. Tutte was a world-renowned expert in combinatorics, an obscure but important branch of math dealing with subjects such as optimization, graph theory and cryptography. Tutte's knowledge went a long way towards drawing some of the best minds in the field to Waterloo and raising the level of scholarship during the twenty-three years he taught there.

But Tutte was hiding a much greater secret than any of the calculations underlying his math theorems. During the Second World War, he had worked at the legendary British code-breaking office at Bletchley Park. Tutte and his team cracked the code behind one of the most important wireless machines used by the Germans to send top-secret messages. And they did it without having a working prototype of the device, known as the Lorenz machine. Unlike his more famous colleague Alan Turing, who used a prototype passed on by the Poles to crack the codes behind the Enigma machine, Tutte and his crew had only intercepted messages to work with. Sifting through those messages over four gruelling months, Tutte slowly pieced together how the Lorenz machine was structured, then created an algorithm used to build an electronic computer called the Colossus. The computer, among the first in the world, was used to break Nazi codes for the rest of the war. Tutte and crew's breakthrough was described as "the greatest intellectual feat" of the Second World War, but in a cruel twist of fate, no one heard about their heroics. After the war, the British government destroyed or classified all records from Bletchley Park and forbade any of its employees to share their secrets.[37]

The story of their work was finally broken in a 1997 article in Britain's *New Scientist* magazine. Minds were aflutter in the UK, and historians rushed to update their accounts of the war. But back in Canada the reaction was . . . silence. Somehow, Tutte's exploits escaped the attention of the media in this country, including Waterloo. But as word circulated throughout UW and the math community at large, members were awed. Tutte was already held in high esteem, but this blew the lid off anything they had imagined about their soft-spoken colleague. Mathematicians began arriving from all over the globe to meet the combinatorialist, said Dan Younger, a retired UW math professor and friend of Tutte's. In retrospect, there were "slight hints" that Tutte had done something unusual during the war, but no one had any idea it was so critical to the war effort, he said. Younger was typical of the kind of academic drawn to Waterloo by Tutte. A native of New York City, he studied math at Columbia and Princeton Universities. In the early 1960s, he heard a lecture by Tutte at Princeton on combinatorics. "It was the best I had ever heard on the subject." Learning that Tutte was teaching at the small backwater of Waterloo, Canada, Younger was incredulous. "I had never heard of Waterloo," he laughed. Nonetheless, motivated by dreams of working with the master, he made his way to Waterloo as a visiting professor in 1967 and never left. Canada was ahead of the US on combinatorics at that time, Younger explained.[38]

Apart from a brief stay in Britain, Tutte continued to live quietly in a village just north of Waterloo with his wife, whom he had met in Canada, until his death in 2002 at the age of eighty-four. The Canadian media finally woke up to the war hero in their midst when Tutte received the Order of Canada in 2001, and his death in 2002 was headline news. The passage of time has not dimmed his accomplishments. In 2017, on the hundredth anniversary of his birth, a street running between two math buildings at UW was renamed in his honour, with Younger delivering a lecture on his work at the celebration marking the occasion.

* * *

Since the deaths of instructors like Tutte and Graham, UW has continued to be among the pacesetters in computer science, math and engineering. "The reputation feeds on itself," says David Yach, a UW grad, former employee of Watcom and chief of software at RIM from 1998 to 2012. UW gets "a lot of the best students in Canada, and increasingly some of the best students from around the world, who come here based on the school's reputation." The university's extensive co-op program also doesn't hurt. It gives students "a path to a great job when they graduate and gives employers visibility to UW," adds Yach, a winner of the Wes Graham Medal in 2004. Many of those same employers have sent their children to UW, he notes.[39]

When Google opened its new office in the university's tech park in 2007, Stuart Feldman, a vice-president of engineering at the search-engine leader, said a key condition for choosing the location was a view of the university.

"I can remember using the WATFOR compiler as a kid and Maple (math software developed by Maplesoft, another UW spinoff) as an adult and know that the University of Waterloo had produced a grand stream of computer scientists and software engineers," he told hundreds of assembled dignitaries.[40]

Mike Lazaridis thought so much of his experience at UW in the early 1980s that he established RIM's corporate campus just north of the university and placed RIM signs on the backs of the buildings facing the university so students could see them. He paid Waterloo the ultimate tribute in 2009 when he told a digital media conference in Stratford, Ontario, that much of RIM's early success could be traced to what he and other employees learned at UW. Students were working with early versions of compilers, local area networks and the Internet and didn't even know it, he noted. One of the projects he worked on was a digital signal processor. It would have a direct impact on the eventual development of the BlackBerry. RIM "really didn't catch on until 1999, 20 years after I first discovered it through the University of Waterloo," Lazaridis declared.[41]

Former dean of engineering and president Doug Wright perhaps said it best when he remarked that the lack of esteem with which Waterloo was held by other universities in the early days gave it "the license to be radical in campus design as well as in new areas of research and new areas of teaching and learning."[42]

Chapter 3
ENGINEERS FOR HIRE

Dale Brubacher-Cressman found himself staring at an office above a Kentucky Fried Chicken restaurant in a bland-looking strip mall just north of the University of Waterloo campus. He had travelled all the way from Ottawa to answer a job ad for a company named Research In Motion, but the drab-looking lodgings almost made him turn around and walk away on this day in 1988. Yet something compelled him to move forward. The ad reminded him of a co-op job he had done while a systems-design engineering student at UW. He was anxious to move back to the area after spending a year working at a software firm in the nation's capital. When he knocked on the door, it swung open and there stood Mike Lazaridis.

After Brubacher-Cressman explained why he was there, the eager-looking Lazaridis pulled him inside. For the next two hours, the entrepreneur perused the applicant's qualifications and laid out his vision for RIM, concluding it with a job offer. Brubacher-Cressman was smitten. He wanted to accept it right away, but didn't want to appear desperate. He went home and thought about it over the weekend. On Monday, he accepted.

Thus began a seventeen-year odyssey for Brubacher-Cressman at RIM, one full of more thrills than he could count. He was employee number five. When RIM started to become famous, he even had his licence plate changed to read "RIM no. 5" For much of his time at RIM, he was director of product development through six different versions of the BlackBerry. "I was a quasi-celebrity," he recalled years later. "I was one of the early guys at RIM. People would ask, 'what was that like?'"[1]

By the time Brubacher-Cressman joined RIM, it was four years old and still struggling. Yet it was not for lack of determination. In reality, Lazaridis was so eager to start his business that he couldn't even wait to graduate from UW before launching his career. In his final year, he began tinkering with cathode ray tubes and computers and came up with a system to display text on a TV screen. Convinced that it would be a cool way for companies to advertise their products, he summoned childhood buddy Doug Fregin from Windsor, and the pair launched their new enterprise in the spring of 1984. Searching for a name for their startup, Lazaridis was idly watching TV one day when he saw a story about football players trying to improve their balance by taking ballet lessons. Printed across the bottom of the screen were the words "poetry in motion." He had an epiphany and the name Research In Motion was born.[2]

Young companies often need a guardian angel to succeed, and that angel came in the form of John Corman. A UW electronics engineering grad, Corman had launched a manufacturing firm in Waterloo in 1976. Lazaridis turned to him to make the first 100 units of what came to be known as the Budgie, RIM's first electronic advertising product. Lazaridis raised $30,000 to pay for the product and RIM's early expenses by borrowing $15,000 from his parents and securing a loan from the provincial government.[3] It was Corman who stepped in and rescued RIM on its next job, a contract to build electronic signs for the General Motors truck plant in east Toronto. Even though the Budgie had not sold well, word spread about RIM's product and it was invited to join a Toronto advertising company on the GM job. When the Toronto company declared bankruptcy part way into the contract, Corman Technologies rode to the rescue, agreeing to manufacture the GM signs for a major cut in sales revenue. The signs were eventually installed in a second GM plant and sold to other factory customers in Ontario and Michigan.[4]

It was Corman who steered RIM to its next contract, one that would offer the first glimmers of glamour and fame that were soon to attach themselves to the Waterloo company. Anxious to broaden RIM's product line, Lazaridis had gone to his colleague to see if he had any ideas. Corman passed him a fax with a National Film Board of Canada tender on it. The government film producer needed an electronic barcode reader for a new kind of film Kodak had developed. RIM won the contract thanks in part to a microprocessor Lazaridis had become aware of that was about to be released by Intel. It enabled the DigiSync, RIM's name for the new device, to find barcodes ten times faster than any other reader.[5] Lazaridis prided himself on keeping abreast of what the original equipment manufacturers (OEMs) were doing and would often take home notices and reports about upcoming chips, microprocessors and other products that RIM might need. For him "it was bedtime reading," said Michael Barnstijn, employee number three at RIM and head of software.[6] Entered by the National Film Board in award competitions, the DigiSync went on to win an Oscar and an Emmy in the 1990s and provided "good steady cash flow" for RIM, which sold it to film-editing companies, said Brubacher-Cressman who took the lead in production and sales. He was hired at a salary of $27,000 a year but did not mind the modest pay and long hours occasionally put in by the RIM team.

"I was excited. We were working on cool stuff."

He had worked with young, driven entrepreneurs on co-op work terms while at UW. In Lazaridis he saw the same passion and drive, "but at a different level of capability."[7]

Corman also played a role in RIM's next contract, its biggest one yet. Sutherland-Schultz, a large industrial contractor in the area, had been searching for a cheaper programmable logic controller to measure how a machine worked on an assembly line. It turned to Corman for help, but when Corman was unable to deliver, he turned to Lazaridis. Not long before, Lazaridis had become aware of a new and cheaper way of making electronic circuits using surface-mount technology. The smaller and lighter surface-mount components could be attached directly onto circuit boards instead of being soldered in place. The RIM chief executive had learned of this new technology from Ernie Davison, who represented the National Research Council in Waterloo. Davison kept an office at UW so he could spot promising young entrepreneurs and steer federal grants their way. Lazaridis would often drop by to bounce ideas off Davison, whose warm Irish sense of humour and down-to-earth personality helped to break the ice. During one of his visits, Davison urged Lazaridis to apply for a federal grant to study surface-mount technology. With Davison's backing, the grant was approved and he began experimenting with the technology with the help of a Montreal manufacturer. [8]

When he learned of Sutherland-Schultz's dilemma, Lazaridis suspected the solution might lie in this new technology touted by Davison. Using the surface-mount architecture, controllers could be built much more cheaply on a card or board using fewer circuits. RIM won the contract and its controllers sold by the thousands. RIM made a $100 profit on the sale of each controller, pushing its annual revenues past $1 million in 1990.

"That was the breakthrough that got me the Sutherland-Schultz contract because we were probably the only company in town that even knew what surface mount technology was," Lazaridis said. [9]

* * *

The contract with Sutherland-Schultz did more than fill RIM's coffers. It also brought to the firm a man who, over the next twenty years, would shape its fortunes more than anyone else except Lazaridis himself. Concerned about the amount of money it was paying to RIM for its programmable logic controllers, Sutherland-Schultz sent in a new vice-president to negotiate a better deal. His name was Jim Balsillie.

Born in 1961, the same year as Lazaridis, Balsillie had grown up in Peterborough, Ontario, where his dad worked as an electrician. Early on he demonstrated an aptitude for business, selling Christmas cards door-to-door at age seven, taking on a bunch of paper routes and working as a student painter. His ambition was sometimes undermined by a tendency to rebel against authority. In Grade 7, he was kicked out of math class for mouthing off to the teacher. "I was always a troublemaker. Mouthy and cocky," he said.[10] Yet he turned around and aced the province-wide math test that same year, finishing first in all of Ontario. Unlike Lazaridis, who enjoyed tinkering with computers and electronics in his basement, the hyperactive Balsillie liked being the centre of attention. In high school, he played basketball, hockey and golf, partied on weekends, worked his part-time jobs and still had time for studies. Near the end of high school, he discovered a book: Peter Newman's 1975 best-seller *The Canadian Establishment*. After reading it, his career path was set. He would earn a commerce degree at the University of Toronto, spend several years at an elite Toronto accounting firm then obtain his Master's degree at Harvard Business School. The goal was a prestigious business job and a life of the kind described in Newman's book.[11]

All went according to plan until he met Rick Brock. A part-owner of Sutherland-Schultz in Kitchener, Brock had come to Harvard in the spring of 1989 to attend the annual conference of the Young President's Organization, an elite group of entrepreneurs who had become corporate presidents before the age of forty. During a reception with MBA grads, Balsillie inquired if there were any Canadians present. He was steered to Brock. The pair hit it off. Several drinks turned into a night on the town. Brock began thinking it might be good for Sutherland-Schultz to have a bright, young, Harvard MBA grad on its executive team. He offered Balsillie a job as vice-president.[12]

For his part, Balsillie was already having second thoughts about a career on Wall Street or Bay Street. It would take years to crack the top ranks of a Fortune 500 company. High-tech manufacturing and factory automation, the kind of work Sutherland-Schultz was involved in, were changing quickly and offered him a faster path to corporate glory. Besides, Brock had sold him on the idea of learning how to run a company, something he could accomplish more easily at Sutherland-Schultz than a large financial institution. And the Kitchener company was no mom-and-pop operation. It boasted 700 employees when Balsillie decided to come aboard.

By the early 1990s, Lazaridis was thinking that his small team of coders and engineers was in need of some help. None of them had much experience negotiating deals, attracting financing or marketing RIM's latest products. Nor did the RIM boss want to take on those tasks himself. He preferred immersing himself in the latest trends in technology. Lazaridis began looking around for someone to take the business-development reins. He had met Balsillie not long after he came to Sutherland-Schultz. Charged with streamlining the company's operations, Balsillie had visited RIM's modest offices in an effort to cut a better deal with the small supplier. Around Sutherland-Schultz, he was known as "the closer" after negotiating some astute deals to dispose of company assets.

Lazaridis gradually became more and more impressed with Balsillie's business acumen, even when he set his sights on acquiring a piece of RIM. In 1992, Sutherland-Schultz was being sold and the new owners made it clear there would be no place for Balsillie. At this point, the ambitious Harvard grad was tired of playing second banana. He wanted to run his own operation and had a severance deal from Sutherland-Schultz to help make it happen. It wasn't quite big enough to purchase all of RIM, but Balsillie at least wanted a majority stake in the company. Lazaridis wasn't willing to give up control of his baby but by this point had decided he couldn't live without Balsillie on his team.

"It was like meeting your future wife. You just know." He felt this way even though Balsillie's reputation at Sutherland-Schultz was decidedly mixed. Fired up by his new bible, *The Art of War*, an ancient Chinese military text that had become popular with executives in the 1980s, Balsillie streamlined operations and pressed suppliers for better deals. Brock thought he was brilliant but other managers at the firm weren't so enamoured of his aggressive style. "He's a shark," Lazaridis's wife Ophelia warned her husband before he brought Balsillie aboard. "Yes, but he's our shark," replied Lazaridis.[13] At first, Balsillie balked at Lazaridis's offer of a 33 percent stake in the company, less than the RIM founder's 40 percent share. But when a backup plan to acquire another company fizzled, Balsillie agreed to Lazaridis's terms in the spring of 1992 in return for an investment of $125,000. RIM would now be led by two chief executive officers. Brubacher-Cressman was surprised when Balsillie came aboard as a co-chief executive. "I assumed he (Lazaridis) would hire a level down. But Jim being Jim, he wasn't satisfied with that."[14]

* * *

Balsillie took a huge leap in leaving a large, established company for what was essentially still a startup. RIM only had about twenty employees when he joined the company. But Balsillie had his antennae tuned to anything that might look promising. And by this time, RIM was on to something. Several years earlier, it had been contacted by Rogers Cantel, the Canadian cable TV and cellphone carrier. Rogers had licensed a new wireless data technology from Sweden called Mobitex, which, like the name suggests, stood for mobile text. Mobitex had been discovered by Rogers chief executive Ted Rogers during a visit to Sweden in the late 1980s, where his telecom supplier Ericsson was based. While riding in a taxi in Stockholm, he noticed a wireless data terminal used to dispatch drivers. Cab drivers were normally dispatched using two-way radios. This text-based system was different, and Rogers, always on the lookout for new technology, knew he had to give it a try.[15]

The advantage of Mobitex was that it relied on packet-switching rather than the circuit-switching used by the cellular phone industry. With packet-switching, data could be broken down into smaller packets or pieces and sent along different wireless streams before being reassembled at their destination. It was more efficient and used up less bandwidth than circuit-switching, which required a dedicated wireless line during voice conversation. Packet-switching was first developed in the 1960s as a way to develop a secure computer network for the US military. It later became one of the fundamental networking technologies behind the ARPANET and its successor, the Internet.

Rogers bought the Canadian rights to Mobitex but didn't know much about it or how to operate the equipment supplied by Ericsson. It put out the help-wanted sign. One of the job applicants suggested a company in Waterloo named Research In Motion.[16] Lazaridis was only too happy to jump at this opportunity. He was already familiar with packet-switching technology from his days using electronic mail in the internal computer networks at the University of Waterloo. Indeed, the forward-thinking Lazaridis included an email address on his first business cards when he launched RIM in 1984. Though email came into popular usage in the early 1990s when the Internet was established and personal computers became affordable, it was still largely unknown to the general public in the 1980s.[17]

After being hired by Rogers as a consultant on Mobitex, Lazaridis and company immediately set about trying to make the technology work. Led by chief of software Michael Barnstijn, they developed ways to send messages between a computer and a Mobitex radio, and tools so developers could write programs. A key hire in 1991 was Gary Mousseau. A UW grad, he had experience working with a packet-switching network used by telephone companies and automated-banking machines. Mousseau figured out a way to move data ten times faster than previous methods and to connect Mobitex with the first commercial data exchange networks on the Internet. Other innovations, fuelled by the efforts of additional recruits, were data compression, a fail-safe method for delivering messages and a way to analyze data traffic.[18]

A sign that the company was doing things right came in the spring of 1993 when RIM attracted $375,000 in financing from Innovation Ontario, an agency of the provincial government with a mandate to help early-stage tech companies. The funds were to be used for marketing, new licensing agreements and joint ventures, the agency said in a news release. The release also noted that RIM, with twenty employees and annual revenues of $2 million, was involved in three main areas of business: the Mobitex data network, surface-mount technology and motion-picture barcode reading.[19] But Lazaridis left no doubt where he was leaning. The year before, in an interview with the Waterloo Region *Record*, the local daily newspaper, he said mobile communications was on the verge of exploding.

"I think that, in another three years, wireless data will be as successful as cellular phones, if not more."[20]

Yet there were still some bumps along the road. A cumbersome wireless device created by AT&T failed to take off, despite a high-profile demo outside the White House by President Bill Clinton in 1993. And Apple stumbled with the Newton, a bug-ridden handset using a pen-like device called a stylus to write messages on a screen.[21] During this period, RIM won several large contracts worth a total of $4 million to supply modems and point-of-sale terminals to Ericsson. The latter would allow customers to make purchases wirelessly with credit cards at outdoor events. They were tested at a National Football League game in Dallas and a Blue Jays game in Toronto, but they were bulky and the Ericsson modems inside them did not work properly. "It was obvious to us that you couldn't rely on those radios. They were terrible," said RIM co-founder Doug Fregin.[22]

Chapter 4
GOING MOBILE

Lazaridis realized RIM would have to start designing and making its own hardware rather than working with Ericsson parts. Modems were the first item on the to-do list, but RIM lacked someone skilled in radio frequency to lead the project. It so happened that Anand Sinha, a software developer at RIM, knew of a person in Hamilton who might fit the bill. Pete Edmonson was a reed-thin, earthy and plain-talking professor of electronics and communications engineering at McMaster University. As a boy growing up in Hamilton, he was fascinated by the CHCH-TV tower and how its signal could be broadcast to the home through walls and bricks. The Apollo space missions and their ability to broadcast from the moon further drove his interest in the direction of wireless communications. But lately Edmonson had become disenchanted with his chosen field. To him, universities and colleges had become more concerned with enrolment than the quality of graduates they were churning out. "In my early days of teaching I felt like a new-car salesman that could stand behind the product. Gradually I felt like a used-car salesman representing a bunch of lemons to unload."

When RIM came calling early in 1994, he jumped. "Mike (Lazaridis) impressed me with his idea of mobile email being done in Canada. He had the money to get it going and needed the people to stitch it together," Edmonson recalls. After arriving at the Waterloo office and getting a feel for what RIM wanted, Edmonson realized he could not do the job alone. An early strength of the company, he believes, was allowing managers to hire people they knew and trusted. Armed with the title of director of research, Edmonson recruited half-a-dozen of his best graduate students to work on the modem project. The first challenge was designing a modem that could be mass-produced. Anybody can build a radio, but the tough part is making one that will be pumped out at the rate of 20,000 a week, he noted. "When a machine assembles it, it's a different beast. We had to go through a good learning curve." Another obstacle was finding suppliers to manufacture parts in the modest numbers required by RIM. "Our quantities were too low," Edmonson explained. Manufacturers wanted runs of 500,000 parts a month, not 20,000.

The "unsung heroes" of this period in the company's history were the assemblers who put together the first modems and BlackBerrys, insists Edmonson. The university-educated designers and software engineers at head office tended to look down upon the assemblers and factory workers at the company. The lack of respect was unjustified. Mostly immigrant women from plants in the area like Babcock and Wilcox and Budd Automotive or Conestoga College, they were great at spotting errors and working quickly. "They had a hard time getting their education recognized, but boy could they work," said Edmonson.

Early manufacturing challenges notwithstanding, RIM was able to build its first modem within ten months. Dubbed "the brick," it was sold to point-of-sale customers for remote purchases. For its next project, RIM set its sights on a slimmed-down version of the brick that could fit into the slot on a laptop computer so users could access their email wirelessly. The slimmer bricks sold well, with RIM landing several big contracts. One reason was their low energy consumption. "We were brutal in searching out and finding the latest, smallest and lowest-power components from several different suppliers," said Edmonson. "The software people at RIM really knew the radio protocols and figured out how to save a lot of battery power with the software." But new problems emerged, not of the company's doing. On some laptops, the slot was located too close to the flip-up screen and would interfere with the antenna in the modem. On others, the processor chip was too close to the modem slot, causing it to overheat and throw off the wireless signal. And then there was the email program itself, supplied by Microsoft. It took ages to boot up. "To check your email was a five-minute ordeal," said Edmonson. "We simply said, what does a laptop provide? A screen, a keyboard and a battery. Why can't we provide these items in a small pocket-size format?" So the team took the brick, slapped a keyboard over it, attached a small, flip-up screen and presto! The Inter@ctive Pager 900, RIM's first pocket device, was born.[1]

Yet the story is a bit more complicated than that. RIM also needed a circuit board that was small enough to fit into the Pager 900. But the chips or integrated circuits that were on the market, the ones that would be laid down on the board to conduct electricity and process data, were too large to cram into a handheld device. A smaller, more powerful chip was needed to get the job done. But where would it come from? RIM didn't have the expertise to do the job in-house. As fate would have it, before Lazaridis and company could go looking for a supplier, one would come to them.

* * *

Graham Tubbs couldn't believe it. He had travelled all the way from Phoenix, Arizona, to check out a little company in the "Toronto area" that was building modems and radios and trying to break into the wireless field. He had heard the company was small, but he hadn't thought it was this small, and it sure wasn't close to Toronto. "If they had 20 employees, I'd be amazed," said the friendly yet outspoken Brit of his first impressions of RIM's office in the spring of 1995. Tubbs thought to himself, "How can these guys establish themselves in the wireless arena?"[2]

Tubbs worked for the embedded products division of Intel in Chandler, Arizona, a suburb of Phoenix. Embedded products were microchips designed for automotive, wireless and industrial applications. In other words, everything outside the company's main line of business — making microchips for personal computers. Sales had been slow lately and Tubbs was eager to find new customers. A colleague at Intel told him about a company he had once worked for in Canada called Research In Motion. Tubbs was skeptical at first, but after a conference call with Lazaridis and someone from AT&T Wireless in Seattle who knew of RIM's work, he arranged a visit while on a business trip to the East Coast.[3] By this time, RIM had moved into an office on Phillip Street, closer to the University of Waterloo, but was still crammed into a small corner of the building. Tubbs's visit could not have come at a better time for RIM. The company had done business with Intel before, buying off-the-shelf computer chips for some of its earlier products, but had never dealt with Tubbs and the embedded products division. Could this be the source for the chip they needed?

RIM's modest size threw Tubbs off at first, but Lazaridis slowly won him over. He passed around mockups of a RIM pager and talked about the wireless email market. Motorola was the dominant player in pagers, but its products were rudimentary at best. RIM had potential customers in the US just itching for a viable product. Email was exploding in popularity on desktop computers. Mobile data was the next frontier. His excitement growing, Tubbs went back to Arizona and put together a proposal with colleague Terry Gillett to build a microprocessor for RIM over the next eighteen months, at a cost of $2.5 million.

Their pitch to Intel brass did not go over well. Their bosses reacted with hostility to the cost of building a product for a tiny Canadian company they had never heard of before. A paltry $100,000 was all they were prepared to approve. Tubbs was furious. By now, he could see that RIM might be on to something big. But once his anger wore off, his team began brainstorming. Rather than build a customized chip from scratch, what if they packaged three existing chips together in an integrated solution?

Such a combination had never been tried before at Intel. "It was quite revolutionary for the time," said Gillett.[4] By using existing chips, they could also save time and money. Adopting this unorthodox approach, the Intel team was able to deliver a prototype microchip within budget to RIM's offices in March 1996, just three months after starting the project.[5]

The chip could not have come soon enough. Lazaridis had promised to demo a prototype of the Inter@ctive 900, which had been named after the 900 megahertz radio band it would use on Mobitex, at the headquarters of RAM Mobile Data in New Jersey that July. RAM, the wireless data division of BellSouth, had purchased the American rights to the Mobitex network. Lazaridis's design called for a black, plastic, clamshell device that would flip open to reveal a full QWERTY keyboard, several navigational buttons and a small display screen with room for up to four lines of text. There were plenty of long days and nights as the RIM crew raced to get the 900 ready. "I fondly remember being there overnight," Brubacher-Cressman recalled with a dose of sarcasm. Even so, they didn't mind the gruelling pace. "We embraced the pressure."[6] The long hours paid off with a prototype that Lazaridis was able to take to RAM. The demo went off with flying colours. Using the 900, he was able to send a message wirelessly to a desktop computer in the same room. RAM officials were impressed. "You should have seen their faces," an ebullient Lazaridis told employees when he returned to Waterloo.[7]

Even so, reviews of the Inter@ctive Pager were mixed after it came out in the fall of 1996. *Corporate User* magazine called it the top wireless product of the year, but *Wireless Internet and Mobile Computer Newsletter*, a widely respected publication, was not impressed. The pager is a good one, but "it's a bit too heavy, bulky and expensive ($675 per unit) to attract many mobile professionals," said Allan A. Reiter. Part of the problem was the spotty Mobitex network.[8]

If Lazaridis and company were discouraged by the cool reception to the 900, they were soon revived by a strange phenomenon. RIM employees began taking 900s home at night to stay in touch with the office. In Arizona, Intel employees and some managers were given 900s and encouraged to use them. When asked to return them at the end of the test period, virtually no one wanted to. "'Over my dead body,' was the typical response," said Tubbs.[9]

* * *

While the market reception to the 900 was discouraging, Lazaridis was already looking ahead. Before it even went on sale, he was making plans for RIM's next pager. It would be smaller, lighter and consume less power. To achieve these goals, it would require a customized, integrated microprocessor from Intel, at much greater cost. RIM began lobbying Intel for a larger commitment of funds and resources, or it would start looking for other chip suppliers. Meanwhile, the brain trust at Intel, still skeptical about wireless, was resisting just as stubbornly. Tubbs and Gillett were scheduled to return to Waterloo in early 1996 to finalize terms of the 900 deal. They were warned by the Intel brass in unequivocal terms not to commit to any more projects with RIM. They did not want to spend any more money on risky wireless projects.[10] Sure enough, Lazaridis didn't beat around the bush when they arrived at RIM. He demanded a better chip and a greater commitment from Intel and he wanted it now. Tubbs and Gillett were dying to say yes. They believed in RIM's vision. They thought it was absolutely the right partnership for Intel. It offered the microchip giant a chance to break into the burgeoning wireless field, a move with almost as much potential as the desktop industry where Intel was a dominant player. But the warning from head office kept ringing in their ears. The pair stumbled their way through a rejection. No we can't do it, the pair stammered.

Lazaridis, Balsillie and the rest of the RIM team got up and marched out of the room. The dejected Intel crew lingered, trying to figure out what to do. As they rose to leave, Gillett was seized by a sudden, implacable urge. With Tubbs in tow, he strode down to the office shared by Lazaridis and Balsillie. Extending his hand to the surprised pair, he offered the commitment RIM was looking for. Gillett knew he was taking a huge risk, one that could end up getting him fired. "To this day, I really can't figure out why I did it, but it turned out to be a good decision," Gillett recalled years later.[11]

At first glance, it didn't seem like much. A handshake deal. A gripping of palms. That was all the two firms had. Nothing in writing. No carefully worded, neatly printed agreement with signatures at the bottom that one would normally expect for such an important deal. Not even a few scratches on the back of an envelope or a rough scrawl on a napkin over drinks in a bar. It seemed like a shaky foundation on which to build a processor for the next-generation Inter@ctive Pager, one that would cost Intel several million dollars and enable RIM to eventually dominate the wireless data world.

Yet the deal turned out to be anything but shaky. When Gillett and Tubbs got back to Arizona and passed on the news, their bosses were irate. They threatened to fire Gillett, then brought in a lawyer to see if they could cancel the handshake deal. Turns out there were precedents for handshake agreements holding up in court. When told it would be difficult to break the agreement, they drew up a plan to build a microprocessor for RIM at the lowest possible cost and an attractive profit margin for Intel. Gillett, relieved that he had not lost his job and happy to have at least something to offer to RIM, presented the plan on a take-it-or-leave-it basis to Lazaridis and Balsillie at a hotel near the San Francisco Airport. The pair "swallowed hard and reluctantly agreed to the terms." Despite their bluster about finding another supplier, the Intel chip was the only real option for their next pager.[12]

Bolstered by the handshake agreement with Intel, Lazaridis was well on his way to planning the next generation in RIM's wireless arsenal, to be called the Inter@ctive Pager 950. This time, the pager would be code-named Leapfrog. The name was no accident. He wanted it to leap ahead of the earlier 900, which had been code-named Bullfrog, and whatever the competition was planning. For starters, he wanted the Leapfrog to be manufactured in-house. RIM had contracted out the fabrication of the first 900s, but there had been problems with the hinges, batteries, screen and other tiny parts. The hinges in particular lost much of their friction and the clamshell device would just flop open after repeated use. Brubacher-

Cressman would take a 900 home or to the cottage and flip it open and closed repeatedly to see how long the hinge would last. Eventually RIM bought a machine to test the hinges.[13] To gain more control over hardware quality, RIM found a manufacturing plant in the south end of Kitchener and began fabricating 900s there at the beginning of 1997.[14]

After the problems with the hinges, Lazaridis decided there would be no flip-open lid on the 950. It would be a smaller, rectangular piece of hardware — three inches by two inches — with a screen at the top able to show six lines of text. Below the screen was a keyboard with letters sweeping in a gradual downward arc to facilitate typing by the thumbs. A track-wheel in the upper right-hand corner allowed the user to scroll through messages. The track-wheel idea had come to Lazaridis after he noticed one on a new VCR he had purchased. Equipped with a more powerful, customized Intel microchip, the 950 would be small enough to wear on a belt and would feature a back-lit LCD display, clock, calendar, antenna and small LED lights to indicate wireless coverage and the arrival of a message. Rather than resembling a fancy personal-digital assistant or a cute little laptop, the Leapfrog would do one thing and do it well: deliver email. And it would sell for under $400. In this simple little package, the 950 would appeal to the 125 million people currently using desktop email and the 40 million using pagers in the US.[15]

* * *

If Lazaridis was bullish about the possibilities of the 950, BellSouth was running out of patience. It had purchased a major stake in RAM Mobile Data and the American rights to the Mobitex network, then spent big bucks to build out the network. Yet it had little to show for it. Sales of RIM's Pager 900 had been poor. In the spring of 1997, the Atlanta-based telecom gave RIM an ultimatum. Unless it could come up with a better device, BellSouth would put the Mobitex network on the market. Lazaridis and company were horrified. Plans for the new and improved 950 were falling into place, but there was no way it would be ready before early 1998. For one thing, Intel would need the rest of 1997 to finish designing and building the new chip for the 950. Worse, if BellSouth pulled the plug on the Mobitex network, RIM's efforts over the past eight years to build up expertise in the data network would be in jeopardy. Lazaridis pleaded for more time. A meeting was set up two weeks later at BellSouth headquarters in Atlanta where he would get a chance to make his case.

Although prototypes of the 950 weren't ready, Lazaridis planned to use two industrial-foam mockups of the device as part of his presentation. But when he and Balsillie arrived for the crucial meeting, they realized that the mockups had been left in the taxi they had taken from the airport. Awkward moments ensued while the embarrassed RIM founder asked that someone call the cab company to retrieve the precious Leapfrogs. In the meantime, he stalled for time by laying out the business plan for the mobile email market and the fact BellSouth had first-mover advantage over its competitors. He described what the 950 would look like and how it would work. Thirty anxious minutes crawled by. The BellSouth executives seemed bored and unconvinced. All seemed lost when a BellSouth employee suddenly walked in with the missing mockups. Their arrival seemed to jolt everyone awake. As Lazaridis extolled the powers of the device, BellSouth executives passed them around. With tangible evidence of the 950 now in their hands, something they could feel and touch and look at, skepticism in the room gradually melted. Lazaridis's confidence was infectious. The telecom bosses were enthralled. Lazaridis "had those guys thinking he would walk on water," said Jim Hobbs, vice-president of BellSouth's mobile data group.[16]

Thanks in no small part to an Atlanta taxi driver, the BellSouth meeting was a turning point in RIM's history. Several months later, in August 1997, the company announced a $70-million deal to supply 100,000 two-way pagers to BellSouth in 1998. It was by far the largest order in RIM's history. The carrier also decided to double its base stations to 2,400 to cover 90 per cent of the US market. On the strength of the BellSouth deal, Balsillie was able to lead an initial public offering of shares on the Toronto Stock Exchange raising $108 million CA so RIM could ramp up production to meet the BellSouth order and boost its workforce, which now stood at about 180 employees.

The Pager 950, as it turned out, would not go on sale until the fall of 1998. In the meantime, RIM was able to make several key improvements. Email arrived on the device by a push mechanism instead of a pull mechanism. That meant users saw the messages when they arrived instead of having to login and download them when they picked up their handsets. The email address on the 950 was also the same as the one on the user's desktop computer. Initially, the 950 featured a different mailbox but Gary Mousseau, the same RIM software engineer who had figured out how to move data more quickly in the early days of Mobitex, was able to solve the two-mailbox problem by installing a piece of software called a desktop redirector on the user's desktop computer. It copied the email, sent it out on the Mobitex network to a RIM relay station and then to the user's mobile device. The system also worked in reverse.[17]

The relay station, or network operations centre (NOC), also enabled RIM to offer an end-to-end solution to carriers and subscribers. BellSouth still wasn't keen on wireless email. Bringing desktop email into the mix boosted the frequency of transmission errors. BellSouth preferred the simpler two-way paging system, yet wanted to charge subscribers $100 a month to use it. Balking at these demands, Lazaridis pitched the idea of buying carrier time wholesale from BellSouth so RIM could resell it at lower monthly prices to subscribers and offer email at the same time. Assured of upfront revenue for its struggling data division, BellSouth agreed to the request, and Lazaridis bought two years of unlimited network time for $5 million.[18] This led RIM to set up its own NOC in Waterloo to encrypt and receive email messages and data and relay them to their destination. More NOCs were set up in other countries as the number of subscribers grew over the years.

The code-name Leapfrog was an appropriate choice for the 950. It did indeed leap ahead of the competition. When it went on sale in the fall of 1998, the device moved briskly. Balsillie's guerrilla sales tactics helped. He preferred young business school grads to grizzled industry veterans. Aided by RIM's desktop-redirector software, they were able to bypass corporate IT departments and go right to the top, hooking up C-suite executives with devices before the gatekeepers at lower levels even knew what happened. Lazaridis got so charged up his wife accused him of being more excited about RIM's pager than the birth of his two children.[19] Momentum picked up in early 1999 when RIM announced a new name for its sizzling wireless device. From now on, it would be called the BlackBerry. The name had come from a California firm specializing in corporate branding. RIM evangelists, as sales people came to be known, whipped out their BlackBerrys in airports and trade shows. Curious onlookers were soon enthralled by a device that could send and receive messages of up to 2,600 words in seconds instead of minutes, all on a battery that lasted up to three weeks. The BlackBerry was truly a data powerhouse.

Chapter 5
RIDING THE ROCKET

Most people in Waterloo Region never saw it coming. Yet, as the millennium turned, it was nearly impossible to ignore. RIM was on a fast track to high-tech superstardom. Suddenly, business and political leaders in the region couldn't stop talking about the maker of this mysterious device about the size of a wallet that could send and receive email. Local tech consultant and blogger Gary Will would later compare it to Liverpool landing the Beatles.[1] Among the most surprised was Rob Caldwell, a member of the University of Waterloo's board of governors and owner of a boutique investment firm in the region with a list of high-end clients.

"It's just staggering," he told the *Record* in a February 2000 story after RIM's share price cracked the $100 barrier on the NASDAQ exchange in the US and fell just short of the $150 level on the Toronto Stock Exchange (TSX). The increase pushed Balsillie into the billionaire category on paper, joining Lazaridis, who had reached that pinnacle just the week before. Billionaires were a rare entity in Waterloo Region. Statistics weren't readily available on such matters, but Caldwell couldn't recall anyone else from the area that had even come close to attaining that status. According to a 1999 poll conducted by *Forbes* magazine, there were only eight billionaires in all of Canada.[2]

Just a month earlier, RIM had rented Lulu's, a sprawling supermarket in the south end of Kitchener that had been converted into a giant nightclub years earlier and had hosted such aging music legends as Jerry Lee Lewis, James Brown and B.B. King. Celebration was on the company's mind after its recent listing on the NASDAQ stock exchange in the US. Popular Canadian rock band Barenaked Ladies entertained employees, friends and investment bankers and lawyers who had made the trek all the way from Wall Street. RIM was rocking and rolling. Free passes were distributed to several hundred math students from the University of Waterloo. Even though the company's workforce now stood at 450, there was no way that would be sufficient to handle RIM's stunning growth.[3]

For Caldwell, it was all a bit bewildering. He had first become aware of the company in the early 1990s when several RIM people attended a tech conference he hosted for investors at the University of Waterloo. Also on the guest list was Gene McBurney, a friend and investment banker from Toronto who was keeping close tabs on the Waterloo company and who would later help to lead a $31-million financing round for RIM that preceded its IPO. Caldwell was impressed with RIM's plucky independence and entrepreneurial spirit. It reminded him of his own firm, Caldwell Capital, which was trying to go it alone against the larger established banks. Some years went by before he would cross paths with RIM again. In the fall of 1997, Balsillie and RIM's chief financial officer Dennis Kavelman showed up at his office door in the Canada Trust Tower in downtown Kitchener. They were seeking investors for RIM's initial public offering (IPO) of shares on the Toronto Stock Exchange. The pair didn't fit the mould of typical corporate financiers. For one thing, Kavelman looked too young to be doing this sort of thing. He was in his mid-twenties and barely out of college, where he had earned a business degree at Wilfrid Laurier University. But his credentials were impossible to ignore. He had placed first in a national exam conducted by the Canadian Institute of Chartered Accountants in 1994.

"He was very, very bright," said Caldwell. Also "calm and organized." In contrast, Balsillie came on aggressively with a hard-sell routine. "He was very, very confident and strong-willed." The pair talked up the prospects for RIM's new Inter@ctive Pager 950. The ink was barely dry on a $70-million deal to supply 100,000 pagers to BellSouth in the US. The handheld device was about to hit the American market in large volumes. Despite their bullish forecast, Caldwell was wary. Most of his clients were blue-chip, long-risk investors. RIM was a new company and its pagers were still unproven. "It wasn't clear they would do as well as they did," he said. "We viewed it (RIM stock) as quite speculative." Still, Caldwell participated in the IPO on behalf of his clients. "It turned out to be an easy sell."

Caldwell's skepticism would eventually turn into full-blown admiration as BlackBerrys started selling like gangbusters, sending RIM stock through the roof. He would become something of an evangelist for RIM and its hometown of Waterloo. At a dinner of the Investment Dealers Association in Toronto, he found himself sitting beside Barbara Stymiest, who was CEO of the TSX at the time. He wasn't normally one to boast, but it wasn't every day he had access to one of the top business leaders in Canada. "Look at this new technology we have from Waterloo," Caldwell exclaimed, pulling out his BlackBerry. He proceeded to type an email and send it to her office. Stymiest, who would later go on to chair RIM's board of directors, called him the next day to say she had received the email. "She was absolutely amazed by this."[4]

One day in 1998, Kitchener Mayor Carl Zehr was sitting beside Balsillie during an event at Federation Hall at the University of Waterloo when he noticed the RIM co-CEO typing away on a little black device. He had met Balsillie two or three times over the past few years and knew he worked for a high-tech company in Waterloo. Peering over his shoulder, Zehr could see that the device had a small, rectangular window with three lines of type on it. Below was a keyboard sweeping in a slightly downward arc. Finally, his curiosity got the better of him and he asked Balsillie what he was doing. The RIM executive said he was testing the company's new handheld pager, which could send and receive email wirelessly. Zehr was intrigued. Cellphones were in fairly common usage by then, and he was used to receiving email on his desktop computer, but this was something completely new. The mayor took pride in being on the cutting edge of change. When he took office in 1997, downtown Kitchener was struggling, decimated by the crack cocaine epidemic, the decline of manufacturing and the flight of retail to the suburbs. In contrast, uptown Waterloo — the city insisted on calling its core by the classier name of uptown — was doing much better, buoyed by the two universities and white-collar industries such as Sun Life and Manulife. Under Zehr's leadership, Kitchener concocted a bold plan to lure the schools of pharmacy and social work from UW and WLU respectively to downtown Kitchener. Tech companies followed, renovating and occupying some of the old factories, kick-starting a downtown revival.

When Zehr saw the little black box Balsillie was holding, the event they were attending suddenly took a backseat. To this day, he can't remember the reason they had come to Federation Hall. What he does remember is that it was the first time he laid eyes on a RIM pager. He made up his mind that he wasn't going to leave until he found out more about the wireless machine. Pointing to the pager, he said, "I don't understand how this works. Can you explain it to me?"

"I'll get one for you," Balsillie replied. Two or three days later, a little white cardboard box arrived on Zehr's desk with "RIM device" written on the outside in black magic marker. It sat on his desk for several weeks while the mayor kept using his day-timer scheduling book and a Palm Pilot digital calendar device that had been issued to councillors several years earlier. Finally, Zehr couldn't ignore the pager any longer. He took it out and started playing around with it. With help from IT staff at the city and RIM, he got it hooked up. It wasn't long before he wasn't using his day-timer or Palm Pilot any more. "I went cold turkey to it," he said of the pager. At a council meeting soon after, Zehr casually pulled out his RIM pager and started to use it. He didn't make a show of it, but it wasn't long before curious glances started coming his way from around the horseshoe. With the RIM device, Zehr could send an email to a laptop on the other side of the council table. "It was still in beta (testing) when I started on the pager. It wasn't even available for sale yet."

Like Caldwell, he became a disciple for the BlackBerry in its early days. "It became a tool to connect with people when I wasn't in the office. That's where I found it most useful." And he had no hesitation in using it to toot the city's horn. Several years after the BlackBerry had been released, Zehr attended a meeting of the Canadian Big City Mayors' Caucus. Kitchener was a member, but with a population of about 250,000, it wasn't getting a lot of respect from larger centres across Canada. Anne Golden, president of the Conference Board of Canada, an economic think tank, and her research assistant were making a presentation on hub cities across the country. Kitchener was not one of them. Nor was Waterloo Region, which boasted a population of more than 500,000 when the adjoining cities of Kitchener, Waterloo and Cambridge were lumped together. Zehr was not happy. It didn't matter that RIM was based in Waterloo and he was mayor of Kitchener. It was all one urban area as far as he was concerned, especially when it came to industry and commerce. Picking up his BlackBerry, he fired off an email to an assistant at Kitchener City Hall requesting statistics on the gross domestic product (GDP) of Waterloo Region compared to other cities in Ontario. After Golden had completed her presentation, Zehr asked those mayors who carried BlackBerrys to put their devices on the table and turn them upside down. Now don't touch them for the rest of the meeting, he instructed. Grumpy looks creased the faces of the Black-Berry-toting big-city bosses. "Now tell me Waterloo Region isn't a hub city," Zehr exclaimed, noting that the BlackBerry was made in Waterloo. During a break, Zehr pulled out his BlackBerry and showed Golden the GDP numbers sent to him by his assistant back in Kitchener. Impressed by his bold attitude and the shiny new pager, she accepted his invitation for a bus tour of Waterloo Region and its star attraction, Research In Motion. "They certainly were the talk of the town," said Zehr, who would progress through a series of BlackBerrys during his seventeen years as mayor, which ended in 2014. "RIM was in the news frequently. People were proud of the fact their technology was home-grown."[5]

Zehr was an early champion of the BlackBerry and the first local politician to actually carry one, recalls Ken Seiling, the long-time chair of Waterloo Region. Seiling was not so sure of the new technology himself. "I remember wondering at the time if this was sort of a fad." Once it proved to be reliable, he started using one. "It altered the way political people operated. Issues became much more immediate." He too was surprised by RIM's rocket-like trajectory and said other communities were envious of Waterloo Region for having a company like the BlackBerry-maker.[6]

* * *

That RIM's stunning success caught much of Waterloo Region napping was not surprising. Many of the company's early successes were carried on the business pages of the *Record* rather than the front page, where RIM regularly landed later in its history. Readers had to flip all the way back to page F4 in the *Record*'s business section to find news of RIM's landmark $70-million deal to supply thousands of pagers to BellSouth, the one signed after the dramatic and nearly disastrous meeting in Atlanta in 1997, and there was no colour about the mock-up pagers left in the taxi.[7] And RIM's initial public offering of shares on the TSX, one that would deposit more than $100 million in the company's bank account, an astounding sum by local standards at that time, was tucked inside the paper, once again in the business section.[8] Even the *Globe and Mail*, Canada's national newspaper, a Toronto-based publication that was widely read in Waterloo Region, was reluctant to give prime real estate to RIM's early breakthroughs. The paper had published several short features on the Waterloo company and the wireless data industry in general through the 1990s. One from 1996 included a quote from Balsillie saying the future of mobile was "going to be colossal."[9] But these stories had been buried inside the "Report on Business" section, and RIM's IPO on the TSX didn't merit more than a spot on page B19.[10] RIM was making news but readers had to hunt to find it.

Even so, by 2000 the Waterloo company was often landing on the front page. One by one, the accolades kept rolling in: the BlackBerry 950 named mobile product of the year by *InfoWorld* and *PC World* magazines; a contract to supply 2,000 BlackBerrys to computer chip giant Intel; more contracts with American Online, Compaq computers, Oracle software, the US Army and the US Defense Department; distribution deals with Rogers, AT&T and Bell Mobility in Canada, Motient in the US and BT Cellnet in the UK; RIM shares cracking $200 on the TSX after being just $10 a year earlier; Lazaridis's donation of $100 million in company stock to launch the Perimeter Institute for Theoretical Physics in Waterloo; Al Gore's use of a BlackBerry in his presidential election campaign; the BlackBerry 957, an upgrade on the 950, winning a spot on *Time* magazine's "best of 2000" list. "Email is still the internet's killer app, and RIM's 957 is the wireless gadget of choice for the on-the-go email addicts," *Time* said at the end of 2000.[11] It was enough to make your head spin.

In his year-end column, *Record* business writer Kevin Crowley actually apologized for devoting so much space to the Waterloo wireless communications company.

"In one four-day stretch," he wrote, "RIM's BlackBerry email pager was selected by *Time* magazine as one of the top ten techno-gadgets in the world, *Maclean's* magazine named RIM founder Mike Lazaridis to its honour roll of distinguished Canadians and the *Globe and Mail* ran a long story on the BlackBerry craze that's sweeping corporate America."

With a workforce of more than 900, a market cap of $9.5 billion, double-digit revenue increases each quarter and ownership of seven buildings locally, RIM was on the road to becoming the most successful company ever to emerge from Kitchener-Waterloo, Crowley said.

"Now and again, gentle reader, a few of you chide me for devoting too much ink to Research In Motion Ltd. But, alas, it's simply impossible to ignore a company that's this hot."[12]

RIM's amazing success was making waves throughout Waterloo Region, but that was nothing compared to the tsunami that some rank-and-file employees inside the company were riding.

Pete Gould was getting frustrated. It was the fall of 1999, and he had been chasing Don McMurtry, the vice-president of sales at RIM, for weeks, but getting nowhere. For the past eleven years, he had been working in sales at Moore Business Forms in Toronto. He had done well at Moore, winning awards and becoming the youngest sales manager in Canada for a company that had been around since 1882 and was the IBM of printing solutions. But the commute from his native Kitchener was wearing him out and besides, Moore was in a "sunset industry." Business forms were being replaced by electronic forms printed on computers. Gould had been "hearing a little bit about this company called RIM" in his own backyard. It was smaller than Moore but with a brighter future. When RIM finally did get back to him, he ran a gauntlet of interviews over a two-week period, seven to eight with different people each time, culminating in a chat with the big man himself, co-chief executive officer Jim Balsillie. When Gould finally got an offer letter, McMurtry told him the tough-love treatment was deliberate to see how tenacious Gould was. He was hired as a national account manager, selling BlackBerrys on his own. Three days later, he was called in and told they really needed someone to manage people, something he had done at Moore. He was put in charge of a sales team and given a territory — the southeastern US including the states of Florida, Alabama, Georgia and Texas. Gould laughs when he thinks back on it. It was a huge area to cover for the thirty-four-year-old business grad from Conestoga College in Kitchener, and RIM had few established customers there. He was being thrown in the deep end.

Gould and his team started by following up on leads picked up from trade shows and chasing after "value-added resellers," a fancy term for businesses that help large companies automate with computers, printers and the like. "They were a natural channel for us." But most of their sales came from cold calls to the chief information officers (CIOs) of companies on the Fortune 1000 list. "Smiling and dialing," Gould called it. Often those calls would lead to a demo. Part of the CIO's role was to investigate new technology. During the demo, Gould would hand out ten BlackBerrys for a free trial period and install software on the company's servers to make them work. "Adoption through addiction," was the strategy. The closest thing to what RIM was offering was the paging business, and it could only send alerts. "We were sending them their full in-box and connecting it to a desktop computer." And the technology was bullet-proof. "Mike (Lazaridis) and the whole product team were crazy about security." Once the trial period ended, "you couldn't get it back from them," he said. The usual response was "give me an invoice." The strategy worked for a while until Gould and others noticed that sales were stopping at the executive suite. The CIOs of these companies were happy to allow senior people to use BlackBerrys but, despite RIM's assurances about security, they were still nervous about the new wireless technology and didn't want to unleash it on the company as a whole. "You're sending data through our firewall," was the usual response.

While RIM was mulling over this dilemma, it stumbled on a "huge sweet spot" — stock brokers and lawyers. On Wall Street, data is gold. Once they had a look at what the BlackBerry could do, analysts and brokers were hooked. And lawyers loved the fact they could use their BlackBerrys in court. "Judges had no idea what they were doing," said Gould. RIM sales teams started targeting legal and brokerage firms. Gould's first big deal was with a law firm based in Lakeland, Florida, called Holland and Knight. After making contact with the CIO, a demo was set up at the firm's office. Rather than launching into a technical discussion about how the BlackBerry worked, Gould would always go right to the demo. "What's your email address?" he would ask. Grabbing his BlackBerry, Gould would send an email to the IT person's computer. In the thirty to forty seconds it would take to arrive, he would explain how the email travelled to RIM's network operations centre in Waterloo and then back to the recipient. It was nerve-wracking at first. What if the email didn't arrive? "I always had butterflies in my stomach." But it invariably did. Gould would then ask the CIO to send him an email. "Literally in two to three minutes you could establish the basis of a value proposition. That was awesome." Once the demo was successfully completed, a flurry of questions inevitably followed from the IT person. In his responses, Gould would always try to shape the conversation around the return on investment. Equipped with a BlackBerry, lawyers could stay in touch better on the road, he kept saying. "We were selling immediacy." At this point he would offer ten or twenty BlackBerrys and a server for a free trial period.

Even after they had a foot in the door, there was still a lot of heavy lifting to do. The security issue was a big hurdle, but so was the scalability question. Having the CIO and twenty executives using BlackBerrys was one thing. It could be handled with a separate server in the IT room. But equipping hundreds or even thousands of lawyers across a number of offices with devices was quite another. And the problem got even more complicated if the firm had offices outside the US. "Infrastructure management becomes a huge issue. You have to talk them through all those things." Lack of precedent was a big issue too. "It was really, really early days. You couldn't point to other big deals. There weren't any," Gould said. The next step was to bring in a bunch of TAMs, or technical account managers as they were known at RIM. A crack team of software engineers, they would explain how the wireless system worked and reassure the IT people at the law firm that it was safe and reliable. "We would use them to break through the objections." In the case of Holland and Knight, it took six to eight months to close the deal for roughly 400 BlackBerrys, Gould said. For him, the payoff was the excited reaction of customers. He would get a call from a lawyer saying he had used his BlackBerry while standing in line with his kid last night at McDonald's. He had responded to an email from a client. "Are you still at the office?" "No I'm using this new thing called a BlackBerry."

RIM was gaining traction with law firms, brokerages and Fortune 1000 companies when an enormous new channel opened up. Wireless carriers such as BellSouth, Verizon and T-Mobile in the US and Rogers and Bell in Canada decided they wanted in on the action by selling BlackBerrys directly. BellSouth had given RIM its first big order, then had balked at the idea of email, preferring a simpler two-way paging system for its RIM handhelds. That had prompted Lazaridis to buy a chunk of air time wholesale and sell it along with the BlackBerry. Initially, the carriers didn't want anything to do with RIM. "They didn't understand the software," said Gould. But as RIM started selling large chunks of the network to BlackBerry users, the carriers realized they had to act. "We were cutting them out of the loop. That drove them bananas." When the large carriers came on board, sales teams had to be reorganized in Waterloo. "It stopped being about geography and started being about each carrier," Gould explained. Large teams of finance, marketing, sales, product and operations personnel at RIM — about 100 employees in total — were assembled around each carrier. Each was a complete profit and loss unit — a business within a business — explained Gould. Chinese walls were erected around each team. Carriers did not want the same team working for two different carriers. Gould was promoted to vice-president and put in charge of the team attached to T-Mobile. Each carrier wanted its own features and apps on the BlackBerry to make them different from the competition. To accomplish this, software teams at RIM had to build a separate applications layer for each carrier's device.

Gould felt excited, even thrilled, to be selling such a cool piece of technology to a lot of high-end American customers, but at the same time it was tremendously stressful. "I was just going, going, going. There was a lot of pressure for results." He was on the road a lot, about 50 to 60 per cent of the time. But Gould and everyone else on team had to be available for the weekly sales and marketing meeting every Monday. It was an ordeal in itself. For years, it was held in the lunchroom, nicknamed the fish bowl, of RIM 2. It would begin at eight o'clock sharp with about 100 people either sitting or standing around a square table with Balsillie and various vice-presidents occupying the most prominent positions. New employees would sometimes make the mistake of sitting at the table but quickly learned the protocol for who got the best seats. As time went on, attendance grew to more than 300 with employees spilling out into the halls. Starting with New York City, marketing people would report their activities from the past week and plans for the week ahead. Sales people would give updates on deals they had closed and deals in the pipeline. Then the mike would be passed around the room. Overseas sales people were expected to call in regardless of what time it was. You had thirty seconds to give your update and Balsillie would hold you to it, Gould said. Balsillie would take notes on a single sheet of paper. If you weren't in the room or answering your phone, he would start pinging you on your BlackBerry. "You had to have your shit together."[13]

The tension would build as the microphone was passed from person to person and gradually came closer, recalls Lindsay Gibson, who worked in marketing at RIM in the early 2000s. She would give her update and then pray that Balsillie wouldn't ask her a question. "I was in my mid-20s at the time so it was like being thrown into the fire to have to talk to the CEO." Though the meetings were stressful, they were effective. "It was Jim's way of keeping a pulse on everything and I do think they worked for a long time."

While Gould pulled out all the stops to get a job at RIM, Gibson stumbled into the company by accident. At their home in the Laurelwood subdivision of Waterloo, her parents had taken in a female boarder who worked in human resources at RIM. The woman lived with them for two years, but her work didn't interest Gibson. "I never once asked her what that little black thing was she was using." One day in 2000, the woman told her RIM was looking for people to work in a call centre it had just opened in downtown Kitchener. A graduate of the print journalism program at Conestoga College in Kitchener, Gibson was having trouble finding a job in the newspaper world and was working at the local ski club. She took the job at the call centre, but it was a small office with just six people and calls were few. Growing bored, she left, saying she really wanted a job in marketing and communications at RIM. Six months later RIM called her back and offered her a job on the marketing team. She moved up quickly, creating promotions for business and retail customers. By this time, RIM was moving to the carrier model and Gibson, assigned to the T-Mobile team, spent a summer travelling from city to city in the US, educating store reps on various BlackBerry models and hyping up the retail experience.

Among the highlights of her early years at the company was an opportunity to work with *The Oprah Winfrey Show*. In 1996, Oprah started doing a show during American Thanksgiving week on her favourite products or gift ideas of the year. The show grew in popularity to become Oprah's most-watched program of the year.[14] By the early 2000s, Oprah and her team were using BlackBerrys through T-Mobile. In 2003, they chose the RIM smartphone as one of Oprah's favourite things of the year, along with about twenty other products. It's hard to believe now, given how popular Oprah's show had become, but the honour did not generate a lot of excitement at RIM. By 2003, the company had become so dominant in its market and had received so many accolades, that a tribute from the queen of daytime TV was greeted initially with yawns. The company had added 96,000 subscribers in its most recent quarter, 10,000 more than expected, pushing its subscriber base to 711,000 customers.[15] BlackBerrys were flying off the shelves. As head of T-Mobile marketing for RIM, Gibson was contacted about the Oprah show. Thrilled at the chance for RIM to go on one of America's most popular daytime programs, she put together a budget for the proposal and took it to the director of marketing. But the director was not impressed when she heard the details. Oprah wanted 350 free Black-Berrys to hand out to audience members along with other gifts from her list of favourite things. When Gibson persisted, the director left the decision up to her. "You will either be the girl who got us on the Oprah show or the girl who wasted a lot of money on the Oprah show," Gibson was told. Worried that it would be a waste of money, Gibson and her team leader had special sleeves made with the words "BlackBerry" and "T-Mobile" clearly printed on them. They were slipped over the phone boxes so viewers could see clearly who made the devices. During the taping in Chicago, Gibson nearly fainted when Oprah said "BlackBerrys for everyone from R.I.M.," pronouncing each letter of the company's name individually instead of saying Research In Motion or RIM.

The BlackBerry's appearance on the show ended up being one of the marketing highlights of the year for RIM. Alerted several days before, executives at RIM headquarters watched the show, erupting in cheers and claps when the BlackBerry was named. Sales of the brand spiked in subsequent weeks. A T-Mobile version of the BlackBerry also made Oprah's list in 2005. It was an exhilarating experience for Gibson, who worked closely with Oprah's producers to ensure it was a success. At one point, two of them asked her how to make the ring tone louder on the BlackBerry. "They couldn't even drive with their radio on at the risk of missing a call from Oprah."[16]

* * *

Paul Lucier's life changed on a golf course. While driving balls and lining up putts at the Elmira Golf Club just north of Waterloo in the summer of 1999, he ran into an old acquaintance from his days studying business at Wilfrid Laurier University. It was Dennis Kavelman, chief financial officer of RIM. It was a fortuitous encounter. The company had been on Lucier's mind lately. He had read some articles in the media about RIM and could see "something was happening." Not only that, he was thinking of making a change. An Elmira native, he was working in business development at Coca-Cola in Cambridge and Mississauga, but wanted a job closer to home. Kavelman told him to send in a resume. Nothing happened. He bumped into Kavelman again on the same golf course. Send in another resume, he was told.

This time it led to an interview and a job. Early employees at RIM often recall the order in which they were hired. Lucier was employee number 407. He couldn't have timed it better. The BlackBerry had just been launched a month earlier. When he walked in the door at RIM he couldn't believe how young his co-workers were. At twenty-eight, he was one of the older people. "I thought wow, I'm working with high school students. It was the opposite at Coke." Lucier's first job was inside sales. The department handled customers who had heard about RIM from trade shows and other sources and wanted to purchase a BlackBerry. Orders would come in on a fax machine, and Lucier's job was to "patch" over the deal — in other words, to complete the sale. One day he pulled an order from the fax machine and did a double-take. It was from Michael Dell, the Texas entrepreneur who had made a fortune selling computers directly to customers by mail, cutting out the retail middle-person. Lucier knew at that point he had come to the right place.

Sometime later, he moved to the outside sales team and was given a wide swath of the American southeast that included Florida, Oklahoma and Washington, DC. His targets were financial and legal firms. As time went by, he found himself spending more and more time in Washington, and could see that the US government was a huge, largely untapped market. He pushed for a job in government sales. There was one problem. Lucier was Canadian, and RIM wanted an American to handle the sensitive job of selling smartphones to US politicians and bureaucrats. The company already had an American sales rep in the US capital, but she was abrasive and not the best at getting along with people. RIM decided to take a shot on Lucier. He got the accounts for the Pentagon, White House and Congress. Not long after, passenger jets hijacked by terrorists hit the Twin Towers and the Pentagon. Cellphone coverage went down, but BlackBerrys miraculously did not, thanks to their packet-switching technology for transmitting data. Word got around and sales of the handheld soared. Lucier was there to ride the wave. He set up or sat in on meetings with key government officials including the top IT brass from the Department of Defense, White House, Congress and three- and four-star generals from the air force, army and marine corps. Lazaridis and Balsillie flew in to close some of the deals.

Typically, the pitch went this way. Lucier would install a light version of BlackBerry desktop software on the user's computer. The software would poll the main servers for emails and send them out to the user's

BlackBerry, or from the handheld back to the server. "It was a rough way of mimicking the key features of our full BlackBerry Enterprise Servers known as BES," he said. At that time, most IT staff knew little about wireless data and were reluctant to put a full BES into their server infrastructure for fear of bringing down the network or causing other problems. Once RIM had their managers hooked on mobile email, "getting the go-ahead to install the BES was easy and it was smooth sailing from there." Military personnel were an easy mark, Lucier said. "Generals don't like to be upstaged. Once we had one three-star or four-star general at a briefing receiving mobile emails, staff from the other meeting participants were soon calling to ensure they could hook up their superior with the same functionality."

Demand spread so quickly that before IT staff could figure out where to draw the line, everyone at the Department of Defense was requesting a BlackBerry. "It was a fun time to be calling on the US government and satisfying to know we were having a positive contribution to the war efforts after 9/11," Lucier recalled. For a guy from Elmira, Ontario, it was an incredible experience. "I had access you'd dream of getting. It was very surreal." Ironically, growing up in a small town of 15,000 people helped him deal with big-time military brass. His parents taught him humility and minor hockey taught him banter. "You had to learn to survive in a hockey dressing room and handle lots of chirping." In Washington, Lucier was thrust into some interesting situations involving people with high expectations. "You learned quickly to survive and thrive or you didn't last long." The US government became RIM's largest customer. More than 40,000 employees at the Pentagon alone were using BlackBerrys.[17]

* * *

While Lucier often had to rely on his people skills to make a deal happen, Pete Edmonson, RIM's director of research, sometimes merely acted as a prop. Part of his job was to act as government adviser. This would entail helping RIM's finance people file claims for tax credits under the federal government's Scientific Research and Experimental Development program, a scheme designed to stimulate investment by the private sector in research and technology. RIM filed some huge claims under the program that helped save the company "a bundle," he said. Occasionally he would travel to Toronto or Ottawa when RIM applied for grants from the provincial and federal governments. Playing the role of "resident PhD," Edmonson sat in on many meetings and quite often never had to say a word. On one occasion he accompanied a RIM lawyer to Washington to argue a patent rejected by the US Patent Office. "I nodded on cue but never spoke other than the usual hellos and goodbyes."

While in Ottawa to meet with the National Research Council, Edmonson went to dinner with federal politicians, including industry minister John Manley. The Ottawa Senators were in the NHL playoffs at the time and Edmonson decided to check the score of the game. Manley, a hockey fan, got really excited. He could not believe Edmonson was actually pulling up hockey scores on his BlackBerry. Though politicians were impressed by RIM's wireless technology, they seemed more interested in how many jobs the company was going to create. "I don't care if you're making anvils or radios, how many people are you going to hire?" Edmonson recalled being asked.[18]

RIM's hot new device was causing a stir in Ottawa and Washington, but back in RIM's hometown of Waterloo Region, the economy was starting to feel the impact of the company's galloping growth.

Wes Graham at the University of Waterloo in the 1980s.

University of Waterloo Archives

(from left) RIM co-founder Mike Lazaridis, employee Chris Shaw and co-founder Doug Fregin display the Budgie, the company's first product, at Fairview Park Mall in Kitchener, 1984.

University of Waterloo Archives

Gerald Hagey, the University of Waterloo's first president, played a key role in launching the university and its ground-breaking co-op education programme.

University of Waterloo Archives

Students and faculty work on the huge IBM computer housed in UW's Red Room.

University of Waterloo Archives

(from left) Jim Balsillie and Mike Lazaridis, co-CEOs of RIM, display the company's first interactive pager and a wireless data modem in the late 1990s.

Waterloo Region Record

Microsoft co-founder and former CEO Bill Gates signs autographs during a visit to the University of Waterloo in 2008.

Waterloo Region Record

Chapter 6
BOOMTOWN

Manfred Conrad could not believe what he was seeing. As he looked out the window of an office building he owned just north of the University of Waterloo, he thought he saw Mike Lazaridis. No, it couldn't be, he told himself. Not the same Mike Lazaridis he had known nearly a decade earlier. That guy was fresh out of university, wearing running shoes and jeans and riding a bicycle to work, the only tenant he had who did not own a car. The person he was looking at now was wearing a suit and driving a shiny new vehicle. Conrad's mind travelled back to those days in 1984 when he owned a small commercial plaza on Erb Street in uptown Waterloo. Lazaridis and his friend Doug Fregin had come to him looking to rent a two-room unit on the second floor. They didn't have much in the way of furniture, equipping the 500-square-foot space with old desks scrounged from their apartment and doors laid over metal trestles.[1]

Conrad was happy to provide the space, though he wasn't sure what kind of business they were involved in, something to do with wireless technology and computers. "I had no idea what these boys were doing. They were always playing on a computer." But he saw something of himself in the two young entrepreneurs. Conrad had immigrated to Canada from his native Germany in 1963 at the age of eighteen, drawn by his older brother who had already established himself in Kitchener. The pair teamed up to start a painting business but, as time went on, Conrad moved into the real estate sector, buying houses, fixing them up and selling them. "I did more and more and realized it was not a bad thing to do." Conrad is soft-spoken and affable. He gives off an almost absent-minded air and has trouble recalling some of the details of his past real estate holdings. But beneath the easy-going exterior lies an astute business mind. By the early 1980s, he was ready to take his small business, which he called the Cora Group, to the next level, but lacked the capital to get into commercial real estate. Fate intervened in the form of a real estate investor from Germany who was trying to sell an apartment building in Kitchener. He was having trouble moving the property until someone gave him Conrad's number. It helped that Conrad spoke German. The pair got talking, and Conrad helped him sell the property. They realized they had similar interests and decided to go into business together. The partnership evolved into a friendship. Bolstered by the money from his German partner and a few other investors he brought in, Conrad was able to make the leap into commercial real estate, starting with a building in north Waterloo and then the small plaza near the city's uptown occupied by the tiny startup, Research In Motion.

Two years after moving into the Erb Street plaza, Lazaridis and his small crew needed more space and moved to another strip mall closer to the University of Waterloo. Conrad didn't give them much more thought. By this time, he had bigger things in mind. Several commercial and office properties in downtown Kitchener caught his eye. At one point, he acquired so much real estate there he was dubbed the King of Kitchener's core. But Conrad was not one to put all his eggs in one basket. By the early 1990s, he set his sights on the growing number of tech companies spilling out of the University of Waterloo. Land at the corner of Columbia and Phillip Streets, just northeast of the campus, was in a great spot to attract some of these startups. "The Waterloo office sector was thriving compared to Kitchener," he explained. He didn't know it at the time, but this would end up being ground zero for

RIM and other companies in the exploding Waterloo tech sector. There, Conrad started erecting his own buildings, a trio of modest, three- to four-storey, concrete-and-glass office structures that would appeal to university grads looking to start their own businesses. He hired local architects and contractors. "I always go local," he said. "There is no shortage of knowledgeable people." He could feel electricity in the air, charged by the bright students pouring out of the doors of UW. "It was an exciting thing to be there. I spoke to the university (administration) quite a bit. We were building adjacent to it."

It wasn't long before Conrad's suspicions about Lazaridis were confirmed. More sightings revealed it was indeed his former tenant from uptown Waterloo. The bushy hair, now sporting flecks of grey, was unmistakable. Lazaridis was occupying a building about half a block away and his company, Research In Motion, was thriving. Film barcode readers, wireless point-of-sale terminals, modems for laptop computers and equipment for two-way pagers made up its product line and its workforce stood twenty-five strong and was growing rapidly. More importantly, RIM was running out of space. Soon after, Lazaridis and Balsillie paid Conrad a visit. They renewed acquaintances. Lazaridis introduced his new co-CEO. Once the pleasantries were done with, they got down to business. "Before we knew it we were dealing," said Conrad. He had an 11,000-square-foot unit at 295 Phillip available for lease. He considered it a large unit, one of four in the building. "They wanted it all."

Soon RIM filled that space and needed more. It gobbled up all of 295 Phillip Street and started moving into one of Conrad's buildings next door. He had other tenants who weren't ready to move. Among them were Open Text and MKS, prominent software companies in their own right. "I had never experienced growth like this," said the startled landlord. He was used to tenants moving in and not needing more space for five years. At one point, RIM needed to open a call centre and fast. Conrad was now their go-to guy, but he'd run out of space at Columbia and Phillip, so he offered a unit in one of his buildings in downtown Kitchener. RIM's rapid growth was starting to stress Conrad out. One day in 2000, he invited Balsillie to lunch. "You should own your own real estate," he told the RIM executive, offering him the three buildings Conrad owned near Columbia and Phillip streets. A short time later, RIM did indeed buy the three buildings for $20 million, along with two other offices nearby owned by businessman Abe Wiebe for $9.6 million.[2] Just like that, it owned five buildings in the heart of Waterloo's high-tech corridor. It was the end of Conrad's involvement with RIM for the time being. The real estate tycoon would eventually sell most of his properties in downtown Kitchener, but double down on his investments near UW, developing more office space in the university's research and tech park, with RIM leasing one of those buildings. "They were a Cinderella story," Conrad said of RIM's early days. "I was very fortunate to be a part of that story."[3]

* * *

From those five buildings at the corner of Columbia and Phillip Streets, backing on to the campus of UW, RIM spread its tentacles through the neighbourhood. Pale blue signs, adorned with the RIM logo and a swooshing wireless wave, began popping up in front of buildings on both sides of Phillip Street and spilling over onto Columbia. The company moved its manufacturing operation from south Kitchener into one of the largest buildings on Phillip Street. That section of Waterloo began to resemble a town in its own right, RIMtown. A few years later, RIM simply ran out of room in the area and began acquiring, leasing or constructing buildings in northeast Waterloo, mid-town Kitchener and northern Cambridge. At its height around 2010, it occupied more than twenty-five buildings in Waterloo Region, an equivalent of nearly 3 million square feet. It was the largest private-sector real estate holder in the region. In 2001, the company even put its name on a giant recreation complex when employees agreed to donate $2 million towards an ambitious project launched by the City of Waterloo to mark the turn of the millennium. Indoor hockey rinks, gymnasiums, soccer fields, outdoor pitches and a golf course sprawled over 200 hectares in the northeast corner of Waterloo.[4] The name would later be tarnished when an investigation by the *Record* revealed that the city had been duped by the financing company into paying double the expected cost of the vast complex. All the same, RIM Park, as the recreation facility is called, is the only building in the region that still bears the Research In Motion name today, as the company changed its name to BlackBerry in 2013.

While Conrad let Research In Motion slip through his grasp, John Whitney did not. For nearly twenty years, from the rise of the company in the mid-1990s, through its middle period when BlackBerry sales stalled but RIM kept hiring and needed more space, he acted as the company's agent on most of their real estate transactions. The ones he didn't work on were handled by RIM without an agent. It was a plum job, one that any agent in the region would kill for. Nonetheless, he is vague about how he landed the coveted position. "I had met Jim Balsillie," he explained. "The company was beginning to grow." It was early days and cash was tight. "They would always remind you they had no money." Other agents might have bailed, but Whitney hung in there. It was a smart move. Like gold records won by a pop superstar, plaques listing the buildings he helped RIM acquire over the years line the walls of Whitney's office in north Waterloo. There is even a picture of him cycling with Lance Armstrong, the Tour de France champion who was hired to promote the BlackBerry. Armstrong was brought to Waterloo Region three times by Balsillie to lead fundraising rides for cancer, before losing his titles in a doping scandal. Apart from RIM, Whitney also kept his fingers on the pulse of the tech sector in general, helping to found Communitech, the association representing tech firms in the region, and serving as its board chair until 2006.

A veteran of more than forty years in the real estate business and the fourth generation of his family to work in the field, Whitney has the inscrutable mien and unflappable temperament of a poker player in a high-stakes game. There were other cards in his hand, but RIM gave him four aces. "They were an awesome client, a fantastic client." He helped engineer the company's first big deal, the acquisition of Conrad's three buildings and the two others owned by Abe Wiebe at Columbia and Phillip streets. Being close to UW and its steady supply of grads was paramount, the need underscored by the signs Lazaridis placed on the back of his buildings so students couldn't miss the RIM logo as they gazed out the window or walked around campus. "They loved being at Columbia and Phillip," said Whitney. The company's strategy of acquiring buildings in close proximity to its headquarters made sense to him. "Whenever you try to create a campus, you want it as close to the mother ship as possible." The university area was suburban with ample parking, another quality sought by RIM as most employees preferred to drive to work. RIM would buy buildings in blocks and if tenants occupied them, it would wait until the leases expired, then move in. It preferred to purchase, but would lease if necessary. Whitney and his staff spent a lot of time analyzing the market. As RIM's appetite for space grew more voracious, an accurate read of the market was essential. "It was fast and furious. They kept on growing." Many layers of staff inside the company were dedicated to handling property matters, including procurement, construction, legal, design and architectural teams. "It was a big organization. They were very corporate about how they did things. Nothing happened overnight." Size brought the need for confidentiality and Whitney handled the deals without revealing the identity of his star client. While RIM was a prize client, he brought the same approach to each deal, regardless of the customer. "Whenever you're working with a client, the strategy is comparable." RIM scrutinized everything. It turned down lots of buildings if conditions such as price or parking weren't suitable, he noted.

As land and buildings grew scarce, Whitney was forced to look farther afield. Northern Cambridge, with its ample supply of industrial buildings and close proximity to Highway 401 was an obvious target. RIM purchased several buildings there, including a plant once used to make solar panels by ATS Automation Tooling, a large factory automation company in the area. Another acquisition was a giant, 500,000-square-foot plant once used to make furniture and shelving products. Purchased in 2009, it was the largest building in RIM's real-estate portfolio and served as a network operations centre to route wireless traffic. In northeast Waterloo near the RIM Park recreation complex, the company purchased fifteen hectares of vacant land in 2008 from Dalsa, another tech company in the city. Dalsa was planning to expand, but changed its mind and decided to sell. On that parcel, RIM erected a cluster of four modern office buildings that serve as BlackBerry's headquarters today. "As RIM continued to grow it needed more than a one-off building," explained Whitney, adding that the Dalsa deal took more than two years to complete. Looking back at that era, he still marvels at RIM's explosive growth. "They were such a big player in the marketplace. The amount of suburban office space they occupied was incredible."[5]

RIM's strategy of locating its main campus on the doorstep of UW with its world-class reputation and enormous co-op program was nothing short of brilliant, said John Lind, a commercial real estate agent with Colliers International in Kitchener. "They were so far ahead of the curve on recruiting talent." Despite their prime location, the buildings themselves were not fancy. Often repurposed factories or offices made of pre-cast concrete, there was a uniformity to them that made it hard to tell which building was the headquarters, if one existed at all. Lazaridis and Balsillie even worked in separate buildings in their later years with the company. The structures were replete with technology, including generators for power backup, wellness centres and heating systems to melt the snow around the entrances, said Lind. A joke used to make the rounds at his office. "BlackBerry's buildings are what happens when you give engineers an unlimited budget."[6]

* * *

While RIM was disrupting the commercial real estate market, employees of the company and other tech firms were also having a major impact on the housing market in Waterloo Region. In the early months of 2000, the biggest worry seemed to be whether Waterloo Region had enough high-end homes for all the employees at RIM about to cash in their stock options and vault into the six- and seven-figure income brackets. Although RIM wasn't the only local company riding the dot-com wave, it was leading the charge. "There are a couple of thousand new lottery winners, so to speak, who are saying there is no place to live in Kitchener-Waterloo," David Gillians, a vice-president of TD Bank, told a housing seminar in the spring of 2000. "A house worth $500,000 is the low end of what they are looking for and there is no inventory out there." At RIM alone, 6.5 million stock options ranging from $3.40 to $13.40 per share were about to vest at a share price nearing $60, he noted.[7] Later in the year, the Kitchener-Waterloo Real Estate Board reported a doubling of sales in higher-priced homes over the previous two years and a surge in construction of custom, estate-style homes.

Gillians was later accused of exaggerating the shortage, but there was no denying that something was happening in the housing market. There was Laurelwood, the wooded suburb northwest of UW where so many RIM employees had bought houses that it was unofficially called RIM wood. Flush with options and good salaries, they could afford to look in nicer neighbourhoods. Buyers looking to upgrade to a home in the $250,000 to $275,000 range were now shooting for something in the $350,000 to $400,000 price bracket, said Helen Alpaugh, an agent with Re/Max Twin City Realty.[8]

Bruce Nicholson started to notice something unusual around 2000. All of a sudden, buyers were coming in with cash offers when normally an offer would be conditional on arranging financing or the sale of their existing home. "It's not like there were hundreds of them," said Nicholson, president of the Kitchener-Waterloo Real Estate Board in 1999–2000. But it was a noticeable trend. He did some investigating and learned many of them were employees of Research In Motion. Many were young, in their thirties and forties, and their demands were as diverse as the people who were making them. One purchaser with options to cash in worked in shipping. "He was looking for a hobby farm west of town." Was there ever a serious shortage of homes? "We saw pockets in the market where inventory got used up, but nothing to the degree of the last few years," said Nicholson, referring to the recent overheated housing market.[9]

Jim McIntyre cashed in more than most real estate agents during the dot-com buying surge of the early 2000s. An agent with Re/Max Solid Gold Realty, he had as many as fifty RIM employees as clients, many of them coming to him in the late 1990s and early 2000s when the company was starting to make a serious dent in the market. "I met my first RIM person at an open house. It just rolled from there by referral, which was huge." If he got a lead from a department head at RIM looking for a house in the $1-million range, McIntyre might end up selling houses to five other RIM employees. Most were anxious to protect their privacy. "They didn't broadcast the fact they were from RIM." McIntyre didn't take those RIM clients for granted. He would take them out for lunch or dinner, give them a tour of the region, even take them to plays in town. "In terms of red-carpet treatment, I did that for everyone. Maybe a bit more for some people, depending on the client." Of the roughly 1,000 agents in the region at the time, about twenty-five got most of the business from RIM employees, McIntyre estimates. "I would say I was in the top 20, maybe the top 10." BlackBerry workers "were part of making the market hot, definitely." There were brief shortages of the kind of housing they wanted, but nothing prolonged. "They brought the inventory down, but not dramatically," said McIntyre.[10]

Stock options allowed many people at RIM to skip buying a starter home and vault right into a more expensive property, said Lucier. They were "pretty lucrative" for a lot of people. "It was a lottery win." It didn't hurt that in the fall of 2000 the federal government lowered the tax on stock-option profits to 50 per cent from 75 per cent just a year earlier.[11] When he started at RIM in 1999, Lucier wasn't even sure what stock options were. Coca-Cola, his former employer, didn't hand them out. Options allow the recipient to buy company stock at a fixed price over a period of time. If the value of the stock goes up, the options are worth money. If the stock goes down, they are said to be underwater or worthless. Typically, options are granted when an employee joins the company, performs well or is promoted. Usually they vest over a number of years, meaning recipients can't exercise them until they have worked at the company for some time. A way for cash-strapped firms to reward employees, they also offer an incentive to work hard so the company's stock will rise. The options he received "made us comfortable," Lucier admitted. "My wife didn't work for 18 years." Employees at RIM in the early years made the most off stock options. Timing was often critical. "The first wave cashed out millions," said Lucier. The money spoiled some people. Corvettes, Maseratis and other fancy cars started showing up in RIM parking lots. "There was a culture of entitlement. There was excess." But it wasn't crazy or out of control. Silicon Valley was worse, and plenty of foreign students at UW drive expensive cars now, he said.[12]

Pete Gould would get an email from RIM payroll telling him his stock option cheque had arrived. When he went to pick it up, envelopes were laid out like Christmas cards on a display case for himself and other employees. "When you open up the envelope and see a six-figure cheque with your name on it, it's a pretty frickin' incredible feeling." Gould sold his house and bought a new home worth about $500,000 before some of his options had vested. The house had a $350,000 mortgage on it. He was nervous about meeting the payments. Six months later, he walked into the bank and handed the teller a cheque big enough to retire the mortgage. "That happened to a lot of people," Gould said. Employees didn't even have to buy the shares. The company would buy them for you at the option price, sell them at the actual price and send you a cheque for the difference, he said.[13]

Most employees didn't have the money to exercise their stock options, said Rob Elder, who started working at RIM in sales in 1999. He paid off his mortgage with his option money, but didn't blow it all. He attributes his prudence to age. Elder was thirty-five when he started working at RIM. "I was one of the old guys." "Plenty of folks made some serious coin" off their options, said Elder. But engineers at RIM did five times better than he did. "They were more important." And if you were in a leadership role, you made a killing, he noted. There was a lot of conspicuous consumption. "Car dealers loved RIM."[14]

Dale Brubacher-Cressman started early enough at RIM — he was employee number five — to get nickel shares. Just like their name suggested, they had a strike price of five cents. He sold them at $50 to realize a thousand-fold gain. With some of his option money, he moved back to his native New Hamburg, a small town west of Kitchener, bought a century-old home and put a $100,000 addition on it. "The cars got a little newer, the houses got a little nicer" for RIM employees, he said, but among his colleagues, spending was not reckless. "Most of my circle were technical engineering types. We were more grounded." He did well enough financially to leave RIM at age forty-two in 2005 to start his own firm with several friends designing and building solar-energy systems. He also founded a community energy co-op that helps average people finance renewable-energy projects. "That was my first retirement," he said. He's now into his second retirement and spends his time sitting on boards and investing in startups.[15]

Levels of affluence can vary widely. There's modest wealth and then there's private-jet wealth. Apart from the founders and a few others at the top of the company, most people at RIM fell into the former category, said David Yach, chief technology officer for software at the company. The vast majority of employees who benefited significantly from stock options either bought a house or paid down a car loan, he said. Options helped to boost the net worth of young people in their twenties and thirties to the level of someone in their fifties and sixties. "It's a huge liberation when you're not stressed out about money," said Yach who worked at RIM from 1998 to 2012. "But it wasn't lifestyles of the rich and famous." Many employees at RIM were math and engineering grads who were not inclined to blow all their money like a lottery winner or Hollywood celebrity living an unsustainable lifestyle, Yach said.[16]

Yach's observation that stock options and RIM shares were heavily skewed towards the founders was evident in how the money was spent around town. Lazaridis poured $170 million in several installments into Perimeter Institute for Theoretical Physics, his think tank in uptown

Waterloo, while Balsillie pumped $100 million into the Centre for International Governance Innovation (CIGI) and the Balsillie School of International Affairs. And Doug Fregin and Balsillie topped up Lazaridis's gifts to Perimeter Institute with significant contributions of their own. Their largesse was rewarded with some of the best real estate in the core. An eye-catching structure with a black façade overlooking Waterloo Park was erected to house Perimeter, and a buff-stone and glass edifice popped up nearby to house CIGI and the Balsillie School, which the RIM boss subsequently launched in collaboration with the two universities. A cluster of high-end condos and a fancy hotel have sprung up around the two think tanks, breathing new life into an area once blighted by empty warehouses and factories. Behind the CIGI building looms an assemblage of boxy, yellow-brick structures with small windows and blue shutters, once filled with Seagram whisky barrels, now tastefully renovated into plush condos.

The Institute for Quantum Computing took root at the University of Waterloo thanks to another whopping donation from Lazaridis and his wife Ophelia — this time $101 million — with Fregin chipping in $35 million of his own cash. And Wilfrid Laurier University decided to name its business school after Lazaridis when he gave $20 million to the institution for a new school focusing on high-tech entrepreneurship. Meanwhile, Michael Barnstijn, employee number three at RIM, and his wife, Louise MacCallum, also on the company payroll, sprinkled a total of $30 million around the area for a variety of causes including the Kitchener Waterloo Community Foundation, a museum in downtown Kitchener and a nature preserve in Cambridge.

The shares doled out to ordinary employees paled in comparison. Yet for young people, it seemed like a fortune. Gibson, who worked in marketing at RIM in the early 2000s, was among a group of employees in their twenties who suddenly had a lot of money in their bank accounts. With $150,000 in options money, she was able to pay off her student loan and put a down payment on her first house. "For a lot of people I worked with, it was a windfall." But the flaunting of wealth and the partying by some employees in her age group soon turned her off. At local bars like the

Flying Dog and Club Abstract, they would walk in like celebrities flashing their BlackBerrys and wallets and "just throw money around." "Guys were showing up (at work) driving Corvettes. It was just obnoxious." At some point, she stopped hanging out with the revellers and the big spenders. "I'm quite introverted." The rock-and-roll lifestyle wasn't unique to RIM. Gibson went to lavish events put on by carriers in places like Las Vegas. The peak in extravagance was an event staged by T-Mobile in San Francisco. The carrier rented Alcatraz island. The Barenaked Ladies and Train performed on a stage that was open at the back so you could see downtown San Francisco. At RIM's annual conference for carriers in Orlando, Balsillie would rent a suite that only certain people were invited to, where the booze flowed freely and the cigar smoke was thick. "It felt like *Mad Men*," Gibson said, referring to a popular TV show of the time. At one point a whole sales crew from Latin America was fired en masse after their spending and revelry got out of control, she said. Not everyone at RIM spent their wealth wisely. Some people lost their jobs and have struggled ever since. "You get accustomed to a lifestyle that's not sustainable."[17]

Edmonson, RIM's director of research, left the company in 2001 and started his own biotechnology company with a friend from Atlanta. "You don't have to hold a collection for me," he said when asked if he benefited from RIM's stock option program. Edmonson saw lots of people, flush with cash, blowing their money. Options flowed freely. "There were wheelbarrows full of them." Some employees bought expensive houses but forgot they had to furnish them and pay taxes on them. One single parent spent her windfall on a $50,000 Volvo. "It was decadence, sheer decadence." The BMW dealership in north Waterloo did extremely well thanks to RIM. "Everyone had a Bimmer. I had a pickup truck," he said.[18]

* * *

Edmonson's observation that RIM handed out stock options by the wheelbarrow was not far off the mark. More than 2,000 employees received options from 1996 to 2006, according to an internal investigation of the company's stock option program conducted in 2007. And employees who took advantage of RIM's option-purchase program were numerous. That was the program, known officially as the "net settlement" feature, in which the company would exercise the options for each employee, sell them at the going price and cut a cheque for the difference. A total of $220 million US was distributed to employees in this manner until the option-purchase program was eliminated in 2002. It's a stunning number, the impact of which meant that millions of dollars were injected into the economy of Waterloo Region and beyond if employees decided to spend it. Surprisingly, RIM failed to account for this expense, known as "variable accounting," in its financial statements. This was okay according to Canadian accounting rules until 2004, but not according to US rules. It forced the company to take a special $220 million US charge against earnings in 2007, lowering its earnings per share and stock price in the process.

The internal review also found numerous inconsistencies in the way stock options were granted. When RIM handed out options to new employees, some got sweeter deals than others. Their options were priced on the date they accepted the job rather than the day before their start date. Or they were based on the lowest trading price between acceptance and start date. In some cases, employees who were promoted got options priced according to an earlier date rather than the date of the promotion. In other cases, new options were granted or re-priced because they were under water; in other words, RIM's stock price had fallen below the option price. Sometimes options were handed out to groups, but the date for pricing them was selected before all the eligible individuals were determined. At times, documentation was so poor that it was impossible to determine the proper measurement date of the options. The stock option program seemed like one giant candy store with few rules on when you could help yourself. Rules were tightened after that so that options were approved on a quarterly basis by RIM's board of directors through its compensation committee instead of being subject to the whims of various RIM executives.[19]

The 2007 internal review also found evidence of stock-option back-dating at RIM, a practice that had sparked the review in the first place. Launched in 2006, RIM's review was an attempt by the company to get out in front of a growing controversy over stock-option back-dating among publicly traded companies in the US. In Ontario, the practice worked this way: Stock options were usually granted at the price of the company's stock on that day. But the options didn't have to be reported to the Ontario Securities Commission (OSC) for ten days. A company could look back over this ten-day window, choose the day when the stock was at its lowest value and claim the options were granted on that day. Prior to 1999, when the regulations were tightened, the window was even wider, as much as forty days. The controversy had erupted in the US when a University of Iowa finance professor named Erik Lie stumbled upon evidence of widespread back-dating during an innocent study of stock options and their impact in 2003. When he took his findings to the *Wall Street Journal*, it launched its own investigation, confirming many of Lie's revelations. The *WSJ*'s stories led the Securities and Exchange Commission (SEC) to launch its own investigation of more than 100 US companies.[20]

While it found evidence of back-dating at RIM, the review committee concluded that it was not intentional. Balsillie, Chief Financial Officer Dennis Kavelman and others who supervised the program thought it was okay to choose any grant date within the allotted windows, the committee said. It also found that the majority of the gains had gone to senior executives such as Lazaridis and Balsillie. No figures were included, but RIM was forced to take an additional $30 million US charge against earnings, on top of the $220 million US for variable accounting violations. To atone for these errors, executives agreed to return any benefit from exercised options and re-price unexercised options granted at below-market value. Balsillie agreed to step down as board chair, Kavelman was moved to chief operating officer and Balsillie and Lazaridis donated up to $5 million each to cover the costs of the review.[21]

Though RIM's committee found no intent behind the back-dating, the SEC and OSC disagreed. Collaborating on their own probe, the two regulatory bodies found plenty of evidence that company executives knew exactly what they were doing in back-dating options and, in some cases, tried to hide it from regulators. "We view the fact that this occurred over a 10-year period (1996–2006) to be a shocking fact," said OSC vice-chair James Turner when the results of the investigation were released in 2009. Balsillie, Lazaridis and Kavelman were ordered by the OSC to reimburse RIM a total of $83.1 million and fined a combined $9 million, including $1 million in court costs. Balsillie was suspended from RIM's board for a year and Kavelman banned from serving on any board for five years. Lest anyone shed a tear for the beleaguered BlackBerry executives over the whopping $83.1 million in penalties, the loss was a paper one only. The three men were allowed to reimburse the company by forfeiting stock options worth that amount.[22]

Sometimes disputes over stock options at RIM ended up in the courts. In 1993, Bryan Taylor was hired at RIM after graduating from the computer engineering program at UW. He rose steadily through the ranks to the position of vice-president of engineering, a title he held through the design and development of the BlackBerry. In 1999, his performance was good enough to earn him a grant from RIM's stock option program. The grant gave Taylor the right to purchase 40,000 shares in 2005 at 1999 prices. For Taylor, it was potential multi-million-dollar windfall. But in 2004, Taylor began missing a lot of time at work to care for a close relative diagnosed with a serious illness. When he asked the company to reduce his hours and the extensive travel required for his job, RIM suggested he retire or take an unpaid leave of absence. Taylor decided to take a six-month leave but when he returned to work, Balsillie told him he would be fired unless he resigned first. When Taylor refused to resign, he was dismissed. He was given eight months' salary as severance pay but denied his stock options. For its part, RIM argued that concerns about Taylor's performance had developed long before the illness of his relative. His duties were gradually reduced to the point where he no longer played a significant role in the company, RIM said.

Taylor was frequently absent from work and RIM officials often didn't know where he was or what he was working on. Taylor filed suit for wrongful dismissal and the case dragged on for several years while lawyers conducted the examination for discovery process. Though none of the allegations were proven in court, RIM eventually agreed that Taylor was entitled to the 40,000 stock options. What neither side could agree upon, however, was the value of the options. RIM argued that Taylor would have bought and sold the shares as soon as the options vested for a profit of $4.4 million. This had been his practice in the past. Taylor argued he would have held on to the shares until they increased in value to $11.6 million. The matter had to be settled in court, with the judge eventually ruling in 2010 that Taylor would have sold three-quarters of the stocks immediately and kept the rest until they increased in value. He also ordered the two sides to settle the amount of damages privately, meaning that RIM would have eventually paid Taylor about $6.2 million.[23]

Chapter 7
SILICON VALLEY NORTH

When Research In Motion held its initial public offering of shares on the Toronto Stock Exchange in the fall of 1997, it was not alone. Five other high-tech companies from Waterloo Region also went public around that time. Open Text Corp. was the first, listing its shares on the Nasdaq exchange in the US in January 1996, raising $60 million US in the process. The company offered two products: a search engine to sort through the public Internet and private intranets shared by companies and organizations; and a software platform that enabled users of private intranets to share, update and organize their documents. Like Open Text, two other companies in the group of six were primarily software businesses. Mortice Kern Systems, later rebranded as MKS, was launched by four UW grads in 1984 and offered tools to make the software development process more efficient. Descartes Systems Group, also founded by grads from UW in 1981, started out developing distribution software for beverage and food companies but evolved into supplying logistics software for shipping and supply-chain management businesses. Two firms in the group were rooted in the hardware space. Com Dev specialized in components for space satellites and was launched in 1974 by an Irish immigrant to Montreal named Val

O'Donovan, who developed a new kind of transponder that combined multiple signals into one data stream. He moved the firm to Cambridge in 1979 to tap into the area's deep talent pool. Dalsa Corp. emerged in 1980 out of research by UW prof Savvas Chamberlain into a microchip that could capture tiny images in sharp and precise detail. Dalsa's image sensors and cameras were used in a range of products including fax machines, machine-vision systems and medical imaging equipment.

There was a seventh company from Waterloo that also went public in the mid-1990s. Certicom, which specialized in data encryption, was created in 1985 by three professors from UW, two of whom were students of William Tutte, the code-breaker from the Second World War. But the company decided to move to Mississauga in the early 1990s to be closer to the larger Toronto tech community. Certicom cryptography would later form the foundation of the BlackBerry's vaunted security system, and the company would be acquired by RIM in a hostile takeover in 2009.

It would be easy to point to this period from 1996–98 when the Waterloo Six went public as the birth of the local tech sector. Observers in the Canadian tech community and business world at large suddenly sat up and took notice. Who were these six upstarts, all from one area, listing their shares on stock markets in Canada and the US? Investors also took notice and snapped up shares. All except Dalsa were valued at more than $100 million. Going public is a way for companies to raise capital to expand their product lines. It's not intended as a means to attract attention to a community. But that was the indirect impact. Waterloo was suddenly on the map as a high-tech hub. Adding momentum was the emergence at the same time of Communitech, modelled on similar tech associations in Ottawa and Boston. A group of tech leaders in the area, including Balsillie and Tom Jenkins of Open Text, had been meeting informally for several years and decided to kick in $5,000 each and turn it into a formal organization. Membership in the local chamber of commerce would not suffice. They wanted a separate voice to share strategy and speak to the policy-makers in government and the wider world.

But declaring this period in the 1990s as the birth of the local tech cluster would be wrong. It was more a coming of age for the Waterloo tech community, observed Gary Will, the writer and startup consultant who followed the Waterloo tech scene closely at that time. Apart from Open Text, which began in 1989, the other five enterprises were all at least ten years old and Com Dev had been in business for more than twenty. All six had gone through long gestation periods, developed and refined their products and services and reached the stage where a springboard was necessary to catapult them to the next stage of growth. Working in their favour as well was the dot-com boom of the 1990s, triggering a wave of IPOs on stock markets. "It was a crazy period," recalled Will. The timing was good, the circumstances were ideal and all six companies were "at the right age and maturity" to go public, he said.[1]

To understand the birth of the Waterloo tech sector, you have to go back 100 years, to the early twentieth century, when Kitchener entrepreneur Arthur Pollock obtained the rights to manufacture a record player without an exterior horn. Calling his company Pollock Manufacturing, he moved aggressively into the production of phonographs, radios, furniture, electric fans and, after the Second World War, televisions. By this time the company was called Electrohome and before long it was pumping out more TV sets than any other firm in Canada. At one point it employed 1,400 people and had ten manufacturing plants in the Twin Cities that also produced radios, organs, stereos, speakers and amplifiers. By the mid-1980s, cheaper products from Japan prompted Electrohome to abandon the TV market. Led by John Pollock, the third generation of the family, it pivoted into projection systems for rock concerts, political conventions, corporate trade shows and control room displays, systems that were produced from its one remaining plant in Kitchener. From there it moved into the production of digital cinema projectors in the 2000s, rebranding itself Christie Digital after forming a partnership with a competing firm, Christie Inc. of California.

Electrohome was not the only firm to play a role in igniting the Waterloo tech sector, yet it has earned the title of granddaddy of area technology firms and for good reason. Apart from its long history in electronics, it has also played a role in other aspects of technology growth in the region. In the 1950s, Carl Pollock, the second generation of the family, persuaded the Massachusetts military contractor Raytheon to open a plant in Waterloo as part of a joint venture with Electrohome. By the 1990s, Raytheon Canada employed more than 600 in the city and was making radar equipment and air traffic control systems for civil and military customers, a business that continues to this day in reduced capacity. Carl Pollock was also among the industrialists who joined the Associate Faculties at Waterloo College, the same group that drove the creation of the University of Waterloo in the late 1950s. From there, UW's trailblazing engineering, math and computer science departments laid the foundation for a blossoming tech sector that emerged in the 1980s with companies such as Watcom, RIM, Dalsa, Open Text and Maplesoft, a company specializing in mathematics software, as well as a slew of smaller startups.

By the late-1980s, Waterloo was already branding itself as Silicon Valley North thanks largely to the efforts of a marketing organization known as Canada's Technology Triangle (CTT). Funded by local governments including the City of Guelph, which formed the third point in the triangle along with Kitchener-Waterloo and Cambridge, the CTT's job was to attract foreign investment and companies interested in setting up shop to the region. But the real coming out party happened in the mid-1990s with the listing of the Waterloo Six on the public stock markets, noted Will. He might have mentioned another sign of the emergence of the local tech community: his blog. Every movement needs an oracle, someone to chronicle the story of its growth and development and no one did it better, longer and in more compelling fashion than Gary Will. He started his online blog in 1996 before blogs were trendy and continued writing a monthly analysis and summary of the Waterloo tech sector for the next fourteen years, attracting more than 5,000 subscribers in the local tech community and beyond, including many RIM employees. For anyone following tech in the area, it was a must-read. When the *Record* started its annual tech supplement in 1998, another signpost on the road to tech-sector prominence, it hired Will to write some of the features. For the second edition in 1999, he wrote nearly every article in the publication and continued to be a regular contributor for years after. Few writers combined his knowledge of computer technology and his later work counselling startups and the ability to convey it all in a clear and readable fashion. During an interview for this book, Will lamented that the fiftieth anniversary of the WATFOR Compiler, the mega-selling educational software program created at the University of Waterloo, had passed in 2017 without any celebration to mark the occasion. "It was a major milestone and a huge deal for the university's reputation." The importance of UW in the creation of the Waterloo tech sector can't be underestimated, he said. Without UW "Waterloo would have been Peterborough." Unlike many, RIM's stunning success did not catch him by surprise. "It happened gradually. I read every single press release."

The son of a civil engineering prof at the University of Toronto, Will earned his BA in applied math and statistics at U of T, then did a master's degree in history and the philosophy of science and technology. Asked where his interest in technology comes from, he shrugs. "My dad was a professor of engineering. That's the obvious answer." Then he adds, "I don't know. I was good at math and science." After graduating from U of T in the late 1980s, he started his own software and marketing business — clients included the Bank of Montreal and the Law Society of Upper Canada — which he continued to run after following a friend, now his wife, to Waterloo in 1992. The Waterloo tech digest, his monthly blog, emerged in 1996 when he signed up for an Internet account with a local service provider and learned he could have his own website. "I had to put something on it." He started by summarizing business news in the *Record* and the weekly *Waterloo Chronicle* and within a few months was generating his own content. "I was very good at finding stuff on the Internet." He wrote the whole thing over a weekend. Before long, Will was generating enough traffic to attract the interest of advertisers. Initially he balked. They wanted a six-month commitment. "I was worried I would even do it next month." In the end he began accepting ads for a three-month period, enough to justify working on the blog two days a month.[2] Will couldn't have picked a better time to start his blog. In addition to the IPOs of the Waterloo Six, there was plenty of other stuff going on, but no company was going through more drama at the time than Open Text.

* * *

Tom Jenkins felt like someone had punched him in the stomach. Open Text's stock was plummeting and there was little the CEO could do about it. The company had explained to investors participating in its IPO that it was facing a difficult decision. It could no longer operate both a public search engine on the Internet and a private search engine for clients behind corporate firewalls. One of them would have to go. Operating both required vastly different rollouts and was draining too many resources from Open Text. And it was looking increasingly like the axe would fall on the public search engine. The competition was just getting too intense. In 1995, the Waterloo software company had signed a deal with California-based Yahoo! to allow it to use the Open Text Index search engine on its directory of websites. The partnership was potentially lucrative for both sides. Yahoo! now had the search technology it lacked and Open Text would get half of the advertising revenue for every page retrieved by its search engine. Bolstered by this new source of revenue, the Waterloo company felt like it finally had the muscle to take on the four other contenders fighting it out for search-engine supremacy on the still-youthful Internet. Like the Open Text Index, which had emerged from the University of Waterloo, three of the competitors had sprung from American universities: Excite from Stanford in California, Lycos from Carnegie Mellon in Pittsburgh and Infoseek from the University of Massachusetts. The fourth, Alta Vista, was developed by computer manufacturer Digital Equipment Corp.[3] But then disaster had struck. In the summer of 1996, just after Open Text had completed its IPO, Jenkins got a call from Tim Koogle, the chief executive of Yahoo! The California web portal had just signed a deal to bring Alta Vista's search engine to Yahoo! Open Text could remain on Yahoo! as well as long as it offered its search engine for free as Alta Vista had done. Once he got over the shock of this news, Jenkins could see the offer made no sense. "We immediately thought that this was crazy since running the site would cost tens of millions of dollars per year."[4] His hunch proved correct. In a filing with the SEC in 1996, Alta Vista revealed its startup costs for the Yahoo! site had soared past $100 million.

The Alta Vista deal made Open Text's decision an obvious one. It would have to abandon the public search engine market and pour all its resources into the private intranet market, where its search engine would operate behind corporate firewalls. The board of directors approved the decision and Open Text made plans to sell off its Internet technology and web traffic. All was going according to plan until Open Text announced publicly that it would no longer have a search engine on Yahoo! Investors reacted with horror. Yahoo! was something they knew and understood. They used it regularly. In their minds, the private market had far less glamour and potential. Intranet? Was that a spelling mistake? A massive selloff began, plunging Open Text stock from $20 to $2 in less than six months. Layoffs soon followed, and the company was forced to close its offices in California and Paris. For Jenkins, it was "a near-death experience."[5] He had been president and CEO for less than two years. Jenkins had the aura of the all-Canadian boy — young, ambitious, good-looking and on the fast-track to success. Now, at thirty-six, it looked as though his career might be in tatters.

A native of Hamilton, Jenkins had studied business at McMaster University, then earned his master's degree in science at the University of Toronto and his MBA at York University. A job as vice-president of sales at Dalsa, the image-sensor startup, brought him to Waterloo in the late 1980s. "You don't forget Tom," recalls Sam Ogilvie, a test technician at Dalsa at that time. "Tom came in with a whole different air. He was the guy with drive. He wanted to go fast, go far and go high." Jenkins would think nothing of calling at three o'clock in the morning, excited about some new idea, Ogilvie said, and then expect you to get right on it. Though he was driven, he had a fun side too. Dalsa was just beginning to make high-precision sensors but didn't have a clean room yet with specialized filters to keep out contaminants. Ogilvie and his colleagues would be "all garbed up" nonetheless, working on the sensors in a separate room with the regular air-conditioning turned on. Jenkins would bring customers or guests through on a tour, crack open the door and in hushed tones say, "you can feel the air pressure." Eyes widening, the guests would nod in wonder. "Tom was always a bit of a spinner," said Ogilvie.[6] At some point, he and Dalsa founder and CEO Savvas Chamberlain had a parting of ways. Dalsa wasn't growing fast enough, and Jenkins soon found a company that was.

Abandoning the Internet search engine was a difficult decision for Jenkins and Open Text. The company's history, its *raison d'être*, its pride and glory were all tied up in its search engine. When the University of Waterloo won the contract to digitize the *Oxford English Dictionary* in 1984 over thirteen other bidders, UW president Doug Wright turned to two computer science professors, Frank Tompa and Gaston Gonnet, to lead the project. They assembled a team of five full-time programmers and a handful of co-op and grad students to begin the enormous task of digitizing the 60 million words and 600,000 definitions filling twenty volumes that made up the OED. It would take the team three years and 400 million keystrokes to finish the job. Each entry had to be tagged, coded and indexed using software developed at UW. Software was created so it could be edited as well. The next step was to build a search engine to find and display any word or string of words within seconds in the massive database. Using two different software programs developed at UW, the team was able to complete this task in about a year. The result was a browser "that was light years ahead of anything on the market in the early '90s in terms of speed."[7]

With the OED project now complete, the team had to figure out what to do next. As it progressed, the project had attracted international attention with scholars and linguists visiting UW or requesting information on the work. UW had also begun selling the search engine software to universities such as Stanford, Columbia and Princeton, earning about $100,000 a year. But government and university funding on both sides of the ocean had now run out. The only alternative was to see if the OED project could be turned into a commercial enterprise. Early in 1990, Open Text Systems opened its doors in a tiny office in Waterloo Town Square, the main shopping mall in uptown Waterloo, with four full-time employees and eight investors. The founders were Tompa and Gonnet, the two profs who had led the OED venture, and Tim Bray, a Vancouver programmer who had joined the OED team in 1986 after spotting a help-wanted ad about the project. The launch looked half-baked at first. Tompa and Gonnet kept their jobs at UW while re-mortgaging their houses to finance the startup. That left Bray as the only full-time employee among the three founders. His investment consisted of cashed-in RRSPs and a loan co-signed by his mother.

Business was slow at first. "The main problem was that our stuff was built for the Internet, but the Internet really wasn't there yet," said Bray. With early sales coming mostly from university libraries, the company decided it needed to break into the commercial market by installing its search and sorting software behind corporate firewalls in the private intranet network. Traction came slowly but surely with customers such as Mutual Life in Waterloo, Grolier Publishing, auto-manufacturer Peugeot, the government of Japan and consulting giant Booz Allen and Hamilton eventually jumping on board. Open Text's search technology was simply better than the rest. Not only could it search words, it could find phrases such as "to be or not to be," something the competition could not do. In the meantime, rumours were starting to circulate about an exciting new thing called the World Wide Web. At a conference in the fall of 1994, Bray heard a speech on the coming web and the need for search technology to find data on it. His mind started racing. Could Open Text's search engine be the answer? It could crawl and parse. The only missing piece was a web server. "It could all be done and it wouldn't be that complicated. I got so excited that I was physically shaking on and off for the next three days." By this time Bray had moved back to

Vancouver but had continued to work full-time for Open Text. He went home and found an Internet service provider — not an easy task as they were scarce in those days — to offer free hosting in return for a share of the publicity if it proved successful. Calling up head office in Waterloo, he requested Open Text's entire engineering team to work on the project. By this time, Jenkins was in charge. He wasn't prepared to devote so much to the scheme, but he gave Bray the green light to work on it by himself full-time. It took three days and the assistance of an expert consultant to get Bray's Sun workstation connected to a modem so it could talk to the Internet. "The software was crawling in January 1995, limping in March, and we unleashed it to the world in April."[8]

Jenkins had good reason not to go all-in on the Open Text Index. The company's intranet business was picking up steam. And much of it was due to his energy. In 1994, Open Text decided to expand into Europe by acquiring a small partner in Switzerland called IntUnix. Jenkins set up a meeting with Marco Palatini, a vice-president with IntUnix, at its Swiss office. There, Jenkins talked about transforming Open Text from a small private Canadian company into a worldwide software business. He talked about plans for a public offering on the Canadian stock exchange within a year, and even a listing on the Nasdaq. "He wanted to conquer the world. And my initial reaction was, yeah sure. His story sounded a lot more like a dream than a realistic plan," Palatini said.[9] Nonetheless the deal went ahead, giving Open Text a jumping off point into Europe. As time went on, however, it was becoming apparent that corporate clients wanted more than just a search engine to find and retrieve documents. They wanted the ability to share and revise those documents from different locations over their private intranets. Open Text didn't have this kind of expertise, known as integrated document management, but as it turned out a spinoff company from Northwestern University in Chicago did.

In the early 1990s, Odesta Systems developed a software product known as Livelink that allowed users to collaborate on documents and manage them from different locations. Once it had the bugs worked out, the company debuted Livelink at a trade show in Long Beach, California, early in 1995. Visitors were blown away and stood five-deep at Odesta's booth to see the software in action. Soon after, the company began considering how to deploy Livelink over the Internet instead of through Microsoft and Apple, its existing distribution partners. By this time, word of Odesta's breakthrough had reached Mike Farrell, Open Text's vice-president of sales. Livelink looked like the kind of software that would take Open Text to the next level. He set up a meeting with Jenkins and Odesta founder and CEO Daniel Cheifetz at the San Francisco Airport. A merger made a lot of sense. Livelink's collaboration and work-flow software could be combined with Open Text's search technology and web savvy to create the killer app of corporate intranets. A merger was eventually put in motion, but using a novel strategy. Since both firms were roughly of equal size, it didn't make sense to move one workforce to the other's hometown. Indeed, their software platform made relocation of one office to the other unnecessary. It was decided that each would remain in place, with Waterloo serving as corporate headquarters.[10] "Odesta was a really important acquisition. They offered the kind of collaboration tools that are common today in Facebook, Dropbox and Twitter," said Jenkins.[11]

In those dark days of 1996 when Open Text's stock went into free fall, the merger with Odesta gave Jenkins hope. Bolstered by an aggressive ad campaign with the letters "ra" highlighted in the word intranet, the company went to market with a more robust document-management platform and began to reel in large, new corporate customers. Among them was the auto behemoth Ford. In the old days, engineering teams from Ford would visit corporate offices in Europe and Asia, bringing CDs loaded with data and diagrams. With Open Text software, they could do it all from head office, said Jenkins.[12] Annual revenues doubled to $45 million in 1998 and the company's workforce jumped to 400 from 200, deployed at ten offices around the world, including Europe, Asia and Australia.[13] Open Text stock recovered and moved well past pre-IPO days. Going the private-intranet route was less glamorous than the public Internet. A consolation prize, but it was the right strategy, said Jenkins. "In this sector, the market capitalizations are much smaller. However, they're much more stable. Business-to-business is based on long-term, decades-long, supply-chain relationships. There was far greater risk in the consumer market — fickle, fashion-and-trend-conscious that it is."[14] Open Text, still based in Waterloo, would go on to become the largest software company in Canada and one of the largest software and cloud-computing firms in the world. Jenkins had survived his near-death experience, but he wasn't the only one in Waterloo to suffer a career-threatening blow during the dot-com mania of the late 1990s and early 2000s.

* * *

As Dave Caputo sat in the comfortable house he had purchased in Colorado he had good reason to be satisfied with his career to this point. At times, it all seemed too good to be true. Just over a decade ago, he was a teenager from the northern Ontario city of Sault Ste. Marie who had been fascinated by computers. Now, in 1998, he was working for one of the largest computer enterprises in the world, the storied and legendary Hewlett-Packard, one of the founding firms of Silicon Valley, in one of the most picturesque and exotic states in the US. He had come a long way in a short period of time. If only his friends back in the Sault could see him now. Computers had enthralled Caputo from an early age. Before he even entered Grade 9, he would sneak into the computer lab at the high school his two older brothers attended. When he did get to high school, he spent a co-op term at a firm selling Commodore and IBM computers, then started working there after school and on weekends. Dark-haired with warm eyes and a radiant smile, Caputo looks back on those days fondly. "It was an incredible time. New computers were coming out every few months."

After earning his BA in computer science at York University in Toronto and his MBA at the University of Toronto, Caputo set his sights on Silicon Valley. His timing wasn't good. In the early 1990s, the cradle of high-tech was in the grips of a recession. Jobs were in short supply. In the meantime, Caputo heard about a job in the Panacom division of Hewlett-Packard, now called HP, in Waterloo. Specializing in data acquisition and control systems, Panacom Automation had been launched in Toronto in 1978, then acquired by HP in 1983. A year later, the computer giant moved Panacom to Waterloo to tap into UW's computer engineering talent.[15] If he couldn't go to Silicon Valley, Caputo told himself, working for one of the pillars of the fabled California region would be the next best thing. During the job interview, he was asked where he wanted to be in five years. His dream job was to lead a team designing a product, deciding what features to put in it, giving it a name, working with the engineers to build it and so on. "I'm a product manager at heart," Caputo said. That's exactly the kind of person they were looking for, the Panacom official told him. He was hired. In Waterloo, HP was manufacturing computer workstations with a staff of more than 100 people. Caputo moved up quickly and in 1995, three years after being hired, he was transferred to Colorado Springs, Colorado, to manage storage and systems for HP there.

The move was a fortuitous one. Three years later HP would shut down its Panacom division in Waterloo, putting more than 100 people out of work. Though Caputo was happy in Colorado, something started to gnaw away at him. Two friends at Panacom in Waterloo had left before the shutdown to launch a startup helping telecoms deliver video over phone lines. With the advent of the Internet and fibre optic cable, the world of video was exploding with more ways to distribute content to the home. On a visit back to Waterloo, Caputo ran into those friends, Marc Morin and Brad Siim. They encouraged him to join their new firm, called Pixstream. Seeking counsel with another friend, he talked about the pros and cons of working at a smaller company. "Wouldn't you rather make a difference?" the friend asked him. "But I'm making an incredible difference at HP," Caputo shot back. Still the question began to haunt him. On a fishing vacation with some pals, he cut the trip short. He was going back to Waterloo. Within three weeks, he sold his house in Colorado, bought a house in Waterloo and moved his wife and two young boys, aged three and one, back to Ontario. Days after arriving at Pixstream as vice-president of marketing, he was on a plane to the National Association of Broadcasters convention in Amsterdam. "It was a whirlwind," he said, recalling those times.

By the time Caputo came aboard in 1998 Pixstream had caught the attention of a key investor. Terry Matthews was a Welsh-born serial entrepreneur based in Ottawa who had made a fortune manufacturing telecommunications switches and networking equipment through his company Newbridge Networks. Matthews had already invested $3 million in Pixstream through his venture capital firm Celtic House International. Over the next eighteen months, Matthews and three other venture-capital firms would pour another $20 million into the Waterloo startup, pushing its workforce to more than 200 people, and attracting interest from phone companies in Canada, the US and Europe. Telcos were jumping on the convergence bandwagon in their battle with cable-TV firms for supremacy in the home-entertainment market. Pixstream had found a sweet spot right in the middle of the conflict. Packaged in a hot box, its technology would enable telecoms to deliver phone, Internet and up to 140 TV channels at a fraction of the cost of the competition.[16] Most of the world's phone companies are dying to get into cable TV, Matthews told Pixstream's annual meeting in Waterloo in May 1999. "Video services are right up there with the gods." Major telcos such as AT&T and Telefonica were seeking the kind of equipment provided by Pixstream. The market was "hot, hot, hot." The combination of Newbridge switches and Pixstream technology meant video service wouldn't tie up phone lines while in use, Matthews noted.[17]

Stoking interest as well was the company's rising valuation. After a third round of financing from the Matthews group put $12.5 million in its coffers, Pixstream was valued at $65 million. Within a month, that figure soared to $200 million just before the company raised another $35 million in special warrants, a dress rehearsal for an initial public offering. Pixstream was caught up in the dot-com mania that was taking the world by storm in the late 1990s. "It was a good time to be raising capital," said Tim Jackson, Pixstream's chief financial officer, who had come on board in 1998 and spearheaded much of the fundraising. All this activity had one other impact. Pixstream was starting to look ripe for a takeover. As the company was getting set to do an IPO, an offer came in from Teryan Communications Systems of Santa Clara, California. While the Pixstream brass was mulling this over, Caputo got a call from Jack Bradley, general manager of video services at Cisco, the networking equipment goliath from Silicon Valley. Pixstream had been working with Cisco on a plan to offer TV services over the Internet. But that wasn't the subject of Bradley's call. His son was getting set to drive in an auto race in Toronto. Would Pixstream be interested in sponsoring his car? As the conversation moved on to other topics, Caputo casually mentioned there was a significant offer on the table to purchase Pixstream. Bradley hung up and immediately called Cisco's corporate development team. "They came in very fast and very hard," said Caputo. Cisco assumed the other bidder was Alcatel, the French telecom equipment company and a major rival. In the late 1990s, Cisco was in the midst of an acquisition boom as it battled for market share in the growing Internet equipment market. In one case, it spent $7 billion to acquire an optical-equipment maker. "If any dog was going to eat a bone, they wanted it," said Siim.

Cisco's interest set off an intense six to eight weeks of negotiations over the summer of 2000, conducted on Pixstream's side with the help of a boutique investment bank. Cisco executives also beat a path to New Brunswick where Pixstream had signed a deal with NBTel to use its routing technology. When the final sale price was announced in late August, it was a stunner: $369 million US or $554 million CA. The transaction was an all-stock deal, with Pixstream exchanging 12.7 shares for every Cisco share. The reaction among Pixstream employees was "rejoicing," said Caputo. Workers had been given stock options over the years and many had invested during the funding rounds. Founders Siim and Morin made $20 million each on paper and the rest of the management team were up $2 million to $6 million each, said Caputo. "Is there a Porsche dealer in town?" quipped Andrew Sage, director of Canadian marketing for Cisco.[18] The announcement was made at the nearby Waterloo Inn where food and drinks were brought in to celebrate. The party continued at the Flying Dog nightclub, where jubilant staff ran up a bar bill of $30,000. In January, the company brought in aging rockers the Guess Who to perform before 800 employees, family and friends in a private concert at UW's Federation Hall. The deal, set to close just before Christmas, made headlines across the country. It was all the more shocking because Pixstream's annual revenues were just $400,000 in 1998, but had jumped to $7 million in 1999.[19] The dollar value of the deal buried any regrets over Pixstream losing its independence. Venture-capital investors could now be paid off. Besides, there was the euphoria of being acquired by the most valuable company in the world at that time. Cisco, whose name comes from the last syllable of San Francisco, built the underlying infrastructure of the Internet and some of its equipment carried Pixstream software. It was the Google and Apple of its day.

After the excitement wore off, Pixstream got the green light to hire fifty more staff and employees went back to work. Not much else changed apart from the cosmetic. "There was a lot of training in the Cisco way," said Caputo. Pixstream remained in its headquarters at 180 Columbia St. W., where it shared space with a booming Research In Motion. But Pixstream's workforce had grown so much that space had to be rented in two other buildings. The first sign that anything was amiss came in March, less than three months after the deal had closed. On the heels of the dot-com crash in 2000 and the first unprofitable quarter in its history, Cisco announced it was chopping 8,000 jobs from its global workforce of 48,000, but did not immediately say where the axe would fall. Cisco CEO John Chambers called it the "100-year flood." Staff at Pixstream were uneasy, but consoled themselves with the knowledge they were not an obvious target. Acquisitions had been numerous in recent years and Cisco had exempted them from its hiring freeze. Moreover, Pixstream had just celebrated the first profitable quarter in its history and was the only business unit at Cisco that had grown. "We thought we were immune to all this," said Caputo.

They weren't. Six weeks later Cisco lowered the boom. Pixstream would be shut down, throwing 210 people out of work. The euphoria that had reigned just eight months ago when the Cisco deal was announced was shattered. No amount of money could make up for the shock and pain of this news. As a member of the management team, Caputo got the word early. Pixstream was being closed, he was told, because the company had to write off more than a billion dollars in goodwill, an accounting term for the difference between the price of an acquisition and the current value of the assets. With the dot-com crash, recent acquisitions by Cisco and other large companies had plunged in value. Caputo was stunned. Pixstream was being closed for accounting reasons? Outraged, he got on the phone with a Cisco official. After a heated conversation, the official called back the next day to say the shutdown was strategic — Cisco was no longer interested in video networking and Pixstream was not located near San Jose, the company's headquarters. "I appreciated him telling me that," said Caputo who, from then on, would think of accounting as "the devil's work."

Looming on the horizon was the thankless and gut-wrenching task of informing employees that the company they had worked so hard to create was history. Lou Santora, an official with Cisco, flew up to Waterloo to help break the news. Caputo was a mess. In the nights leading up to the announcement, he couldn't sleep. Just before workers arrived to receive the terrible news, he went into the cloakroom and wept. The announcement was greeted with stunned silence. One hundred and seventy workers would lose their jobs immediately. Forty would stay on for four months to wind down the business. "Cisco is going through a tough patch," Caputo told them, noting that other Cisco divisions were being closed as well. As workers digested the news, some were not surprised. They had feared the worst after the Cisco cutbacks announced six weeks earlier, and some had sensed that something was wrong. "My sense was there was a bit of a leak," Caputo said of the closure. "That was a good thing." Amid the shock and pain, he could feel "a remarkable level of empathy" from the team. "We were in it together."

Later that day, Caputo went for a walk with his two children to find some peace amid all the turmoil. It felt like the worst day of his life. His cellphone rang. On the line was Matthews, the venture capital investor. After commiserating with the embattled Pixstream boss, his tone changed. "Dave, you've got to start another company. You can't let everyone scatter to the four corners of the earth." Caputo was taken aback. "But Terry, I just fired all my engineers today." "Well, you've got their fuckin' phone numbers, don't you?" Matthews went further. He had made millions on the Cisco deal. If Caputo and crew took up the challenge, he would back them with a $10 million investment. Caputo felt his spirits start to rally. That evening, he set up a conference call with a cadre of Pixstream leaders, including Siim and Morin, to discuss their next move. Reaching Siim was a challenge. Knowing there was no way Pixstream could be saved, he had departed to the big island of Hawaii on a seven-day bike trip planned earlier. Yet Caputo wanted him on board. Siim, Pixstream's vice-president of engineering, has a tougher and grittier edge than the more genteel Caputo. In football terms, he is the linebacker while Caputo is the quarterback. When they finally did reach their colleague, Siim had to perform some contortions to make the call happen. Standing on a chair to pick up the signal on his cellphone, he was asked if he was in or out. "With the money from the Pixstream sale, I could stay in Hawaii for the rest of my life or I could do another startup with you guys," Siim said. "Doing another startup sounds like a whole lot more fun."

In the meantime, Pixstream had to endure the public embarrassment of defeat so soon after victory. This time the media response was more muted. *Canadian Business* magazine summed it up best with a simple headline: "Pixstream's Waterloo."[20] The company was the Canadian poster child for the wild exuberance and myopia of the dot-com era. It had gone from rags to riches and back to rags. Behind the scenes, Caputo, Siim, Morin and two other Pixstream leaders, Don Bowman and Tom Donnelly, quietly got down to the business of pulling something from the wreckage. Rolling up their sleeves, they brainstormed ideas for their new startup. They soon got some good news. Matthews and some of the same Pixstream investors, were ready to kick in another $9.5 million, allowing the new company to bring on about twenty more Pixstream employees. Breaking into groups, they considered four options: voice over the Internet, storage-area networks, fibre to the home and value-added services such as call-waiting and call-display over the Internet. The last option was the winner. By adding a layer of intelligence to the Internet, carriers and Internet-service providers could offer different plans depending on the service. Siim compared it to the delivery of water or hydro to the home. In the beginning it was all-you-can-eat. Then utilities started offering value-added services such as smart-metering. It was all about making Internet traffic better and more efficient. Network-equipment management was a niche market, perhaps, but there was demand for this kind of service. "When people deployed our technology, they generally were the best operators in their region," Siim noted. Calling their new company Sandvine,[21] they opened for business in September 2001, four months after Cisco shut down Pixstream and just before planes hit the Twin Towers in New York City. If their financing had closed two weeks later, there would have been no Sandvine. "You have to be good but you also have to be lucky," said Caputo.

Over the next decade and a half, with Caputo as CEO and Siim as chief operating officer, Sandvine would grow into the largest global producer of hardware and software to help carriers manage their Internet networks, boasting annual revenues of $120 million US in 2016 and a workforce topping 700. A highlight on the road to success came in 2006 when they decided to turn themselves into a public stock company to raise more capital. No investment bank would take them on in North America so they turned to the Alternative Investment Market in London, England. Nonetheless, they still had to find investors in North America. On the first day of their road show in Silicon Valley, a meeting was set up with Jon Gruber, a legendary curmudgeon in the Valley. Gruber walked into the meeting, threw Sandvine's prospectus in the air and said, "That's the biggest piece of shit I've ever seen." Warned ahead of time of his irascible nature, Caputo and Sandvine's chief financial officer plowed ahead with their presentation. When they finished, Gruber said to an aide, "Make sure I get $4 million," and walked out. By the time they landed in London, they had already met their target of $40 million.

In 2017, after hitting a wall of $120 million in sales and needing a major injection of capital to get to the next level, Sandvine was sold to a Silicon Valley private equity firm for $562 million. The purchaser, Francisco Partners, merged the company with the number-two player in the market.[22] Sandvine just didn't have enough money to build a worldwide infrastructure, explained Siim. He compared the business to an amusement park. "You need to have new rides every year."[23] The majority of its workforce remains in Waterloo and the company retained the Sandvine name. Caputo stepped down as chief executive officer but moved over to chair Sandvine's board of directors.

It wasn't just Sandvine that rose from Pixstream's ashes. Pixstream employees who did not join Sandvine went on to start a slew of other tech firms in the region. Despite years in the trenches helming a global Internet company, Caputo has not lost his competitive fire. There's still another startup in him, he said. The success of the company that sprang out of Pixstream has caused him to view the Cisco debacle in a new light. "When I think back to the worst day of my life, I now think of it as one of my best."[24]

* * *

As time went by, Will continued writing his tech blog and working as a self-employed marketing and software consultant. But he found himself paying more attention to the local startup ecosystem, or the lack thereof. The launch of Communitech was a "big milestone," he noted, but it was trying to be all things to all people. Its only revenues were the $5,000 annual fees provided by members. "There wasn't much going on for startups." In 1998, Will started doing his own thing, moving away from established clients to focus more on early stage companies emerging from UW and the local tech sector. Business models, investor-pitches and go-to-market strategies were the kind of things he taught them. Bolstered by funding from Tech Capital Partners, a venture-capital firm launched by former Pixstreamer Tim Jackson, and other cash cadged from local law and accounting firms, Will's venture evolved into a more formal organization named WatStart in 2004. Around the same time, Communitech hired a new president with a background in branding and marketing at a disparate group of employers including Nortel, Ontario Tourism and CBC. His name was Iain Klugman. Klugman saw what Will was doing with startups and brought him on board at Communitech. "And then things went insane after that," said Will.[25]

Iain Klugman's first impressions of Communitech were not good. Compared to the vast bureaucracy of CBC where he had worked as executive-director of communications, it was tiny. Ensconced in a small office at Jim Balsillie's think tank, the Centre for International Governance Innovation, Communitech's membership had grown to 400, but it had a budget of less than $2 million and fewer than ten employees. And some of the people hanging around were former tech leaders who appeared to be past their prime. It looked like a place you went to when you retired. Yet Klugman wasn't ready to turn on his heel and go back to Toronto. He wasn't happy at CBC. It had too many bosses, and at the age of forty-one, he'd been used to being his own boss as CEO at Ontario Tourism. He had only joined the government broadcaster a year before, but now he felt like it was a mistake. When Bob Crow, an old friend from the Information Technology Association of Canada, called about a job opening at Communitech, he was curious. The two had met when Klugman was director of global branding and advertising at Nortel Networks in the late 1990s. They had stayed in touch after Crow was hired as director of government and university relations at RIM in 2001, and then tapped to represent the firm on Communitech's board of directors. The tech association needed a new president and Crow thought he had a good candidate for the job. "Iain is incredibly creative and bright. He has immense energy and he's a leader," said Crow.[26] After spending a day making the rounds at Communitech, Klugman went home to consider his options. The association was small, but had a lot of potential. And it was located in a dynamic area. There was a history of entrepreneurship in the area, and a handful of local tech companies led by RIM had accomplished amazing things. Moreover, the University of Waterloo had opened a forty-hectare research and technology park just north of the campus two years earlier, with the aim of attracting more. Klugman began to get a sense that something special was going on. "And if I'm not part of it, I'm going to kick myself in 10 years."[27]

With the help of Will, he began beefing up services for tech startups. One of his first moves was to bring in people who had run companies before. These so-called entrepreneurs in residence would advise young firms on marketing, raising capital, hiring and compensating employees, closing deals and protecting intellectual property. But they couldn't be just any entrepreneurs. They had to be good teachers as well. "Some of the best hockey players aren't the best coaches," Klugman said. They would be paid with $1 million in funds secured over three years from the province. Volunteer coaching will only take you so far, he reasoned.[28] Like other tech hubs, the local sector had taken a drubbing after the dot-com collapse, but had emerged relatively intact. There were about 250 tech firms in the area, many of them small, with RIM overshadowing everyone else. There was a foundation to build on. Klugman moved the Communitech office to UW's research park to partner with a tech incubator launched by the university called the Accelerator Centre. Hackathons, pitch competitions and workshops were held throughout the year, and tech celebrities and thought-leaders were brought in from Silicon Valley and other tech hubs to inspire the troops during the annual Entrepreneur Week. The seven-day extravaganza also featured a film fest with documentaries and movies about the dot-com craze and tech luminaries such as Steve Jobs and Bill Gates.

Klugman was a big believer in the mythology and culture of tech as well as the toil. Part of his appeal was his colourful personality. Of average height and build with closely cropped grey hair and a jovial manner, it was rare for him to deliver a speech without inserting a few jokes or wisecracks. Typical was the time that one of his entrepreneurs left for another job. Klugman summoned him to the stage before hundreds of people at a Communitech conference, made him don a funny hat, handed him a bottle of whiskey and presented him with the Order of Communitech. For the interview for this book, scheduled on Halloween Day, he showed up dressed like Patrick Stewart on *Star Trek*. He was quick to adopt the geek wardrobe of jeans, running shoes, T-shirts and a sports jacket to dress things up a bit. Formal dress was a no-no. "Burn your ties," Communitech urged young techies on its website.[29]

Klugman thought he was doing a great job until he met with Tom Jenkins, the same Tom Jenkins of Open Text and a member of Communitech's board of directors. The tireless Jenkins had also played a major role in launching Communitech, recruiting its first president in 1997. "We need to be thinking about a $10-million strategy," Klugman told him. "Not $10 million, it has to be a $100-million strategy," Jenkins fired back.[30] As he pondered that challenge, Klugman thought back to something Bob Rabinovitch, chief executive of CBC, told him while he was at the public broadcaster: It's important to bring everything together under one roof.

The Lang Tannery building in downtown Kitchener was in sad shape. Sprawling over an entire city block just west of the core, the five-storey brick building erected in the 1850s had seen better days. In its heyday during the First World War, it had made more soles for leather boots than any other company in the British Empire. During the Second World War, leather linings for aircraft fuel tanks kept the factory humming. But peace and changing times did not bring prosperity and the tannery closed in 1954. For the next fifty years or so, a motley collection of small businesses moved in, and the massive building — actually a warren of connected buildings — slowly deteriorated until it resembled a giant eyesore, a huge slab of obsolescence on the urban landscape. The dilapidated state of the Lang Tannery had not gone unnoticed at city hall where Carl Zehr was mayor. In 2004, a pair of city managers came up with a plan to create a $107-million economic development fund to attract investment and stimulate downtown renewal. Thirty million dollars was soon earmarked by council to help the University of Waterloo build a school of pharmacy just a block away from the Tannery. Another $6.5 million went to renovate the former St. Jerome's High School nearby so it could house a school of social work affiliated with Wilfrid Laurier University. In the same neighbourhood, the old Kaufman rubber plant had been converted into lofts. All this activity soon caught the attention of a Toronto developer. Late in 2007, Cadan Inc. purchased the Tannery from a Kitchener construction company. After spending $30 million to clean up and restore the massive building, the company hoped to attract tenants seeking funky office space with hardwood floors and exposed rafters.

Cadan didn't have to spend a lot of time looking for tenants. With Jenkins's challenge still ringing in his years, Klugman realized he couldn't launch a bold expansion plan without a larger space to house it. The UW research park, where Communitech was located, did not hold much appeal. The buildings were shiny and new but spaced far apart and surrounded by fields and parking. He needed something with character and history, a building close to other structures to provide the necessary critical mass and appeal to stimulate entrepreneurship. The Tannery building, now undergoing a restoration five kilometres to the south in downtown Kitchener, seemed to fit the bill. Here was the perfect place to establish his dream, a new entity called the Communitech Hub. The Hub would house a large and full-service incubator — the biggest in the area — for tech startups, firms looking to scale, mentors, support staff, investors and established firms serving as advisers. Resources from the UW Accelerator Centre and the Velocity Garage, an innovative incubator created around the same time in a UW student residence, would bolster the startup team. Also housed in the Hub would be a digital media centre, featuring state of the art equipment to link tech hubs in other parts of the country. To finance the whole venture, funding would be sought from both the federal and provincial governments and cash or equipment from tech companies in the area.

It sounded like an audacious plan. Yet somehow it worked. With the city, UW and local tech firms such as Open Text backing the venture, $5 million was lined up from the feds and $26 million from the province. It didn't seem to hurt that the Tannery was located in the riding of John Milloy, Kitchener Centre MPP and provincial minister of research and innovation. The grand unveiling in 2010 saw Communitech move into a 30,000-square foot space in the Tannery building. "This will absolutely put Waterloo Region on the map as being a major digital media centre in North America," said Klugman.[31] Among the features in the Hub were a 3D-immersive environment donated by Christie Digital, state of the art labs, a prototyping and virtual-conferencing facility and premier event space. Everything would be geared to startups in the hope they would come up with the next big thing. "This is their sandbox," said Kevin Tuer, director of the digital media network. "This is where they can bump into each other often and have those conversations that will accelerate the entire commercialization process."[32]

The momentum ramped up even more when two big name tech companies — local standout Desire2Learn, which was doing well in the online education field, and search engine giant Google, which had opened an office in Waterloo several years before — set up shop in the Tannery too, transforming the once-moribund leather factory into a citadel of innovation in downtown Kitchener. Like a magnet, it would start to attract tech entrepreneurs from UW who fell in love with the tougher, grittier, blue-collar feel of central Kitchener with its abundant supply of aging factories and empty warehouses, structures that were not plentiful in more genteel Waterloo. As time passed, a second tech cluster would start to emerge in downtown Kitchener to rival the first near the University of Waterloo. "Place matters," Klugman said, reflecting on the birth of the Communitech Hub. Some places are just a building. Others are a gathering place, a club house and "a strategic tool" to normalize the "often weird career choice" of tech entrepreneurs.[33] When Klugman first arrived in 2004, Communitech's annual budget was a paltry $2 million. By 2018, it had soared to $25 million and its workforce to ninety employees. More than half its funding comes from government and the rest from a cross-section of nearly fifty private investors or companies, of which twenty-one have a physical presence in the building to provide support and mentoring to tech startups. The trade-off is the opportunity to tap the minds of the talent residing in the Tannery. The association now occupies a total of 120,000 square feet in the Tannery and a second location called the Data Hub in uptown Waterloo, and says it supports more than 1,400 companies — from startups to scale-ups to global corporations.[34] "Iain brought government support to the table at all levels," said Randall Howard, co-founder of MKS and a local tech investor. It would not have been possible, however, without a foundation of private-sector and institutional participation, he noted. "If government starts it, it doesn't work as well." Since Klugman's arrival, Communitech has made "a quantum leap," Howard said.[35]

While central Kitchener was enjoying a revival thanks to the influx of tech workers and students, a run-down section of uptown Waterloo was experiencing a turnaround of its own with the help of philanthropic money from RIM's two CEOs.

Chapter 8
SHARING THE WEALTH

Michael Duschenes makes no bones about the fact he doesn't know much about theoretical physics. As the second-in-command at Perimeter Institute for Theoretical Physics, it's not his job to explain what goes on inside the finely tuned brains of the researchers and post-doctoral fellows who wander the halls there. Nor does he even want to try. Theoretical physics is intimidating stuff, the kind of discipline pursued by some of the most accomplished minds in human history, people like Albert Einstein, Sir Isaac Newton and Stephen Hawking. Duschenes, the managing director and chief operating officer at Perimeter doesn't have to know how it all works. He just has to know why it's important and how the research carried on there has some value for the betterment of society. "It's not such a bad thing having someone not from a physics background in my job," he said. In that way, the self-described "generalist" is better suited to explain what goes on at Perimeter to the average person who walks through its doors.

Duschenes was about as far from physics as you can get before joining the staff at Perimeter in 2004. The Montreal native came to Kitchener to manage the symphony orchestra before launching his own consulting firm specializing in turnaround work for arts organizations. During this period, he met Howard Burton, founding director of Perimeter and a member of the symphony board. Burton encouraged him to apply for the COO position at the physics institute. "It was complete luck," he said of landing the job. When he does get into a discussion about the importance of research at Perimeter, he adds a big qualifier. The results won't be seen anytime soon. Perimeter is not in the business of instant gratification. Long-term gratification, extremely long-term, is what one can expect from the work coming out of the Waterloo institute. There is no way James Clerk Maxwell, the inventor of electro-magnetism, or Einstein, a giant among physicists, were thinking about magnetic resonance imaging machines while doing their research more than 100 years ago, yet the MRI would not be here today without them, said Duschenes, a slim, balding, fifty-something man with a close-cropped grey beard. Nor was Einstein thinking about quantum computing, one of the holy grails of modern-day tech, when he was playing around with the theories underlying quantum mechanics.

The time frames may be long, but the value of theoretical physics cannot be underestimated, Duschenes said. "This is the most prolific science. It produces more wealth and knowledge creation than any other science." Another thing about Perimeter: it's into quality, not quantity. Duschenes brushes aside questions about the volume of research papers pumped out by Perimeter scholars or the number of times it is quoted in the media. It's all about the grand slam home run, the long-term breakthrough. "We tend to measure peaks, not volume." And staff at Perimeter toss around names of famous physicists like sports fans chatting about the latest young phenom, though you won't find any trading cards to help you keep track of who discovered what. On the topic of breakthroughs, Duschenes casually drops in a mention of the Higgs boson and the Large Hadron Collider. The existence of this important particle, or boson, in physics was first proposed by British theoretical physicist Peter Higgs in 1964. Its existence wasn't confirmed until 2012 when physicists ran tests in the particle collider, the world's largest machine, buried in an underground tunnel near Geneva, Switzerland. For his discovery, Higgs was awarded the Nobel Prize in physics in 2013, nearly fifty years later.[1] The time frames are getting shorter, Duschenes said, but not a lot shorter judging by how long Higgs had to wait for his recognition.

Though huge breakthroughs don't tend to happen too often in theoretical physics, everything at Perimeter is designed so that if they do, there is a place to write them down or record them in some fashion. Blackboards are sprinkled generously throughout the building and the aluminum-clad exterior wall on the front of Perimeter, pockmarked with small windows and mirrors, is black to symbolize a large blackboard covered in equations. Even some of the tables in the cafeteria, named the Black Hole Bistro, double as blackboards. Such surfaces are a tradition in physics dating back to when pre-historic peoples used soft rocks to carve out messages on harder rocks. Wood fireplaces have a prominent place in Perimeter, often in nooks between floors where the 150 permanent researchers and the 1,000 visiting researchers who study at Perimeter each year can sit on couches or easy-chairs, converse with each other, stare into the flames or gaze out onto the four-storey atrium in the middle of the structure. Small rocks painted in different colours are attached to a large black wall at one end of the atrium to symbolize stars in the night sky. Quirky accents abound, including manual typewriters in several lounges and old hockey sticks doubling as pointers in lecture rooms, a reminder of Perimeter's early days in the old Waterloo post office when researchers had no laser-pointers and found old hockey sticks to use instead. "This is a purpose-built facility for theoretical physics. I don't think that's ever happened before," Duschenes said of the design. Other physics institutes tend to have utilitarian layouts where work is done in offices at the end of sterile corridors. While the wood fireplaces add warmth to the place, he bristles at the cliché that they often spark epiphanies. In the 2014 Hollywood biopic *The Theory of Everything*, Stephen Hawking has a sudden inspiration about a difficult problem while staring into the flames of a fireplace.

"It's so wrong and so insulting," Duschenes notes, adding that years of mental toil and sweat are behind all breakthroughs.[2]

Mike Lazaridis had only a vague notion of what he wanted to create while pondering a use for his sudden riches after torrid sales of the Black-Berry pushed him into the billionaire class. As Howard Burton relates in his entertaining 2009 book, *First Principles: The Crazy Business of Doing Serious Science*, he had no idea a desperate email he sent out in the summer of 1999 to twenty CEOs across the continent looking for a job would lead to the top position at Perimeter. A native of Toronto, Burton had earned his MA in philosophy at U of T, then done a PhD in theoretical physics at the University of Waterloo. Worried about the job prospects in physics and needing a decent salary to support his wife and new family, Burton landed a job on Wall Street at a time when math and physics grads were thought to have some insight on how to manipulate financial instruments. But the cold-blooded pursuit of money and the boring nature of the work turned him off of Wall Street, so he was pleased and intrigued when Lazaridis was one of the few CEOs to get back to him. Burton had found RIM's name in a business directory, but knew little about the Waterloo company apart from the fact it had two CEOs and made wireless devices. It seems that he had earned his doctorate at UW without hardly setting foot in Waterloo, retaining his residence in Toronto during this time.

When they finally met at a restaurant in Brampton, Lazaridis rambled on for three hours about wanting to devote a substantial chunk of his wealth towards something worthwhile in the realm of science and phys-ics and how they could be harnessed to improve communications. As he waxed enthusiastic, Burton wondered if the RIM boss was naïve or just plain off his rocker. Nor was Burton sure he possessed the right skills to tackle the vague challenge Lazaridis was offering. But the thirty-four-year-old was desperate to escape Wall Street and something about the RIM boss appealed to him. "The man had charisma, it was undeniable." He also exuded "an honesty, a fundamental decency that pervaded all of his discourse and made him, well, likable."[3] After accepting the pos-ition, Burton's friends back in Toronto wondered if he had lost his mind.

Lazaridis was just a rich eccentric who would one day lose interest, wasting Burton's time in the process, they told him. Nonetheless, he plowed ahead, deciding that a physics institute was the right solution and that it should be called Perimeter. It was pushing towards the perimeter of research, and the acronym PI also stood for pi, the famous mathematical constant. He began researching other physics institutes, then embarked on a tour of some of the leading ones, starting with the Institute for Advanced Study at Princeton, where Einstein himself had studied in his latter years. Burton felt a little like a used-car salesman touting the vague idea of a physics institute up in Canada, whose benefactors could not be identified yet. With high hopes, Burton entered the office of one of his heroes, physics pioneer Freeman Dyson, only to be told that the best advice Dyson could offer was "keep things fresh." He was getting on in years and probably should have been booted out years ago, but his family liked Princeton and wanted to stay, Dyson told him.[4]

In the meantime, stock markets were tanking as the dot-com bubble started to lose some of its air, turning Burton into a nervous wreck as he worried that Lazaridis's gift of $100 million in RIM stock would no longer be possible. There was also a problem with the donation itself. According to Canadian law at the time, no single individual could contribute more than 50 per cent of the funding to a registered public charity. The aim was to prevent the wealthy from avoiding taxes through donations to dubious causes. It was decided that Lazaridis would donate $20 million at the outset, with the remaining $80 million in stock flowing in subsequent years as more funding was raised from government and private donors. In the meantime, Balsillie and Doug Fregin, RIM's co-founder, would kick in $10 million each, giving Perimeter an initial stake of $40 million.[5]

Perimeter Institute would need a home, but this ran into flack as well. The city was naturally thrilled when it was told confidentially how much Lazaridis was willing to donate. It offered free land at four possible city-owned locations, three in suburban wooded areas and one near the uptown on a site occupied by what was left of the Waterloo Memorial Arena. The aging facility had been declared unsafe in the 1980s, but to keep it going the city had torn down most of the structure and replaced it with an inflated bubble. The only remnant of the original structure was the front wall and entrance. Lazaridis immediately preferred the arena site. It bordered a small lake and Waterloo Park, the city's largest uptown green space, and was close to shops and restaurants. The city was happy to oblige, but then realized veterans might object. Even though it was scheduled to close in 2001, the arena held a special place in their hearts. It had been built after the Second World War and named in honour of local soldiers who had died in the two world wars. When told of the snag, Lazaridis, never a fan of hockey or sports in general, said in exasperation, "What does a hockey rink have to do with the war?" A compromise was eventually reached whereby a nearby recreation centre built by the city a few years earlier would be renamed and a monument erected to honour the fallen.[6]

Somehow RIM stock recovered and it all came together in a grand announcement in the fall of 2000 that made headlines across the country. The institute would open its doors a year later in temporary quarters in the old post office nearby with an initial complement of ten to fifteen resident researchers and plans to increase the number to forty within five years.[7] In the meantime, construction would begin on a permanent home slated to open in 2003. When the new facility finally did open in 2004, 8,000 people attended the two-day ceremony with Prime Minister Paul Martin cutting the ribbon. Lisa Rochon, the *Globe and Mail*'s architecture critic, praised the new structure but enraged local leaders and residents when she noted that Perimeter was "surrounded by a city of surpassing ugliness," the result of too much "car-dominated planning."[8]

David Johnston, UW's president and Canada's future governor-general, was thrilled that Perimeter was located in Waterloo, but miffed that it was not part of the university. Lazaridis wanted Perimeter to be free of the bureaucratic shackles and teaching responsibilities of a university. There was also concern that UW was not involved in quantum information theory, a new branch of physics that had sprung up in the 1980s and 1990s. Under this theory, computing and cryptography could be made much faster using the principles of quantum mechanics.[9] But

Johnston showed some willingness to back an endeavour in this field, prompting Lazaridis to offer a donation of $33 million in 2001, on the condition it be matched two-to-one by the university through private fundraising and government donations. The matching funding was eventually raised — including $150 million in government support and $35 million from RIM co-founder Doug Fregin — and Lazaridis and his wife, Ophelia, later bumped their contribution to $100 million.[10] The Institute for Quantum Computing opened its doors in 2002 and moved into a new building on the UW campus in 2012.

As the calendar turned over to 2007, Burton had every reason to be proud. Perimeter housed ten full-time faculty and eight associates from regions as divergent as California, France, Germany and Australia. Fifty post-doctoral students and forty graduate students had studied there since research began in 2001. The institute had produced more than 700 scientific publications and hosted more than thirty international conferences. It had also received high marks in a recent review by the Natural Sciences and Engineering Research Council of Canada. "PI has been a great success on a world-wide scientific scale," the council said.[11] Based on these accomplishments, Burton was confident his contract as executive director would be renewed after eight years at the helm. It was not. Angered and worried about the book he was working on, the board of directors chaired by Lazaridis decided to let him go. The official reason was failed contract negotiations, but Burton believes the real reason was his decision to write about his journey launching Perimeter. "Bizarre as it may seem, it appears that a major preoccupation of the institute's board of directors for the first six months of 2007 was what to do with this pernicious book, followed closely, presumably, by how to get rid of its author who had the brazen temerity to once again bring the dark story forward publicly," he writes in *First Principles*.[12] Far from a hatchet job, the book was an enlightening, self-deprecating account of Burton's struggles to get Perimeter off the ground. After its release, *First Principles* was hailed by noted Canadian science writer Peter Calamai as an "astonishing" work offering rare insight in this country "into how smart people have fun in the theatre of scientific ideas."[13] In an interview when Burton's departure was announced, Lazaridis praised his contributions, but would not say why contract talks broke down. The split was not acrimonious, he said. "The best way to describe it is unfortunate."[14] A lack of oversight of Perimeter's board may have played a role in his departure too, Burton speculated. Neither he nor the provincial or federal governments, which gave generously to the institute, had seats on the board.[15]

Burton was eventually replaced in 2008 by South African physicist Neil Turok, who had taught at Princeton and chaired the mathematical physics department at Cambridge University in Britain where he also worked with the renowned physicist Stephen Hawking. Hawking himself served as a distinguished visiting research chair at Perimeter from 2009 until his death in 2018 and came for six-week study visits in 2010 and 2012. A $30-million addition, which opened in 2011, bears his name. In February 2019, Turok stepped down as director and was replaced by long-time Perimeter physicist Robert Myers.

The fact that Perimeter is not affiliated with any university makes it unique among physics institutes, said Duschenes. When Burton initially went looking for donors and support, he was regarded with some skepticism because of the institute's independence. And yet Perimeter works "very, very closely" with universities across the country and beyond, and some of its faculty teach at universities. Every year, thirty master's students from universities around the world come to the institute to study for a year under its Perimeter Scholar's International program. "Our tentacles are spread widely across the country," said Duschenes. "There is never a day when people from another institution are not here." Collaboration with other researchers, wherever they are located, is how science gets done. "There is no IP (intellectual property) here. Papers are posted on the archive as soon as they are written." Perimeter has a library of 12,000 lecture videos available to students and researchers in other locations. It also runs a public-lecture series distributed on the Internet. A lecture by Turok in 2018 on black holes and the Big Bang theory attracted 500,000 views on YouTube.

Perimeter doesn't worry about how it ranks among other theoretical physics institutes. "It's not an extremely valuable exercise to be honest," said Duschenes. Hawking called Perimeter one of the leading centres for theoretical physics and that's good enough for him. With government contributing two-thirds of its annual $32-million budget, scrutiny is heavy. An advisory committee made up of international scientists reviews research at Perimeter, and budgets are checked by outside auditors. One area where Perimeter doesn't take a back seat to anyone is in attracting talent. "We are extremely competitive on recruitment. We have to be," said Duschenes. For example, Perimeter gets 800 applications for the fifteen post-doctoral positions it offers each year. These are students at the height of their learning power with multiple offers from other institutions, said Duschenes. "We set the bar very, very high." Research at Perimeter spans the gamut from "quantum to cosmos," or infinitesimal to the infinite, and physicists are given total freedom. "If we point them in one direction, they might miss the boat." Perimeter doesn't think of itself as a think tank. It's not trying to influence public policy as traditional think tanks do. Duschenes prefers the term "research accelerator."[16]

∗ ∗ ∗

Research In Motion had two CEOs, both of whom wanted to use their wealth in some worthwhile fashion. So it's no surprise Waterloo also has two research institutes. The second is located less than a block away from Perimeter in a four-storey, glass and buff-stone edifice called the Centre for International Governance Innovation. And its boss has no problem calling CIGI (pronounced *see-jee*) a think tank. Think tanks have a long and noble tradition dating back to 1831, when the Duke of Wellington created the Royal United Services Institute to study naval and military issues in Britain, wrote Rohinton Medhora in a 2017 magazine article.[17] Medhora writes about think tanks, he does interviews about think tanks, he quotes rating services on think tanks, he cites transparency figures on think tanks. He embraces the word think tank. "We are a think tank, and we want to be nimble," said the president of CIGI, the Waterloo-based research institute on global affairs founded by Jim Balsillie in 2001. While the history of think tanks dates back to the 1800s, the term wasn't invented until after 1950, when "policy wonks," as people at think tanks are often called, started gathering to discuss strategy and influence government, especially in the US where they initially took off. Today there are more than 6,500, with about 2,000 located in the US and 2,100 in Europe, according to the University of Pennsylvania, which studies think tanks and is considered the authoritative voice on this societal niche. While think tanks have been denigrated as "talk shops" in some circles, most notably by former Prime Minister Stephen Harper in 2011, they have played a role in some epic changes. A report by the Brookings Institution laid the foundation for the Marshall Plan to resurrect Europe after the Second World War. And a study by the RAND Corporation eased the admission of former Soviet states in Eastern Europe into NATO.[18]

Canada has about 100 think tanks, including familiar names such as the C.D. Howe Institute and the Fraser Institute, but the actual number of reputable policy institutes is closer to 25, said Medhora.[19] Beyond the numbers, think tanks range widely in the type and quality of work they do. Some are just "convening tanks" that hold meetings and bring people together for talks. Others are tied to political parties, ideologies or rich benefactors with an axe to grind. Some do research but don't have the resources to do much with that research. The ideal think tank is one that does research and then moves it into the public domain to effect change. CIGI aspires to the latter category. "We have content and we want to make something of that content," said Medhora. "From contact to impact" is another phrase he likes to use. Impact is something Medhora wanted to have when he took the helm of CIGI in 2012. After earning his doctorate in economics at the University of Toronto, he taught there for four years, then spent the next twenty years at the International Development Research Centre in Ottawa, a Crown corporation that funds research in developing countries. A friend of John

English, CIGI's first director, Medhora was appointed to the centre's board in 2009. When the top job came open three years later, he leapt. "It was a once in a lifetime opportunity," said Medhora, who is in his late fifties, with thinning grey hair and an earnest gaze.[20]

Despite its short history, CIGI is long on ambition. It aspires to be the world's leading think tank on global governance. Three areas — the global economy; global security and politics; and international law — are the focus of its research. In aspiring to be number one, CIGI faces a daunting task. The global governance field is littered with big, important-sounding names — the Council on Foreign Relations in New York City; the Brookings Institution in Washington, DC; the Peterson Institute for International Economics, also in Washington, DC; and the Royal Institute of International Affairs, also known as Chatham House, in London. Among this glittering cast, CIGI is the only one based in a smaller non-capital city. In that sense, it is unique, said Medhora. It has a roster of 140 researchers and experts, a veritable house of wonks — schooled in everything from conflict analysis to climate change, Indigenous law to Arctic governance. Half are based at CIGI, with the rest spread around the globe. "The bulk of the work is done by fellows" or "part-time stringers," as Medhora sometimes calls them. Retired diplomats and academics who are eminent in their fields, they come together to write on issues, work on projects or attend conferences on CIGI's behalf. At the 2018 G20 summit in Buenos Aires, CIGI had "a spokesman in the media tent," he noted.[21]

The mention of G20 is apropos. In its early years, CIGI tried to make its mark by focusing much of its research on the Group of Twenty. Founded in 1999 by then-Canadian finance minister Paul Martin and US treasury secretary Larry Summers, the G20 brought together finance ministers from nineteen leading nations and the European Union to discuss ways to improve global financial stability. In 2008, heads of state began attending G20 summits, and CIGI helped to smooth the transition by contributing research papers or "soft capital," as Medhora calls it. "The early days of CIGI were all about the G20," he notes, but in recent years, the centre has embraced a new cause — technology. Artificial intelligence, cyber crime, financial technology, big data and the like are impacting global governance, and CIGI wants to be in the mix. "Our overall chapeau is still the G20," said Medhora,[22] but the centre has tried to shift away from traditional diplomatic work to explore new worlds. It has also done work on the refugee crisis, forming the World Refugee Council in 2017, led by former Canadian foreign affairs minister Lloyd Axworthy. In a January 2019 report, the council called for a major overhaul of the global refugee system, including the prosecution of perpetrators and the creation of innovative financing systems to assist refugee-hosting states.

* * *

It all started with a run in the snow. Jim Balsillie had invited a cast of movers and shakers in diplomatic and educational circles to his cottage on Georgian Bay early in 2001 to do some brainstorming. Among the group was Paul Heinbecker, a WLU grad and former Canadian ambassador to the United Nations; John English, former MP from Kitchener, UW history prof and author of biographies on Lester Pearson and Pierre Trudeau; and UW president David Johnston. Balsillie had already been thinking of donating some of his wealth to an endeavour in global relations, but wasn't sure what that endeavour looked like. After several hours of debate, the group was stuck. As Rod McQueen relates in his 2010 book *BlackBerry*, Balsillie decided to go for a jog in the snow even though the flakes were falling fast and furious. After two hours, just when the group was thinking of sending out a search party, the RIM co-CEO burst through the door, covered in white. "I've got it! I've got the theme!" he shouted to the stunned and relieved crew.[23]

Thus was born the New Economy Institute, as it was first called. The name soon gave way to CIGI, a somewhat cumbersome but apt moniker because it married Balsillie's two passions — international governance and innovation, his bailiwick at RIM. As soon as the City of Waterloo got wind of Balsillie's plans, it rolled out the red carpet regardless of who was in the way, much as it had for Perimeter. The RIM boss wanted to install CIGI in the Seagram Museum, the yellow-brick heritage structure built in 1878 and purchased by the city from the Seagram Distillery. It was now occupied by Waterloo Maple, a UW spinoff specializing in math software. Maple was part way through a ten-year lease with first rights to buy the property should the city put it up for sale. After convincing Maple to waive its purchase rights and vacate the building within a reasonable time frame, city council agreed to sell the museum building to Balsillie for $2.5 million, about $2 million less than its assessed value and to split the costs of any repairs or environmental remediation required to the site. The objections of several councillors were swept aside in the excitement over Balsillie's $20-million gift to CIGI, the prestige it would bring to Waterloo and the strong possibility of more money coming from senior governments. "We are witnesses to an exceptional act of individual philanthropy," said Waterloo Mayor Lynne Woolstencoft.[24] In the meantime, the RIM chieftain needed a temporary home for CIGI until Waterloo Maple could find another location. An empty train station stood across the street. It had been built in 1996 by a tourist-train operator, then purchased by the city after the business failed. Council agreed to lease it to CIGI for six months even though the city had already been approached by a bakery-owner offering to lease the station for ten years with a $100,000 down payment. "It appears CIGI is being treated as a preferred party and this is not fair," said bakery-owner John Bergen.[25]

By the fall of 2003, Waterloo Maple had vacated the Seagram Museum and CIGI was able to move in. In the meantime, more donations rolled in — $10 million from Lazaridis, in return for Balsillie's gift to Perimeter, and $30 million from the federal government. Flush with cash, John English, CIGI's executive director, got busy hiring researchers and fellows, including Heinbecker and Louise Frechette, former deputy secretary-general of the UN. Meanwhile, political and diplomatic bigwigs who rarely set foot in the city began beating a path to Waterloo for splashy CIGI conferences.

Among them were retired US army general Wesley Clark and former prime ministers Brian Mulroney and Joe Clark. For those who couldn't make it to Waterloo, a private intranet portal called Igloo was set up so CIGI could share research with other clients across the globe. Igloo got so busy, its workforce was soon surpassing thirty people and was eventually spun off into a separate company.

As CIGI expanded, Balsillie began thinking it should align with the local universities in some way. Neither had any kind of program in international relations. So, in 2007, he unveiled a major new venture called the Balsillie School of International Affairs. It would offer graduate programs in global governance in a three-way partnership among CIGI, UW and WLU. A new building costing nearly $8 million would rise up beside CIGI on land leased from the city for $1 per year. The school would be financed with a $33-million donation from Balsillie and $25 million each from the two universities. CIGI would get more money as well, a $17-million endowment from Balsillie and $17 million in matching funds from the province. Once again the city ran into flack over arrangements with the RIM boss. Among the critics was Councillor Ian McLean. He came from a blue-blood political family in town. His father, Walter McLean, had served in the Mulroney cabinet in the 1980s. McLean, who would go on to lead the local chamber of commerce, didn't like the way local developers were being shoved aside in the Balsillie deal. The city had promised dozens of them that the property, located on prime downtown land acquired when Seagram closed in 1990, would be sold through an open process. One developer was prepared to pay $3.5 million for the land, but the city was giving it to Balsillie for free and the school would pay no tax on the property, McLean pointed out. But his objections were overruled by other councillors who felt Balsillie was offering something extraordinary. "I'd always felt that this 3.5 acres had to be something special," said Councillor Jan d'Ailly. "Not just a hotel or a commercial building but something that makes Waterloo a unique place."[26]

The skirmishes with local councillors were minor compared to the pier-six brawl that broke out between CIGI and the Canadian Association of University Teachers (CAUT), the body representing professors across the country. It all seemed to start with the mysterious departure of English, the centre's first director and the man who had built CIGI from the ground up. He resigned abruptly in 2009 without explaining why he was leaving. A year later, the first director of the Balsillie School, Ramesh Thakur, was fired after complaining that his academic freedom was being curtailed. A former assistant secretary-general at the United Nations, Thakur's hiring two years earlier had been hailed as a coup. An inquiry by CAUT found that Thakur had been fired unfairly and that his dismissal had been part of a wider purge that started with English. Moreover, Waterloo's two universities had failed to educate Balsillie about his proper role in the school. CIGI and the two universities disagreed, saying Thakur was fired over performance issues.[27] Matters reached a climax in 2012 when York University pulled out of a plan to establish an international law program with CIGI. In doing so, it was walking away from big bucks. The program would have been funded with $30 million from Balsillie, matching dollars from the province and $3 million from York. Two-thirds of the twenty-two PhD students and ten research chairs would have been based in Waterloo. York walked away at the urging of CAUT, which felt CIGI and Balsillie would have too much influence over hiring and curriculum. The sticking point was a hiring committee of five, with CIGI getting two seats at the table. Fred Kuntz, CIGI's director of public affairs, tried to explain that public-private partnerships were the new normal, that private donors deserved a seat at the table, that all they were concerned about was good governance.[28] In the end, the centre backed out of the hiring committee, but it didn't matter. The damage had been done. Osgoode Hall, York's law school, wanted no part of Balsillie and his millions. CAUT next turned its sights on the Balsillie School. It wasn't happy with the way CIGI was throwing its weight around. It called for a boycott of Waterloo's two universities by every professor in the land. The dispute prompted Thomas Homer-Dixon, author of books on the environment and CIGI's chair of global systems, to fire back in an op-ed article. CAUT holds itself up as the sole arbiter of academic freedom, Homer-Dixon wrote, while unfairly targeting Balsillie over his style. "Balsillie is a sharp-elbowed, brusque, American-style capitalist who's largely disdained by Canada's business and cultural elites and intelligentsia, because he often doesn't play by their unspoken rules."[29]

CAUT eventually backed off on the boycott and a truce was called after the two sides reached an agreement that satisfied both sides. After the smoke cleared, CIGI decided to offer an international law program of its own featuring research done by its fellows. Today it is one of three core programs at CIGI along with the global economy and global security and politics. Meanwhile, enrolment at the Balsillie School grew to ninety-five students in 2018, of whom fifty-five were in the doctoral program and forty in the master's stream. Medhora, who took the reins at the tail end of the battle with CAUT, said CIGI does not participate in hiring or curriculum decisions at the Balsillie School. "We have zero say over faculty and research." The two institutions now share the same building after CIGI vacated the Seagram Museum in 2014 and moved next door.

Though Duschenes isn't overly concerned about how often Perimeter is mentioned in the media, Medhora keeps tabs on CIGI's mentions. Promotion of CIGI's research is a primary means of effecting change, he said. CIGI fellows churn out 100 to 115 research papers a year and they often find their way onto the desks of journalists. "Not a day goes by when someone from CIGI is not quoted in the media," Medhora said. The centre also ranks highly for quality and financial transparency by independent groups rating such issues, he noted.

Together, Perimeter and CIGI have brought many foreign researchers, scholars and students to Waterloo Region. The same scenario played out at Research In Motion. As RIM grew into a global corporation with the best-selling smartphone on the planet, international talent seemed to beat a path to its door.

Chapter 9
THE IMPORTS

As the BlackBerry took the business world by storm and Research In Motion grew into a global corporation in the late 1990s and early 2000s, it was inevitable that the culture, camaraderie and ambience within the company would change. RIM was no longer a startup, propelled by a small, plucky crew of engineers, designers and sales people all pushing towards the same goal. Nor was its workforce largely home-grown. More people started showing up in Waterloo from other parts of Canada, the US and even Europe, people with accents and attitudes and different ways of doing things. And oh, how its workforce grew. In 1992, it stood at around twenty. By 2000, it was more than 700. By 2005, it had exploded to 3,500. Everybody, it seemed, wanted to climb aboard the RIM rocket ship. The Waterloo smartphone-maker was the Apple of the early aughts and the hottest ticket in tech. As RIM's workforce took off into the stratosphere, some of the early employees looked around and didn't like what they saw. Some of the magic was gone, replaced by a more mercenary attitude.

Among them was Rob Elder. A native of Richmond Hill, Ontario, just north of Toronto, he joined the sales team in early 1999 when RIM was in "crank-up mode." For a number of years, life was fantastic, beyond his wildest dreams. At his previous job, he had travelled throughout south-western Ontario, selling hardware and software for a small distributor. Now he was flying around the American Midwest, flogging BlackBerrys to such Fortune 500 companies as aircraft-manufacturer McDonnell-Douglas and brewery goliath Anheuser-Busch. At one point, he even sold BlackBerrys to August Busch IV and celebrity-cleric Jesse Jackson. But gradually things started to change. RIM brought in people from outside at higher levels, people from companies like Nortel Networks, which was downsizing. "They brought politics to the company. Early on there wasn't politics. It was all about chasing the same goal," said Elder. And many of these people started doing things based on their personal agendas or to advance their careers and fatten their paycheques. The added layers made it harder to get the ear of RIM bosses. Messages were being massaged. Mini-empires were being created. "Mike and Jim were getting more and more insulated." Elder knew the company needed help, especially at the management level. "RIM was flat for a long time. You couldn't have that many people reporting to Mike and Jim." But he felt the hiring process beginning to slip. It wasn't as rigorous as it used to be.[1]

Pete Edmonson, RIM's director of research in the 1990s, noticed it too. In the beginning RIM didn't go through employment agencies. It hired a lot based on referrals and word-of-mouth, people inside the company who knew of talented, selfless colleagues working elsewhere. "We were looking for that unique individual." And Lazaridis and Balsillie would at least let Edmonson and others talk to candidates before hiring them. But slowly, as sales surged, the standards started to slip. Motorola and Nortel were imploding, their executives were on the market and a few senior people were brought in without the usual "what do you think of them?" said Edmonson. These executives in turn brought in others from their old company, some of whom were considered the "B team" from that firm, he added. At one point, "a whack of guys were hired from Nortel as it was spiraling down." The same scenario was being played out at Motorola, the Chicago-area cellphone giant whose sales began to tank in the early 2000s.

So many of its employees were jumping to Waterloo that RIM acquired a new nickname — "RIMorola," said Edmonson. In 2008, Motorola launched a lawsuit against RIM, claiming the Waterloo company was improperly poaching employees from Motorola offices in Illinois and Florida. According to the suit, RIM rented a truck and parked it outside a Motorola plant in Illinois. Attached to the vehicle was a billboard advertising jobs at RIM.[2] People with experience running large companies were in short supply in Waterloo, Edmonson admits. "We did need outsiders, but quality outsiders."[3] The new recruits at senior levels made it hard on ambitious people inside the company, veterans who had paid their dues and had aspirations of moving up. When promotions went to outsiders, Brubacher-Cressman, director of product development and an employee since the 1980s, felt "a little bit dissed." He was ready to move up and take on a new challenge. "On one level I understood. On another level it stung."[4]

Not all of the early cohort resented the new recruits. RIM needed to hire people from bigger firms, managers who knew how to deploy large groups of employees or oversee sophisticated manufacturing operations and move product quickly through global supply lines, said Paul Lucier, who joined the RIM sales team in 1999. Many insiders were under the illusion they had the necessary skills and experience to take the company to the next level. In reality, much of their success was based on luck and being in the right place at the right time, he said. "A lot of them had no business doing what they were doing." Many were young. Their job at RIM was the first major position of their career. "They rode up in the rocket." It's easy to sell a product when it's hot, Lucier noted. Robust sales hide a lack of skill and experience. Some insiders really blossomed, said Lucier, citing Patrick Spence as one example. Spence joined RIM right out of Western University in London, Ontario, in 1998 and rose through the sales ranks to senior vice-president of global sales before leaving in 2012. He is now CEO of Sonos, the California-based manufacturer of wireless home-sound systems with annual revenues of $1.2 billion US in fiscal 2019.[5] Lindsay Gibson was another. She stumbled reluctantly into a call-centre job at RIM in 2000 after graduating from the journalism program at Conestoga College. By the time she left sixteen years later, she was vice-president of manufacturing and supply chain, responsible for delivering products on-time to carriers and launching new devices. Gibson is now chief operating officer at TextNow, a texting and calling service that is one of Waterloo's most successful, next-generation startups.

David Yach, RIM's chief technology officer for software from 1998 to 2012, believes the outsiders changed the company for the better. "There was a ton we didn't know about the cellphone industry." Global manufacturing, high-volume production, patent licensing and the like were issues RIM had not grappled with yet. RIM had a lot of smart people who rose up through the company. Many, including Lazaridis, thought they could handle the growth in-house, "but you don't know what you don't know," Yach said. He singled out Larry Conlee, who came from Motorola to be chief operating officer for manufacturing at RIM in 2001. Conlee had a great mind and "had been around since the cellphone industry was born," said Yach. Conlee immediately started looking around for people who had done this before from companies such as Motorola, Ericsson and Cisco. Though a UW grad, Yach was technically an import as well, having joined RIM from the Waterloo office of Sybase, formerly Watcom. "From my perspective it was necessary," Yach said of the recruits from other companies. RIM wouldn't have grown like it did without them.[6]

Though RIM went looking for many of the talented people it brought in, some didn't have to be recruited. They were dying to be part of the hottest tech company on the planet.

* * *

Dietmar Wennemer was sitting in his Munich office one day in 2005 when he took a call from a fellow Siemens employee in San Diego. The two had met when Wennemer did a three-year stint in California in the mobile phones division of the German industrial giant. As the conversation continued, the friend mentioned a job opening he had heard about at Research In Motion. The friend wasn't interested, but

Wennemer's ears immediately perked up. A native of the German state of Westphalia, he had studied mechanical engineering at university then joined Siemens in 1994 at the age of twenty-five. After a year at the German company, he concluded that his best path forward lay in mobile phones. For the next decade he remained in the mobile phones division, working his way up to a job leading new-product concepts. Among the highlights had been the California posting. Siemens had opened a design centre in San Diego and Wennemer was assigned to go there to build up the mechanical team. While he enjoyed the work, the relentless sunshine bothered him. Lean and fit with short dark hair and a broad smile, Wennemer loved cycling and cross-country skiing. He missed the snow and the change of seasons back in Germany. But the San Diego stint was also his first tour of duty outside Germany and it gave him a taste for more.

As he pondered his options, Wennemer was not impressed with the progress Siemens was making in mobile phones. At one point, the German company was the number-two cellphone maker in the world, behind Nokia of Finland. But Siemens was a huge company, with 450,000 employees worldwide and a history stretching back more than 150 years. The cellphone division was just one among many, including power-generation, renewable energy, auto parts and computer chips. In recent years Siemens hadn't been pouring much money into its wireless division. Its software and display screens were looking out of date. Meanwhile, RIM was on a tear. It was blowing away the competition with its durable BlackBerry featuring the killer app, push email. By the spring of 2005, 3 million people were using BlackBerrys, up from 1 million just eighteen months earlier.[7] Various models of the device were being sold in more than fifty countries by over 100 carriers.[8] Unlike Siemens, mobile data was RIM's only division. All its resources went into making the various models of the BlackBerry the best on the planet. Even so, as Wennemer took a closer look at RIM's flagship device, he could see room for improvement. The mechanical design needed some upgrades and the displays were monochrome. "My skill is smartphone housing and surface decoration," he said. When Wennemer contacted RIM about the job opening, he was invited to Waterloo for an interview. He brought several phones with him to show Lazaridis how the Black-Berry could be improved. A day later he was offered a job as director of mechanical engineering. Moving his wife and two young boys to Wat-erloo in the fall of 2005, Wennemer thought it was a good omen when they found a house they liked in the northwest part of the city backing onto some woods. It was on a street called Munich Circle.

Wennemer didn't have to wait long for his first test. Within a week of starting at RIM he was on a plane to Fort Worth, Texas. A company there was making plastic display windows for the upcoming new BlackBerry 8700, 8707 and 7100 devices. But something had gone wrong during production and most of the screens were coming back with flaws in them. After checking out the supplier in Texas, Wennemer decided RIM needed a more capable supplier. From his days at Siemens, he knew of a few in Germany and Singapore. He called chief operating officer Larry Conlee and got the green light to switch suppliers. Flaws in the screens dropped dramatically. "We retooled the parts," he said. Sometime later he was in a meeting with Lazaridis. The co-CEO had always resisted the idea of putting a camera in the BlackBerry because business customers, RIM's core audience, did not want people taking pictures in corpor-ate offices and manufacturing plants. Proprietary technology might get stolen. Attempts had already been made by smartphone competitors to email pictures as attachments, but the practice was not widespread. Wennemer felt strongly that RIM should add this function so business users could email pictures to customers. He conveyed his feelings to Lazaridis. A camera was later added to the Pearl, the first BlackBerry to offer that feature. Wennemer was also worried about the trackball on the Pearl. Previous BlackBerrys had a track-wheel on the side of the handset to move the cursor up and down. With the Pearl, RIM was switching to a trackball in the middle of the device just below the screen so the user could move the cursor left and right as well as up and down. The silver trackball looked like a Pearl, hence the name. But it tended to collect grease from the fingers. Wennemer didn't like that. There had to be something better. When told the trackball had to stay, he argued that users should be able to remove it and clean it. A snap-in silver ring was added so customers could perform those functions.

Over his nine years at RIM — he left in 2014 — Wennemer was in the thick of nearly every major development on the mechanical-engineering and product-design sides of the company. The Pearl, Storm, Curve, Bold, Torch, Porsche Design and BlackBerry 10 phones all have his finger-prints on them. The Storm, RIM's first response to the iPhone, was widely panned for its clickable touchscreen that mimicked a physical keyboard. Typing on the edge of the screen was more difficult than in the middle. Most were returned. Wennemer remembers Lazaridis coming to his office. "Can we do something with a keyboard under the screen?" he wondered. "It was one of the biggest challenges you can come up with," said Wennemer. Though he didn't lead the overall design, Wennemer was part of a team that worked sixty to seventy-hour weeks on the device. Fuelled on adrenaline, he didn't mind the long hours. "It was fun." Looking back, the Storm was too rushed, he said. "We needed more soak time to get it right." Soak means allowing engineers to play around with the device for a period of time to detect its flaws. The iPod gave Apple a huge head start on touchscreen technology, Wennemer said. He didn't take the iPhone lightly when it came out in 2007. "And neither did Mike (Lazaridis), otherwise he wouldn't have pushed so heavily to get the Storm out." The Android phones, not the iPhone, are what really killed the BlackBerry, he went on. "They allowed the Asian manufacturers to get in the game." A favourite memory during this period involves soccer. Wennemer was playing one rainy day after work when he stopped to check his BlackBerry at halftime. There was a message from Lazaridis about an urgent problem. He drove straight to Lazaridis's house and showed up at the door covered in mud. The chief executive was surprised but ushered him in to carry on the dis-cussion. "Mike was into every detail, but he respected you."

Wennemer started RIM's first product-design team outside Waterloo. "It was a bit of a challenge finding talent in Waterloo. They didn't have the knowledge of smartphone architecture and high-precision, plastic-part design," he said. RIM had a legal office in Dallas. Wennemer had been down there and heard that Nokia was shutting down its mechanical-design team in the city. He scooped up a bunch of its designers. Over the years, the Dallas office grew into a full-blown design operation with 200 engineers. Wennemer also added mechanical and product-design teams in Florida and Germany. The Florida team came about when Motorola shut down an office there while the German crew emerged out of a former Nokia operation in Bochum. After leaving BlackBerry, Wennemer eventually landed at a Waterloo drone-maker called Aeryon Labs, founded by two former employees of Pixstream, David Kroetsch and Mike Peasgood. They are considered pioneers in the unmanned aerial-vehicle world and high-end drones.[9] As chief product officer, Wennemer is bullish on Aeryon's drones. "They're like flying super-computers." A Canadian citizen now, he has no desire to move back to Germany. "My kids were 3 and 5 when we moved here. It's their home, and we feel very welcome too."[10]

Not long after joining RIM, Wennemer noticed a big influx of work-ers from Motorola. They brought some of the culture of the American cellphone goliath to Waterloo. They were "more aggressive," even "a little hostile." He was used to the more polite style of Canadian and European workers.

Among the Motorola cohort who came north was a research director who had done so much work on wireless technology and standards, earning numerous patents along the way, that he was awarded the title of Motorola Distinguished Innovator.

* * *

When a colleague suggested to Mark Pecen in 2005 that he consider apply-ing for a job at Research In Motion, he scoffed. "I dunno. I don't know anything about Canada." Yet, he had to admit to himself that he needed a change. He was fifty years old and had been at Motorola for nine years.

Prior to that, he had done consulting work for the telecommunications giant stretching back into the 1980s. Radios and wireless technology had fascinated the Chicago native from an early age. He earned his master's degree in engineering at the University of Pennsylvania, then studied technology management at the Wharton School, Penn's prestigious business school. Moving back to Chicago, Pecen started working as a consultant. "In the 1980s, anybody who knew about computers and wireless was rare. I could consult and do well." He did so much work for Motorola that the Chicago-area company became his biggest customer and then his employer. Thereafter he focused on developing new technology and protocols for the Global System for Mobile Telecommunication (GSM) network, the most widely used wireless network in the world today and the one on which third- and fourth-generation wireless networks are based. Motorola was attempting to expand its reach in Europe, and Pecen worked on the first digital cell service there. Technologies he invented were later adopted as parts of global standards. "The internals of the system that make it work," is how he describes his contribution, but adds that hundreds, if not thousands, of researchers contributed to the creation of GSM. "I like to work on hard problems," said Pecen. "Easy problems are boring. No one will pay you to solve them."

At Motorola in the US, he worked on radio and antenna technology and multiplexers that bunched and filtered various digital signals. He was interested in the big picture and how all the pieces fit together. Understanding how it all worked, not memorization, was the key. Patents rolled in until they numbered more than fifty. The more difficult the problem, the more interested he got. Cheerful and easy-going with a neatly trimmed beard, he downplays his accomplishments. "There weren't really many people interested in this stuff," he said. Despite his reservations about working at RIM, Pecen thought he should at least travel to Waterloo and have a look. What was there to lose? Befitting his lofty status at Motorola, he landed a meeting with Lazaridis himself. The two talked for several hours, and Pecen explained the intricacies of CDMA (code division multiple access), the other major wireless network besides GSM. A whiteboard in the room soon filled up with math equations and diagnostics. As they chatted, Pecen found himself warming up to the RIM boss. "I thought, what an interesting character." Eventually Lazaridis cut to the chase. "You should work with us," he told Pecen. "But what would I do?" the Motorola innovator asked. "We'll think of something," Lazaridis replied confidently. As they were concluding the meeting, Pecen had a sudden inspiration. "Who is your head of advanced technology and research?" "We don't have one," replied Lazaridis.

Pecen had found his niche. In addition to reporting to Lazaridis directly, he became RIM's vice-president of advanced technology and research and later senior vice-president of research and development. "I built out a separate little division," Pecen said, that eventually grew to about 300 researchers spread over four cities — Waterloo, Ottawa, Chicago and Dallas. "You have to go where the talent is. It's not realistic to expect top-level researchers to come to Waterloo." He also brought in some of the best people he could find from Motorola, about twenty to thirty researchers. But the team wasn't assembled overnight. Finding good researchers takes time, he noted. His group worked on multiple-band antennas, tunable antennas, radio-stack components, technology that went into wireless standards and so on. It was stuff that all smart-phones use and manufacturers have to pay for. Nokia and Apple, to name two, licensed some of their creations, Pecen said. For the most part they worked separately from the rest of the company. "We were a little upstream in the value chain." That meant it would take some years before product groups would need their technologies. By 2008, he had a millimeter-wave lab installed at RIM to develop wireless sub-systems at higher frequencies, offering the potential to transmit more data using less bandwidth. In doing so, he was thinking about the future. Developers only began incorporating millimeter-wave technology with the arrival of 5G wireless networks in 2019. Eight years was not unusual for how long it took to see the fruits of their research.

Pecen found he could get things done more quickly at RIM. Motorola had 220,000 employees when he was there, while RIM had 20,000 at its peak around 2011. Motorola was a mature company saddled with a big bureaucracy and slow, formal procedures. RIM was younger and more agile. "I never considered RIM to be a big company," he said. At one point he was assigned to look into a customer's problem in Germany. He went to the appropriate department at RIM, talked with engineers, then flew to the customer's plant. "The problem was solved in two to three weeks."

As time went on, Lazaridis wanted a separate facility at RIM dedicated to research and to house Pecen's department. A 90,000-square-foot building rose up several blocks west of the main RIM campus on Westmount Road overlooking a wooded area called Laurel Creek. For a number of years, there was no sign on the three-storey building indicating what was going on inside or who owned it. Some speculated it was RIM's new headquarters. Pecen didn't see the need for signage. "It was a research building," he said. When RIM downsized in 2013 and sold off most of its real estate, Lazaridis and Fregin bought the building for $15 million. It now houses Quantum Valley Investments, the venture capital firm they started to invest in startups in the quantum-computing field. One of those startups is Isara Corp., where Pecen works as chief operating officer. Isara specializes in cryptography to protect clients against cyber attacks from next-generation quantum computers. Its office is also in the Westmount Road building.

Pecen left RIM in 2013. His whole department was eliminated. Thorsten Heins, who took over as CEO when Lazaridis and Balsillie departed, decided to switch from a vertically integrated structure where everything is done under one roof to a horizontal structure where much of the work is contracted out. When a company goes horizontal, it's harder to connect the other pieces, said Pecen. The other problem was the departure of the man who hired him. "Mike was gone. There was nothing for me to do." After leaving RIM, Pecen did some consulting work for tech startups, law firms and private equity firms. He also kept busy serving on the board of the Institute for Quantum Computing, the UW faculty started with a generous donation from Lazaridis and his wife, Ophelia. One day Pecen was chatting with Ray Laflamme, the institute's executive director at the time. How can quantum computing be made more relevant in today's world? Laflamme asked him. "You need to get involved with industry," Pecen quickly replied. But he knew it was more complicated than that. After taking some time to ponder the question, he had an epiphany — quantum cryptography. Tomorrow's quantum computers will be able to slice through today's firewalls like butter. Criminals could save and store encrypted data now, then break into it down the road when quantum technology makes it possible. Work must begin now and standards developed on an international level to prevent this from happening, Pecen reasoned. To this end, he founded the first industry-based working group on quantum-safe cryptography standards at the European Telecommunications Standards Institute, a global organization that develops safeguards and benchmarks for the high-tech sector. In doing so, he helped spawn a new industry in quantum cryptography.

It also led to his employment at Isara in 2015. The company had nearly fifty employees by the end of 2018, all of whom are younger than Pecen. He describes Isara's workforce as "mostly a bunch of twenty-somethings. I try to help them avoid the same beginner's mistakes the rest of us made." Founded by two former BlackBerry encryption specialists, Isara has raised more than $20 million in financing, including $11.5 million from Quantum Valley Investments. After leaving RIM, Pecen decided to stay in Waterloo and he and his wife are now Canadian citizens. It's a lot easier to get things done in Canada, especially when you're dealing with government, said Pecen, who serves as an adviser to the feds on wireless communication, research and technology standardization. Progress is much slower in the US by comparison. With more competing interests, it's like many different countries in one. Canadians are also more collaborative than Americans, he said. He's bullish on the Waterloo tech sector. "Waterloo could be the next Silicon Valley." The cost of living has soared in the valley. "It's a bit played out." Waterloo, on the other hand, has a solid foundation in a number of key disciplines including physics, biotechnology, computer science, business and quantum information, he said. "There is world-class talent here." Among them is the man who brought him to Waterloo. At Penn, Pecen learned a lot about Benjamin Franklin, who founded the university in 1740 and later helped to launch the US as a country. Franklin believed that the best dividends are paid when you grow people's minds. "Mike (Lazaridis) kind of reminds me of this guy."[11]

While imports like Wennemer and Pecen made significant contributions to the success of RIM, the company's relationship with the media would enter choppy waters thanks to the efforts of another import.

Chapter 10
MUZZLING THE MEDIA

In the beginning, it was mostly sweetness and light. As RIM emerged in the early 1990s as a company that was going places, its relationship with the local media was a friendly one. There was the usual cat-and-mouse game of RIM trying to attract headlines and coverage for its accomplishments, and the media not being sure of what to make of this upstart company that was into the nebulous world of wireless communications and gadgets. Winning a contract to make the Digi-Sync film-editing reader was a story that local journalists had a hard time resisting, especially when the device was used on such Hollywood films as *Home Alone* and the TV series *Road to Avonlea* and would later lead to Oscar and Emmy awards for the company. As RIM's new co-chief executive officer in charge of marketing and business development, Balsillie went out of his way to drum up coverage. The *Record*, the area's largest daily newspaper, profiled him in a short piece in 1993. "Workaholic stick-handles Waterloo firm's finances," read the headline as Balsillie expressed relief that he had ended up at a company like RIM. "It's a game for me," he said of work in general. "And technology is a more complex game. What worried me most a year ago was whether I would get a new game to play." He also couldn't resist a little boasting. "It's a bit conceited, but Mike (Lazaridis) believes there isn't a technology issue he can't solve, and I believe there isn't a business issue I can't stick-handle my way through."[1]

Balsillie even went so far as to write a number of op-ed pieces for the *Record*'s editorial page. Prior to landing at RIM, he had joined a Kitchener industrial coalition of business, labour and political leaders trying to revive a local economy reeling from the global recession of the early 1990s. One of the pieces defended the coalition's call for a freeze on industrial development charges while others endorsed the free trade and deficit policies of the federal government under Conservative Prime Minister Brian Mulroney.

But gradually, as RIM started inking big contracts for its paging device and lining up capital through IPOs to pay for its expansion in the late 1990s, there was no need to court the media any longer. Journalists from Waterloo and beyond started lining up to chronicle this amazing new success story. Despite its growing importance, the company seemed happy to be profiled in the local press. In May 1999, four months after the unveiling of the first BlackBerry, Lazaridis and Balsillie sat down for an interview with Susan Chilton, the *Record*'s business editor at the time. The BlackBerry had just received a rave review in *Business Week* magazine in the US and RIM had won an award for Canadian-American business achievement after forging a partnership with microchip-maker Intel, but the two CEOs seemed more excited about an upcoming showing of the new *Star Wars* movie, *The Phantom Menace*, Chilton wrote. As a gesture of appreciation from management, more than 300 RIM employees were being given the afternoon off and bused to a Waterloo theatre to see the movie. "This is a fun, creative, intense and inclusive corporate culture," Balsillie said.[2] RIM was the flavour of the month in the local press.

The love-in continued into the early 2000s as it soon became apparent that the BlackBerry was a device for the ages. In the fall of 2002, as RIM's user base soared past 400,000 and fifty carriers were distributing its messages around the world, a headline in the *Record* proclaimed, "Competition? Bring it on!" It almost seemed as if the BlackBerry story was too good to be true, that it wasn't possible for a Canadian company to beat Silicon Valley at its own game. "Hardly a week goes by without a stock market analyst suggesting that a competitor is going to put a major dent in company sales," wrote reporter Ron DeRuyter. "The list of the competitors runs the gamut from upstarts such as Danger Inc. and Good Technology to corporate giants such as Microsoft and Nokia." Far from being worried, RIM welcomed the competition with Lazaridis suggesting that it merely corroborated what the company was doing. "I was worried three years ago when we were alone in the business," he said. "I thought maybe we were missing something because no one else was doing it. So it's great that now there is competition. It validates our innovation and entrepreneurship." If anything RIM was ramping up its game with plans to add colour displays, access to multiple email accounts and the ability to read and modify email attachments to the BlackBerry. Earlier in the year, it released its first voice-enabled handset called the BlackBerry 5810. Security was also being tightened with software that would allow IT departments to wirelessly disable BlackBerrys, erase data and remotely set or change passwords. "So while analysts speculate on the latest competitor, RIM and its 2,200 employees will focus on moving forward with the BlackBerry," DeRuyter wrote at the conclusion of the feature.[3]

Even so, there were some early signs that RIM was not a company to be trifled with when it came to tough coverage. *Record* reporter Terry Pender was among the first to feel the company's wrath in 2002. The Waterloo City Hall reporter had been tipped off that the city had struck a deal to sell the former Seagram Museum to Balsillie at below market value. The RIM boss wanted it to serve as the home for his Centre for International Governance Innovation. When Pender called Balsillie for comment, he threatened to take the matter all the way up to the Torstar board of directors (Torstar owned the *Record*) if Pender went ahead with the story. The story would "ruin the *Record*'s relationship with RIM," Balsillie warned. When Pender refused to spike the story, Balsillie wouldn't let him off the phone, and the conversation continued for half-an-hour, with the RIM executive alternating between threats and favours to bring Pender onside. Among the favours were insider tips about RIM business and the possibility of having a "fruitful and ongoing relationship" with him. "It was a transparent attempt at manipulation," Pender recalled. Eventually he did hang up without agreeing to Balsillie's demands and the story was published.[4]

Later in 2002, the *Globe and Mail* broke a story that Lazaridis's pledge of $100 million two years earlier to launch Perimeter Institute was not all it appeared to be. Most of the donation had to be delayed until 2004 or 2005 because RIM's stock had fallen sharply during the dot-com meltdown. Lazaridis could have donated all the money up front, but that would have turned the Perimeter into a private charity and he would not have qualified for a generous tax deduction.[5] Instead he had kept his donation at no more than 50 per cent so Perimeter could qualify as a public charity. That was the reason he pledged just $20 million up front with Balsillie and Fregin matching that amount. The rest of Lazaridis's money would flow a year later when more funds were raised from other donors and governments. But RIM's fluctuating stock price was now throwing some doubt into his generous gift, the *Globe* reported. Howard Burton, Perimeter's first director, confirmed the complicated structure of the donations and the concern over RIM's stock price in his 2009 book. But the *Globe* story pointed out that other donors and the general public were kept in the dark about the delays in the gift.

Lazaridis was livid when the story was published and vented his frustrations in an interview with the *Record*. He admitted that much of the story was true but that RIM's fluctuating stock price had not put the donation in jeopardy. Though RIM shares were worth almost $190 per share when the pledge was announced in 2000, the gift was actually promised in private a year earlier when RIM shares were trading in the $20 range, he said, adding that it would eventually be delivered in full. Lazaridis worried that the *Globe* story would have a chilling effect on private donations to the Perimeter and other such causes.[6]

Instead, the only thing that got chilled was the relationship between

RIM and the *Globe*. For the next five years, *Globe* reporters were given scant access to RIM executives and even the company's public relations department, according to the *Ryerson Review of Journalism*, which explored RIM's rocky relationship with the media in a 2014 feature. Balsillie went so far as to threaten *Globe* reporter Simon Avery in 2006 that "your editors are watching you like a hawk" and ripped into editors John Stackhouse and Edward Greenspon at face-to-face meetings. In the meantime, he fed scoops to the rival *National Post*.[7] It wasn't just the Perimeter story than rankled RIM. Even when RIM was doing well in the early 2000s, business columnist Mathew Ingram wrote a number of negative pieces suggesting it was only a matter of time before competitors overtook the Waterloo company.

The *Globe* wasn't the only paper to be frozen out by RIM over aggressive coverage. The *Record* would soon find itself facing the same dilemma, but it was a young reporter fresh on the staff that would feel the sting of RIM's lash.

* * *

Record business editor Kevin Crowley was going through a stack of job applications in the fall of 2005, when one in particular jumped out at him. It was from a journalist who had grown up in Ohio, studied journalism at the University of Maryland, edited the campus newspaper there and then spent several years working at a daily newspaper in Warren, Ohio, south of Cleveland. Not only that, he had done internships at the *Pittsburgh Post-Gazette* and at a news service on Capitol Hill in Washington, DC. Crowley scratched his head. The *Record* was a respected, medium-sized, regional daily in the Canadian newspaper pantheon with a long history dating back more than 100 years. It boasted a daily paid circulation of around 68,000 subscribers, a staff of more than thirty reporters and had won its share of journalism awards, including several national prizes. By American standards, it might be considered the *Des Moines Register* or the *Toledo Blade*. But it was minor league compared to the large dailies about an hour down the road in Toronto, influential and powerful papers such as the *Globe and Mail*, the *National Post* and the *Toronto Star*. Why in the world would a reporter from Ohio want to work in another country and in Kitchener of all places?

Yet, as Crowley looked through the clippings that Matt Walcoff had submitted with his application, he was impressed. The stories were filled with numbers, financial information and data culled from various Internet sources. Clearly the twenty-eight-year-old Walcoff knew how to cover business and, better yet, extract interesting information from obscure Internet databases. Those were the kinds of skills Crowley wanted. He knew this was going to be an important hire. He was thinking of making a change in how the paper covered RIM. For the past five years, the *Record* had been using a committee approach in its coverage of the BlackBerry-maker. Crowley and reporters Ron DeRuyter and Rose Simone had split up the assignments. But DeRuyter's background was labour, Simone liked to cover science and Crowley was busy running the department. He wanted someone new, a reporter with fire in the belly to take over the RIM beat.[8]

It was always a bit of a mystery why Walcoff came to Kitchener-Waterloo. Of medium build with short, dark hair and glasses, he was not one to make small talk, preferring to elaborate on some aspect of his work, the quirks of Canadians or the Cleveland Browns, his favourite football team. His mother, Cindy Glazer, said he wanted to live in another country, yet not be too far from his Ohio home. On a road trip through Southern Ontario in 2002, he found Waterloo to his liking and, after handing in his resignation at the *Warren Tribune Chronicle*, enrolled in the master's program of the political science faculty at Wilfrid Laurier University. His performance there was nothing short of dazzling. Professor Barry Kay, a frequent and astute contributor to the *Record*'s op-ed pages, called him the best student he had taught in the past twenty years. Another professor, Debora VanNijnatten, was awed by some of the work Walcoff did while assisting her with a research project. He put together an equation comparing after-tax social assistance benefits in Canada and the US that a manager in the US social security administration had never seen before. "He was an excellent writer and his research skills rivalled those of the faculty in the department," said VanNijnatten.[9]

Though covering RIM was not a full-time job, it was nevertheless considered the most important part of Walcoff's beat when he joined the business department. For the first few months, he busied himself with routine stories about RIM. Among them was a feature on a curious grassroots phenomenon that had sprung up around the BlackBerry. Websites such as BlackBerry Cool, BlackBerry Blog, BBHub and RIMarkable were created by obsessive fans of the device and featured tips, forums and blogs on everything from what to do if your BlackBerry falls in the toilet to how to brighten the screen on the handheld. Unsanctioned by RIM, the "fan sites" also offered clues on the release of upcoming BlackBerrys, and Walcoff used one of those tips to get the scoop on the unveiling of the BlackBerry 8700c in New York City on November 1, 2005. The event was a glitzy affair featuring Tour de France cycling champion Lance Armstrong, who had been hired by RIM to promote the device.[10] The fan-site feature was interesting and informative, but it was nothing compared to the thousand-pound gorilla of a story that was about to be dropped on Walcoff's plate. Looming on the horizon was the possible conclusion of a bruising, four-year patent lawsuit between RIM and Thomas J. Campana, Jr.

A Chicago inventor who had built a wireless communications system for the Chicago police force and a pager using a rudimentary form of email for a Miami paging company, Campana had been forced into bankruptcy in 1991. Proud of his wireless research and eager to salvage something from his tattered career, Campana hired a former patent examiner and lawyer named Donald Stout of Washington, DC, and filed for patents for his technology. Together, the two formed NTP Inc. (New Technologies Products) to hold the patents and recruited other investors to back their efforts to secure licensing fees if anyone tried to copy their technology. RIM came into their crosshairs in the spring of 2001 when Stout noticed a story in the *Wall Street Journal* about a patent suit launched by the Waterloo company against an American electronics firm. Balsillie's bombastic quotes added fuel to the fire. "The amateurs out there have to stop," the RIM boss warned, adding that any imitators of RIM's wireless technology would need a licence from RIM or they'd be talking to a judge.[11]

Campana's firm was often dismissed as a patent troll, an enterprise that had only created something on paper, filed a patent for it, then used the threat of litigation to extract licence fees from imitators. But based on the work he had done in Chicago and Miami, Campana believed he was more than just a troll. There was no evidence to suggest RIM had stolen or copied any of his ideas to create the BlackBerry. Nonetheless, the patents owned by Campana were awarded before RIM's pager was launched and he felt they deserved some recognition.

NTP's patent lawsuit against RIM was filed on November 13, 2001, in a Richmond, Virginia, court known as the "rocket docket" for the speedy way it handled patent suits. The case caused barely a ripple in the media with newspapers running briefs or ignoring the filing altogether.[12] Later, the headlines would get much bigger. Despite hiring some of the best legal talent in the business, RIM proceeded to make a number of unforced errors. In the lead-up to the trial, the company delivered documents slowly and failed to work co-operatively with NTP to speed the process up. At the last minute, RIM cancelled a deposition in Waterloo, upsetting travel plans by NTP and making the examination for discovery process unnecessarily difficult. When the case went to trial before a jury in November 2002, Judge James Spencer was already seething about RIM's haughty behaviour.[13]

Matters only got worse. During the thirteen-day trial, RIM's lawyers treated NTP with disdain, calling it no more than a "file drawer" in a lawyer's office. The BlackBerry-maker claimed to have conducted an exhaustive study of NTP's patents, but was unable to produce any evidence that it had done so, nor did it offer any real defence against Campana's infringement claims. A key point came when RIM botched a demonstration of a wireless messaging system developed by a small Arizona company in the late 1980s before Campana had registered his patents. Though a wireless message was sent successfully, NTP lawyers noticed that the transmission used software files from the mid-1990s. Spencer ruled the entire demonstration out of order.[14]

Not surprisingly given RIM's behaviour, the jury found the BlackBerry-maker guilty of infringing all five NTP patents when it issued a verdict on November 21, 2002. Jurists were also swayed by the David vs. Goliath nature of the battle. Big bad RIM was beating up on the poor inventor, Thomas Campana, who was suffering from cancer to boot and would die in 2004 before the case concluded. Spencer assessed a fine of $23 million and ordered RIM to pay royalties of 5.7 per cent on all US sales until the NTP patents expired in 2012. Nine months later, when NTP sought enhanced damages, he more than doubled the fine, hiked the royalty rate to 8.5 per cent and issued an injunction on all BlackBerry sales in the US. The injunction was stayed while RIM appealed the jury's verdict.

Over the next three years, RIM fought the verdict in the US Court of Appeals while at the same time seeking a re-examination of NTP's patents with the US Patent and Trademark Office. By the time Walcoff came on the scene in the fall of 2005, the patent office had rejected only some of NTP's claims, and the upstart Washington company was appealing each one. A negotiated settlement was reached in the spring of 2005, calling for NTP to receive the shocking sum of $450 million US, but it fell apart when Stout and company didn't like some of the terms. It seemed as though the only people getting rich were the lawyers.

The next step in the case was a hearing on February 24, 2006, when Judge Spencer was set to rule on NTP's request for an injunction on all BlackBerry sales in the US. In the weeks leading up to the hearing, Walcoff got down to work on a major background feature about the case. He contacted tech analysts, patent lawyers, law professors and sources at RIM and NTP. The result was a story and sidebar that swallowed up the top half of the front page on the day of the hearing. Topping it all was the ominous headline: "RIM's day of judgment." In the body of the main story, Walcoff didn't hesitate to shine a light on RIM's mistakes. In doing so, he brought up the dreaded "H" word. Was RIM guilty of hubris — exaggerated pride — in letting the case get to this point? Lazaridis can be extremely confident, he wrote, quoting Steve Carkner, a RIM executive who had worked at the company from 1993 to 2002. "He (Lazaridis) believes that the success of the company was predestined by God . . . He is chosen." In a phone interview with Balsillie, Walcoff challenged the RIM boss on whether anger at NTP had gotten the better of him when many felt RIM should have settled the case years ago for much less money. "This is not an emotional issue for me whatsoever," Balsillie insisted. "This is not an indulgent exercise. At the end of the day, we're a company that has a lot of stakeholders we have to look after, and we like to think we look after them responsibly and to the best of our ability."[15]

In the sidebar, Walcoff explored some of the nuances of the injunction and patent issues in the case. Much had been made of the notion that the looming injunction would not apply to US government users, enabling RIM to retain a significant chunk of subscribers in the event of a shutdown. But Walcoff blew a giant hole in that argument. Quoting RIM's own court filings, he pointed out that it would be nearly impossible to keep the system functioning while separating government and private-sector users. As for RIM's much touted software workaround, he noted that the company had admitted it would be "burdensome" and complicated for customers. Should Spencer lift the injunction if a final ruling — expected soon from the US patent office — went in RIM's favour? Walcoff found a New York patent lawyer and a University of Pittsburgh law professor who disagreed on the matter. Lawyer Mark Montegue doubted Spencer would lift the injunction because he thought NTP would appeal, but Prof. Michael Madison countered that a ruling against NTP's patents would undermine the legitimacy of the injunction.

The next step was the February 24 hearing itself. Hopping on a plane to Richmond, Virginia, Walcoff arrived to a mob scene. Reporters, lawyers and spectators were so numerous, many had to watch the proceedings in a separate room on closed-circuit TV. He astutely interviewed the first person in line, learning that he was an employee of Linestanding.com and had arrived at three a.m. The *Washington Post* had paid him $300 to ensure its reporter had a seat in the courtroom. The hearing stretched on for three hours, but in the end proved anticlimactic. Judge Spencer put off his decision on whether to issue an injunction against BlackBerry sales in the US. Even so, there was plenty to write about. Spencer blasted RIM for not having settled the case yet and mocked its contention, backed by dozens of affidavits from high-level BlackBerry users, that the injunction would damage the US economy and national security. If you believed RIM, "the very foundations of Western civilization would be shaken," the judge said.[16]

With RIM backed into a corner and facing a shutdown of sales in the US, the only solution appeared to be a negotiated, out-of-court settlement. It took just a week and several marathon bargaining sessions between the two sides in New York City. On March 3, 2006, a $612-million US settlement was announced, giving RIM and its partners unrestricted use of the company's wireless platform in the US. The amount was astonishing, but Walcoff pointed out it was less than the $1 billion proposed by NTP lawyer Donald Stout late in 2005. Not only did RIM's stock jump 18.3 per cent in the hours after the announcement, the settlement would enable the company to finally turn its full attention back to products rather than legal bickering, Balsillie declared.[17]

With the five-year legal battle with NTP finally over, most reporters would have gladly moved on to other stories. Not Walcoff. It was time to get down to the real business: mining data. He filed Freedom of Information requests with the US Patent and Trademark Office to see if he could uncover anything about RIM's challenge of the NTP patents. The probe snagged a big fish. RIM had hired none other than former Canadian Prime Minister Brian Mulroney to lobby on its behalf. But the Americans weren't swayed by Mulroney's legendary Irish charm and over-the-top blarney. In late 2004, he tried to talk to US commerce secretary Don Evans about the patent office's review of the NTP patents, according to emails obtained by Walcoff. Mulroney didn't get far. His request was forwarded to the legal department, which advised Evans not to talk to the former PM because it would violate patent regulations. Walcoff also learned that RIM was sometimes its own worst enemy in trying to speed up the review process. Re-examination requests were filed improperly, and RIM tried to submit new evidence when it learned of wireless technology from Norway that preceded NTP's patents. All these legal moves slowed down and complicated the review when getting it done quickly was urgent. Walcoff even unearthed an embarrassing incident that resembled something out of an Inspector Clouseau movie. RIM lawyer David Stewart was found snooping around the hallways of the patent office's Alexandria, Virginia, headquarters in 2004 without an appointment or checking in with the receptionist. When asked what he was doing, Stewart said he just wanted to make sure the patent office had not lost any files on the NTP re-exam. He was escorted from the building.[18]

Over the past six months Walcoff had aggressively challenged RIM's handling of the NTP case. He had strongly questioned Balsillie on his defiant attitude, hinted at Lazaridis's outsized ego, poked holes in the company's legal approach and uncovered embarrassing information about the conduct of one of its employees. If RIM wasn't aware of the *Record*'s BlackBerry reporter before, they certainly were now.

* * *

On September 15, 2006, the *Pittsburgh Post-Gazette* broke a story of significant interest to hockey fans across Canada. Balsillie was the leading candidate to purchase the Pittsburgh Penguins hockey team, which had been on the market since January. The scoop was based on unnamed sources familiar with the sale process. Balsillie had submitted a bid of $175 million to $180 million USD in July to purchase the

National Hockey League team but had backed off when he learned it would be difficult to move the team to Hamilton, Ontario, the paper reported. Now he was back in the picture. When the story moved on the wires, editors quickly sent it over to Walcoff's desk. His reporter's instincts kicked in. A response of no-comment or silence from RIM's public relations department would not suffice. The only way to move the story ahead and beat the competition would be to talk to Balsillie himself. Rumours had been circulating for several years that the hockey-loving businessman had been interested in purchasing an NHL team. Here was the potential proof. But how to snag an interview with the mercurial and increasingly inaccessible RIM chieftain? As luck would have it, a two-day conference was underway at the Centre for International Governance Innovation in Waterloo. The invitation-only conference was being held to study rapidly growing economies such as China and India and issues facing fragile countries. A star-studded list of guest speakers was on tap, including retired US army general Wesley Clark, former UN deputy secretary-general Louise Frechette and one-time Canadian Prime Minister Joe Clark.

Acting on a hunch that Balsillie would be there, Walcoff hopped in his car and drove from the *Record* office in downtown Kitchener to CIGI in the hopes of grabbing a quick quote from the RIM boss as he emerged from one of the conference sessions. Sure enough he was there. When Walcoff confronted the surprised Balsillie with the Pittsburgh story, his response was firm and unequivocal. "No, it's not true," he insisted. Walcoff pressed the RIM leader about where the *Post-Gazette* had gotten its information. It may have come from Mario Lemieux, the former Penguins star and co-owner of the team, Balsillie speculated. The two had met on several occasions. Then he abruptly ended the interview. Walcoff was puzzled by the denial. The *Post-Gazette* was a reputable paper. By coincidence, he had worked there as a summer intern while attending the University of Maryland. It wouldn't publish such a bold story without solid evidence to back it up. What was going on? He hurried back to the *Record* building to file his story. But Balsillie wasn't happy. He didn't like being taken by surprise while clinking glasses and schmoozing with international guests. Since the story first broke that morning, he'd been trying to avoid the media while mulling over a proper response. Now a nosy reporter from the local paper had ambushed him, and he had blurted out a denial. And it wasn't just any reporter. It was the same journalist who had been rattling RIM's cage for the past six months about the NTP case. Even worse, Walcoff's story was picked up and published in larger media, including the *Globe and Mail* and the *Toronto Star*.[19]

The day after Walcoff's story ran, Crowley was contacted by Mark Guibert, RIM's director of corporate marketing. He was cordial but firm. Balsillie wasn't happy about the Penguins story. What did Walcoff think he was doing, walking into a conference on government relations and asking a question about hockey? It was inappropriate and out of line. RIM was also unhappy about recent coverage in general. It was too negative and Walcoff was the "worst offender," Guibert said. Many RIM employees lived in the area and read the Record. It was painting a negative picture of the company's performance and embarrassing the front office. Balsillie wanted the business editor to come to RIM's offices to discuss the matter further. Crowley dug in his heels. In his view, Walcoff was just doing his job. "Matt wasn't asking a trick question. He wasn't being deceitful." Crowley told Guibert he would be happy to sit down with Balsillie, but the meeting would have to be held on the *Record*'s turf. "I wasn't about to go cap in hand" to RIM headquarters. To him, that would have been admitting that the paper was subservient to the wireless company. Guibert did not sound pleased by Crowley's response. Now he would have to go back to his boss and tell him there would be no meeting unless it occurred on the *Record*'s terms. With both sides at an impasse over the location, the meeting never took place.[20]

In the ensuing days Balsillie tried to do some damage control. During a speech in Toronto to promote the Pearl, he was asked to confirm the story that he was indeed the front-runner to buy the Penguins. This time he offered a firm "no comment." In attempting to explain his previous denial, Balsillie said if he had refused to comment it would have suggested there might be some truth to the story. "The problem is you're in for a penny, you're in for a pound in answering those kinds of highly speculative questions," he told a *Canadian Press* reporter.[21]

Less than two weeks later, RIM dropped a bombshell. During its quarterly financial release on September 28, 2006, the company announced it was launching a voluntary investigation into its stock-option granting practices from 1997, when it became a publicly traded company, to 2006. The back-dating of stock options had recently sparked an uproar south of the border. Seventy companies had been slapped with shareholder lawsuits over their stock-option granting practices. Twenty executives and directors had resigned and 117 companies had announced investigations into their option policies. To ensure objectivity, RIM said its probe would be conducted by independent lawyers and accountants chosen by RIM board members who were not employed by the company. By announcing the probe on the same day as its quarterly release, RIM hoped its stellar financial results would overshadow the stock-option controversy. The strategy worked. Most analysts focused on the impressive numbers. "If the guidance had been lower, the options thing might have been more of an issue," Barry Richards of Paradigm Capital in Toronto told Walcoff. "But to be honest, the numbers are pretty much immaculate." Walcoff went with a double-barreled lead, starting with the good news. "Shares of Research In Motion Ltd. shot through the $100 US-a-share barrier last night as surprisingly strong profits and projections for the rest of the year offset news of a company-initiated investigation into RIM's accounting practices," he wrote.[22]

The stock-option announcement left a bunch of unanswered questions. RIM didn't say why it was investigating its granting procedures. What had it done to spark this voluntary probe? Who was involved? It was a giant red flag, but before Walcoff could start digging, the Penguins story erupted again. Less than a week later, on October 5, 2006, a second Pittsburgh paper reported on its website that Balsillie would indeed be the new owner of the Penguins. The sale of the team to the

Canadian tech billionaire for $175 million US would be announced by the Penguins the next day, said the *Pittsburgh Tribune-Review*, quoting anonymous sources close to the team. A key condition of the deal was that the city come up with a plan to replace the team's creaky forty-five-year-old Mellon Arena. If no plan were in place, Balsillie would have an opening to move the team to Hamilton. Walcoff knew he would have to act quickly. He felt strongly that the *Record* should be at that Pittsburgh news conference. Seeing Balsillie celebrating with former Penguins superstar and team co-owner Mario Lemieux was something he did not want to miss. *Record* readers would not want to miss it either. Crowley agreed and when he went to editor-in-chief Lynn Haddrall, she quickly approved the trip.

Walcoff filed a story based largely on the *Tribune-Review*'s report, then caught an early flight to Pittsburgh the next day to cover the news conference announcing the sale. "It's a great hockey town," Balsillie told reporters as a smiling Lemieux looked on. "I'm just enormously thrilled to be here. I'm very excited about the game, and I'm very excited about the city." But when pressed, Balsillie would not commit to keeping the team in Pittsburgh without a new rink. "We're a heartbeat away from 50 years old, and you deserve better," he said of the aging Mellon Arena. The plan to finance it was aimed at avoiding the use of public funding. Isle of Capri Casinos Inc. would pony up $290 million to build the new arena in return for a licence from the state of Pennsylvania to erect a slot-machine facility nearby. A decision on the licence was expected by the end of the year. Before the news conference, Walcoff sought local reaction from rank and file Penguins fans. Wandering into the nearby Steelhead Restaurant, he found several fans that were willing to embrace the new owner — as long as he kept the team in Pittsburgh. "We're optimistic people, and we don't believe they'll take our Penguins away from us," said fan Kim Kieser. Others quoted in his story, compiled with material from wire services, weren't so sanguine about the new owner. "Here's a guy who wanted to buy the Penguins with the specific goal of moving them," said Mark Madden, a host on ESPN Radio in Pittsburgh.

"Now he says he's looking forward to keeping them in Pittsburgh. I don't know which Jim Balsillie to believe."[23]

With the Penguins story on hold pending closure of the deal with Balsillie, Walcoff was free to turn his attention back to the stock-options issue. An obvious first step was to find documents indicating when and how RIM had doled out its options. RIM was not about to hand these over on a silver platter, but Walcoff knew of another place to find them — the Ontario Securities Commission. The OSC and the Securities and Exchange Commission in the US had announced their own investigations of RIM's accounting practices, but in the meantime, Walcoff wanted to do his own digging. As a publicly traded company, RIM was required to file disclosure forms for stock-option grants to the OSC. The *Record* reporter strongly suspected RIM was guilty of back-dating its stock options to make them more valuable to the recipient. More than 100 American companies were under investigation for that very reason.

Walcoff could have looked at options distributed to all RIM employees, but they would have numbered in the thousands. Instead he decided to focus on the juiciest target: RIM's top executives. He went to the online database of the OSC and started reading. He entered Balsillie's name and clicked the box marked stock options. Up popped a list showing options granted to him or exercised between 2003 and 2006. The RIM boss had been granted options on several dates, including April 7, 2005, when he received 150,000 options to purchase RIM stock. Balsillie had reported this transaction to the OSC on April 11. Walcoff went back and studied RIM share values for the preceding ten days, the legal time frame allowed for choosing an option date. On April 6, RIM's stock had closed at $89.20 per share on the Toronto Stock Exchange. That was the exercise price on the options granted to Balsillie the following day. It was also the lowest trading price of RIM stock during the ten days preceding the April 11 filing date. If Balsillie had waited two more days to receive his options, they would have been priced at $94.75 per share. By choosing the April 6 date, he had realized a gain of $832,500. Lazaridis had been granted 150,000 options on the same day as well and made a similar bonus. The same pattern emerged for options granted to RIM's top two executives in April 2004.

But the OSC's electronic database only went back to 2003. Walcoff wanted to see whether options were granted as far back as 1997, when RIM first went public. What to do? A potential solution lay with the Ironworkers Ontario Pension Fund, which owned more than $2 million in RIM stock and had launched its own probe of the company's stock-option practices. When Walcoff contacted the Ironworkers, he learned that fund managers had been able to purchase older disclosure records from the OSC going back to 1997 and would be willing to share them with him. Fund lawyer Michael Wright told him that the Ironworkers had noticed three examples of suspiciously well-timed option grants handed out by RIM to senior executives during this earlier period.

Just for good measure, Walcoff also contacted Erick Lie, the University of Iowa professor whose 2003 study of stock options in the US had ignited the whole back-dating controversy in the first place. "This doesn't appear to be a random pattern," Lie said after looking at how RIM timed its options. In all, Walcoff was able to determine that RIM had granted stock options to top executives on ten dates since 1997. On nine of those dates, the exercise price matched the stock's lowest value during the official disclosure period. Sometimes it was even lower. His story was splashed over the top of page one with an attention-grabbing headline: "Cloud over stock options."[24] The *Globe and Mail* did its own investigation of option back-dating at RIM and other Canadian companies around the same time, finding that Balsillie and Lazaridis had each realized a gain of $1.64 million for back-dated options in 2001.[25]

With the stock-option controversy causing numerous headaches at RIM, the purchase of a long-awaited NHL team should have been a good-news story for the embattled Balsillie. It was not to be. On December 15, news broke that Balsillie had withdrawn his offer for the team just before the sale was about to close. The deal had fallen apart over the NHL's insistence that he agree in writing to keep the team in Pittsburgh regardless of whether it got a new arena or not. Making matters worse, Penguins officials lashed out at the RIM boss for his unpredictable behaviour during the sale process. Co-owner Lemieux said he was "shocked and offended" that Balsillie would pull his offer at the last minute, just days before the team was about to hear whether the slots licence was approved for Isle of Capri Casinos, a key to financing the new rink. The move so angered Lemieux that he declared the team would not return Balsillie's $10-million deposit on the purchase. The NHL insisted that it had been clear with the RIM executive all along that relocating the team was never an option. In any event, the financing deal for the new arena appeared dead when Isle of Capri's application for a slots licence was rejected by the Pennsylvania Gaming Control Board. In the meantime, the Lemieux group decided to pull the team off the market to give everyone a chance to clear their heads. In 2007, team owners reached a deal with city, county and state officials and another casino operator to finance a new arena, with the Penguins contributing $4 million per year. The new facility opened in 2010.[26]

* * *

On January 10, 2007, Apple made its first foray into mobile computing when chief executive officer Steve Jobs unveiled the revolutionary iPhone at the annual Macworld trade show at the Moscone Center in San Francisco. Like the BlackBerry, it offered email, contacts and calendar, but delivered messages through regular email providers such as AOL and Yahoo rather than its own company servers, as was the case with RIM's BlackBerry. What really set it apart, however, was its larger screen, touchscreen functionality, bigger operating system and more powerful web browser. Contrary to popular opinion, Apple did not invent the touchscreen. It had been around since the 1960s when it was first used in air-traffic control screens, elevators and musical synthesizers, according to Brian Merchant's book *The One Device: The Secret History of the iPhone*.[27] Palm had employed touchscreens with a stylus in its Pilot and Treo devices, but no one had used the technology to type on a digital keyboard or pinch and spread the screen with the fingers to zoom in and out. Equipped with an accelerometer to detect gravity, the iPhone screen could switch from vertical to horizontal mode depending on how it was held.

Apple had been considering a phone since the release of its iPod music player in 2001. But Jobs was reluctant to go ahead with the project for several reasons. Microchip technology and bandwidth capacity were not advanced enough to allow effective surfing of the Internet or the ability to download videos or games. Moreover, the wireless email market was dominated by RIM, and Jobs did not like playing a subservient role to wireless carriers.

By 2004, things had changed. Sales of the iPod and its iTunes music library began to take off, chip technology had improved and Apple started to worry that cellphone makers would put music on their phones. Eager to cash in on the popularity of the iPod and Jobs's growing celebrity, wireless carrier Cingular approached Apple with a special offer: It would give Apple more freedom to develop the kind of phone it wanted in return for an exclusive deal to sell the product. Late in 2004, Jobs green-lighted the project. Under heavy secrecy, engineers and designers built three different prototypes before Apple chose the one on display in San Francisco. Engineers had to simulate chip speed and battery-drain because the necessary chips were not ready yet. Extensive testing was done with LCD vendors before Apple found a touchscreen technology that worked, and Jobs had to rush a special order with Corning to get the kind of hard gorilla glass he wanted for the screen. According to Fred Vogelstein's book on the battle between Apple and Google for mobile supremacy, the project was so intense and drained so many resources from other programs that it threatened the stability of the entire company.[28]

The novel digital gymnastics required to navigate the iPhone seemed strange at first and critics wondered if it would be too awkward to catch on. Most alarming for Lazaridis, however, was the iPhone's robust web browser.[29] Up until that point, RIM's carriers had not allowed the company to put a browser with that kind of horsepower on the BlackBerry. Doing so would overload and crash the wireless networks. Besides, microchips that could run an operating system and browser of the kind in the iPhone didn't exist until around 2005. Clearly, Jobs had been given a special deal by AT&T, which had acquired Cingular in 2006 and was the exclusive carrier of the iPhone in the US. He had put a smaller version of OS X, the operating system in every Macintosh computer, into a phone. No one had ever installed a desktop operating system on a phone chip before.[30]

Sensation or dud? It was too early to tell. The iPhone would not go on sale until June 2007, but Walcoff realized almost immediately the importance of the iPhone. The day after the product announcement in San Francisco, he rounded up four technology analysts to comment on Apple's trailblazing device. They were inclined to give RIM the benefit of the doubt when it came to competing with the iPhone. "You could say the iPhone is multimedia first, and the phone is almost an afterthought, whereas it's central to the (BlackBerry) Pearl," Todd Kort, a smartphone analyst with Gartner, told Walcoff. "It's possible this may not be a zero sum game for RIM," Mike Abramsky of RBC Capital Markets said in a research note sent to the *Record* reporter. "The high-value smartphone consumer segment is early and growing, offering room for RIM, Apple and Microsoft, all of whom remain strong contenders, and whose offerings, pricing and positioning may appeal to different users."[31]

Walcoff had another reason for relying on analysts a lot more. Sources inside RIM had suddenly dried up. Phone calls weren't being returned. Emails weren't being answered. The stonewalling could be summed up in one word: Balsillie. The mercurial RIM boss had had enough of the feisty *Record* reporter. Walcoff was already in RIM's cross hairs over his aggressive coverage of the company's patent battle with NTP. But the way he had confronted Balsillie back in September about his rumoured bid for the Penguins — eliciting a blunt denial that wasn't true and embarrassing him in the process — had pushed Balsillie to the breaking point. And Walcoff's subsequent stories exposing back-dating in RIM's stock-option grants had only made matters worse. Mark Guibert, RIM's vice-president of corporate marketing called, emailed and met with Ron DeRuyter, who had taken over as business editor at the beginning of 2007 after Crowley left for a public relations job at Wilfrid Laurier University. The talks were cordial but the message was clear: The company wanted Walcoff banished from the BlackBerry beat. And if that didn't happen, it had a second ultimatum: No one from RIM would be allowed to talk to him. He would be shut out and blacklisted.

DeRuyter was surprised and puzzled. Walcoff could be an aggressive reporter who sometimes lacked sensitivity in his approach. "He could be confrontational without knowing he was." Yet there was no malice in Walcoff's reporting or intent to deliberately harm RIM, DeRuyter believed. "Matt was also very respectful of people. He wasn't out to slam people." Moreover, there were no factual mistakes that RIM could point to. The complaint would not likely have stood up to scrutiny before the Ontario Press Council, the body that examined complaints about newspapers at that time. The business editor was well aware that RIM wasn't happy with Walcoff's reporting. "There was a general feeling that Matt was looking for negative stories to write about RIM . . . There was a feeling that Matt was out to get them." But DeRuyter felt differently. "My feeling was that Matt was doing a great job. He was aggressive in the sense of digging and not giving up."

After conferring with senior editors, DeRuyter decided he would not give in to RIM's demands. Walcoff would remain on the beat. "I made it clear they could not dictate to us," he said.[32]

If the *Record* caved in to RIM's demands regarding Walcoff, the newspaper's integrity and autonomy would be undermined, DeRuyter felt. In his view, the reporter had done nothing wrong. RIM was overreacting. In the meantime, a solution was hatched. DeRuyter would personally edit all copy submitted by Walcoff to ensure the utmost fairness and objectivity, but Walcoff would stay on the beat. RIM was still not satisfied. Balsillie wanted the annoying *Record* reporter punished. He demanded a meeting with editor-in-chief Lynn Haddrall and publisher

Dana Robbins. This time there was no standoff over the location. Held at RIM headquarters, it was a stormy one, and the pair have refused to comment on what was said. But they held their ground. Walcoff would continue to cover RIM. Balsillie would later say his anger was a byproduct of the stress involved in running a global corporation and needing to keep everyone sharp and focused. "I'm not perfect. Sometimes you go too far," he said in *Losing The Signal*.[33]

In the wake of the meeting with Balsillie, the moratorium on Walcoff remained in place. No one at RIM would be allowed to talk to him. If he called looking for comment on any story, however small or routine, he would be greeted by silence. It put the *Record* in a difficult position. The paper's main BlackBerry reporter, covering one of the most important beats in the newsroom, was being stonewalled. RIM's power play also ratcheted up paranoia in the newsroom. For some time after that, Haddrall insisted on seeing every local story and headline about RIM before it went into the paper. DeRuyter also felt the heat. Readers would contact him saying the paper was being too hard on RIM. At other times, they would urge the *Record* to keep the pressure on. If RIM stock was down, they wanted to know what was wrong. He felt pulled in two directions.

It certainly wasn't the first time someone had had a beef with a *Record* reporter. If a paper doesn't stick its neck out once in a while, it is not doing its job. Comfort the afflicted and afflict the comfortable: the slogan is hammered home in journalism school. Over the years, the city's Junior A hockey team, the Kitchener Rangers, the marquee athletic team in the region, was known to grumble a little too frequently if coverage wasn't laudatory enough. And the usual allotment of local politicians was not known for having thick skin. But RIM's iron-fisted approach took things to a new level. One of the highest-profile companies in town, the toast of the Canadian business scene — not to mention Wall Street and Washington — was directing its might against a lowly reporter plying his trade at a small, regional daily. None of this was officially shared with *Record* staff, but word gradually filtered out. Tension ran high in the back corner of the newsroom. I had joined the business staff shortly before Walcoff had in 2005. My desk was not far from his. There was no outward reaction from Matt. It was like it didn't happen. He just went about his business as if getting stonewalled by the most important company in town was an everyday occurrence.

Yet he did share some of his thoughts with his boss. The gag order took Walcoff by surprise, said DeRuyter. His initial reaction was that it was "not a smart thing to do" to go to war with the hometown paper. At the same time, he was not intimidated. "He knew we weren't going to pull him" from the beat. Rather than letting it get him down, he took it as a challenge. "Matt believed strongly in his integrity. He took his role as a journalist very seriously," said DeRuyter.[34]

Should the *Record* have gone public about RIM's egregious power play in muzzling Walcoff? The paper was later criticized by the *Ryerson Review of Journalism* for not doing so. Christina Pellegrini, who wrote the article on RIM's tense relationship with the media, argued that it was symptomatic of the company's arrogance, a flaw that later played a part in its downfall in the smartphone race. Going public about the matter was never discussed at any management meetings, said DeRuyter. "It was deemed to be an internal matter, not one for public airing." If the *Record* had reported on the issue, "many of our readers would have been less than sympathetic and would have seen us as being whiners." The best strategy was to have Walcoff continue to cover RIM and report that it refused to comment, DeRuyter said. "That told people a lot about the company and its approach to communications, and shed light on its defensiveness."[35]

Walcoff's plan to cover RIM by getting reaction and comment from analysts worked well for the unveiling of new BlackBerrys and the iPhone. But it would not pass muster for a more complicated and controversial story. And that story came just a few weeks later. On February 27, 2007, RIM announced that its stock-option review was nearing completion. It would be presented to the board on March 2 and, following approval by directors, released to the public on March 5. The *Record* had less than a week to plan coverage of this bombshell of a story, one that its lead BlackBerry reporter had played a major role in covering. It was obvious a second reporter would have to be brought in to assist Walcoff. That reporter ended up being me. I had already conveyed my interest in helping with RIM coverage if the need arose. DeRuyter came to me a couple of days before to explain how the two of us would handle the story. Walcoff would direct coverage and write the main story. To circumvent RIM's communication ban, I would act as intermediary between Matt and RIM. He would feed me questions to send to the company either by email or phone. I would get the answers and relay them back to him. If needed, I would also write a sidebar. DeRuyter looked embarrassed and uncomfortable as he explained how it would work. It wasn't unusual for reporters to team up on a big story. It was unusual that the lead reporter would be unable to talk the most important source. But with Walcoff wearing a muzzle, there was no alternative.

When the day of reckoning came, RIM's gag order turned out to be mostly a non-issue. Apart from a few routine questions that I relayed to RIM on Matt's behalf, most of the material was self-explanatory. There were no lengthy newsroom strategy sessions on the wording of key questions or the substance of our coverage. For the most part, Matt hunkered down and banged out the main story while I worked on a sidebar on changes to board governance. As expected, RIM had rejected our request for an interview with the top brass, forcing Walcoff to scalp some quotes Balsillie had made to *Canadian Press*. The internal review found evidence of stock-option back-dating, but said company executives did not know they were violating securities regulations. A major charge of $250 million US would be assessed against past earnings, but that was mostly because RIM had not accounted for its program of exercising options for employees who could not afford them. Later probes by the SEC and OSC found the back-dating was intentional, and Lazaridis, Balsillie and chief financial officer Dennis Kavelman were assessed heavy fines.

Over the next two years, Walcoff would share coverage of RIM with

Mike Hammond, a business reporter from Ottawa hired in the spring of 2007. Hammond handled face-to-face interviews, annual meetings and other stories requiring direct contact with RIM, while Walcoff tackled assignments that could be covered with reaction from analysts and other outside experts. The two also split coverage of the company's quarterly financial reports. Even with Hammond acting as the face of the newspaper, RIM continued to give the *Record* the cold shoulder. Gradually the communication ban was relaxed to the point where Walcoff was able to write a major feature on the tenth anniversary of the BlackBerry early in 2009, quoting sources inside the company who had worked on the device. In the spring of 2009, the *Record* laid off half-a-dozen reporters in an effort to cut costs during the global economic downturn. Walcoff and Hammond were among those who lost their jobs. The *Record* was a unionized paper, and the contract required it to lay off employees with the least amount of seniority. Walcoff eventually found work as a stock market reporter with *Bloomberg News* in Toronto. By all accounts, he did his job well, even filing a story when Tim Hortons surpassed RIM in market value. "Tim Tops RIM," read the headline.[36] When Balsillie resigned as co-CEO of RIM early in 2012, Walcoff wrote a tough analysis of his old adversary that was sent out on the Bloomberg wire and published in the *Record*. Sadly, in March 2012, he was found dead in his Toronto apartment at the age of thirty-four. His family did not release the cause of death, but no foul play was suspected. "I valued his work ethic, talent and abilities, but more than that I valued his curiosity, his integrity, his character and his unique way of looking at the world," said DeRuyter, Walcoff's boss at the *Record*.[37]

As chief executive officer of Open Text in the 1990s and early 2000s, Tom Jenkins built the company into a global powerhouse in business software.

Waterloo Region Record

(from left) Brad Siim and Dave Caputo founded network equipment-maker Sandvine in 2000 after Cisco closed up their previous startup, Pixstream.

Waterloo Region Record

(from left) Mike Lazaridis, founder of Perimeter Institute of Theoretical Physics, and Howard Burton, executive director, toss apples in an experiment to demonstrate gravity in 2001.

Waterloo Region Record

Matt Walcoff, a business reporter at the Record, *was blacklisted by RIM after covering the company aggressively from 2005–07.*

Iain Klugman, CEO of Communitech, built the association representing tech companies in Waterloo Region into a major force in the local and Canadian tech community.

Dietmar Wennemer, a native of Germany, worked at RIM from 2005–14 in mechanical engineering and product developments.

Gary Will works in his Waterloo office in the late 1990s. Will wrote a blog about the Waterloo tech sector and helped to build the local tech ecosystem.

Waterloo Region Record

Mike Lazaridis shows off RIM's latest smartphone, the BlackBerry Pearl, in 2006. It was RIM's first handset designed specifically for consumers.

Waterloo Region Record

Jim Balsillie cools off after cycling in a cancer fund-raising ride with Tour de France champion Lance Armstrong in rural Waterloo Region in 2009.

Waterloo Region Record

Lindsay Gibson started working in a call centre at RIM in 2000, then rose through the ranks to become vice-president of manufacturing and supply chain.

Photo taken by Aaron Summerfield

(from left) Michael Litt and Devon Galloway, co-founders of the video marketing firm Vidyard, are among a new breed of tech entrepreneurs in Waterloo.

Waterloo Region Record

The former Lang Tannery in downtown Kitchener is the headquarters of Communitech, where it runs the largest tech incubator in Waterloo Region.

Waterloo Region Record

Gary Will, executive director of Google's office in Kitchener, has built the company's local operation into the largest in Canada.
Waterloo Region Record

(from left) Doug Fregin, Ophelia Lazaridis and Mike Lazaridis at the opening of the Quantum-Nano Centre at UW in 2012, home of the Institute for Quantum Computing.
Waterloo Region Record

Chapter 11
WARNING SIGNS

Mike Lazaridis was feeling good. It was the fall of 2004 and everything, apart from the patent lawsuit with NTP, was going RIM's way. Black-Berry sales were shifting into overdrive. It had taken the company five years to reach the 1-million subscriber mark. Now, just ten months later, it was about to crack the 2-million subscriber barrier. The Black-Berry was being sold in more than thirty countries by close to sixty carriers. Revenues were also surging. They had topped $300 million US in the most recent quarter and were expected to shoot past $400 million US per quarter in the next six months. The company's manufacturing plant in Waterloo was working overtime to meet the demand, and a second plant in Hungary would open soon to assemble BlackBerrys for the European market. RIM was the undisputed king of the corporate email space, but now it appeared as though it were making a play for the consumer market. The company had recently taken the wraps off a sleek new model called the BlackBerry 7100t. Geared to the US market, it was about half as wide as the traditional, boxy BlackBerry. A smaller keyboard, with two letters on each key, made it possible. All BlackBerrys until then had featured a full QWERTY keyboard. But on the 7100t, the user could begin typing out a word and intuitive

software built into the device would predict which letter on the key to use. "It's a brilliant innovation," Mark Guibert, RIM's vice-president of corporate marketing, said of the software called SureType.[1] With the slimmed-down form factor and a spiffier grey colour scheme, the new 7100t looked almost like a cellphone. RIM had added voice to the BlackBerry in 2002. Now with a thinner, candy-bar shaped device capable of sending email, browsing the web and making phone calls, RIM was poised to bust down the doors of a whole new market.

Yet it wasn't just the numbers and the technology that were boosting Lazaridis's spirits. RIM had celebrated its twentieth anniversary earlier in the year with a concert for employees and guests at the Kitchener Auditorium, the region's biggest hockey arena, featuring rock bands Aerosmith and the Barenaked Ladies. And in October, Perimeter Institute of Theoretical Physics had marked the grand opening of its permanent new home beside Silver Lake in uptown Waterloo. More than 8,000 people attended the gala event, including community leaders, scientists and two Nobel Prize winners. "This is a great day for Canada, and you are a great Canadian," Prime Minister Paul Martin told Lazaridis before cutting the ribbon at the black-tie event. Guests had even been sent home with little Albert Einstein action figures armed with pieces of chalk.[2] It all made Lazaridis feel bullish about life and the company's prospects as he sat down for an interview with reporter Ron DeRuyter for a story in the *Record*'s annual tech supplement.

But when DeRuyter, taking his cue from the 7100t, suggested that RIM was making a big push into the consumer space, Lazaridis objected. "I have never said we are going after the consumer market," he said. If RIM wanted to court consumers, it would have put a camera in the BlackBerry, but kept it out deliberately because cameras aren't allowed in corporations and manufacturing plants. If RIM targeted the cellphone market, dominated by consumers, "we would all of a sudden have to be all things to all people . . . we would end up compromising our product." Market dynamics would determine when RIM made a bigger play for the consumer market, he went on. In the meantime, the company would continue to target its customer base in the enterprise and "prosumer" markets, a vague term RIM preferred to describe small business owners and consumers using a smartphone for professional purposes. These are markets where "security and reliability trump glitz and features," Lazaridis noted. The consumer market isn't really any different than the business market, he emphasized. Consumers want security, reliability and convenience too. "If you throw too many bells and whistles at them, all it does is complicate the experience and make it unreliable."[3] The BlackBerry 7100t would lay the foundation for the Pearl, released two years later. But the rollout of the Pearl would not go as smoothly as hoped.

* * *

Lindsay Gibson was puzzled. As part of the sales and marketing team attached to the T-Mobile business unit, she was asked to look into a spike in returns of the BlackBerry Pearl as the US carrier was rolling it out in retail stores in the fall of 2006. This had not happened when the BlackBerry was sold to corporations and business customers. What was going on? Was T-Mobile messing things up? Lazaridis had finally given up his opposition to putting a camera in the BlackBerry, and the Pearl was the first model to carry one. It also boasted a music player and other features designed to attract consumers. The handset was making its debut in retail stores in the US, so it was important to get to the bottom of the problem and fast. Gibson visited T-Mobile retail stores and call centres in Allentown, Pennsylvania, and Albuquerque, New Mexico, where most of the BlackBerry agents were located. She talked to the agents and listened to the complaints of customers. Technicians from software, battery, user-experience, keyboard and other departments at RIM were brought in to hear the problems. Focus groups were also set up with customers. They were observed taking new Pearls out of the box and trying to get them to work. The results startled Gibson and her RIM crew. The Pearl simply wasn't easy to use without a corporate IT person walking you through the process. But these were former cellphone users. There was no IT person to show them how the device worked. "People going from a traditional cellphone had no idea what all the icons were, how to make a call, how to email, text because it was a huge leap," Gibson said. The engineers designing the hardware and software on the BlackBerry were not in touch with consumer needs and how they went about using a mobile device, Gibson said. In one case, participants were asked to set up the Bluetooth wireless connection on the device. One woman kept confusing the Bluetooth key with the menu key. Others had trouble getting the music player to work. Apple had not run into the same problem with the iPod. When it launched, consumers found it simple to use. To alleviate the problem, Gibson and others on the RIM team worked to simplify the user-experience, improve customer-support and ensure that all agents had a BlackBerry and knew how to use it. Return rates dropped and Gibson was asked to start a global team to look at customer churn in other countries.[4] She would soon have a much bigger problem on her hands as RIM got ready in 2008 to launch its answer to the iPhone — the BlackBerry Storm.

Over the same period, the competition was heating up as well. All the attention heaped on the iPhone caused many to overlook an announcement in November 2007 — search-engine leader Google would offer a free wireless software platform called Android to hardware-makers such as Motorola, Samsung, HTC and LG Electronics. Google's entry into the smartphone market did not happen overnight. The success of the BlackBerry and the growing market in mobile data had spurred the desktop search-engine leader to turn its attention to the wireless world. If it did not get its search engine and other programs onto mobile phones, the company feared it might open the door to other competitors, particularly Microsoft. Google co-founder Larry Page had been an early admirer of Andy Rubin, who installed Google as the default search engine on the T-Mobile Sidekick, a phone he designed and built in 2002. Though customers balked at its cumbersome design, the Sidekick earned a cult following for its fluid browser, instant-messaging capabilities and ability to download games. Page and Google co-founder Sergey Brin even started carrying them around.

Few in Silicon Valley knew more about wireless than Rubin. He had worked in the field since the early 1990s for Apple and Microsoft before co-founding Danger Inc. in 1999, makers of the Sidekick.[5] By 2003, he had come to the conclusion that the future of wireless lay in software rather than hardware. That same year Rubin and several colleagues launched Android to build mobile operating systems for hardware-makers. When he pitched Android to Page at a meeting at Google early in 2005, Page stunned him by offering to buy the company. The acquisition gave Android instant credibility. Just weeks before, Rubin had been laughed out of the room when pitching Android to the South Korean hardware-maker Samsung. For the next two years Rubin and his Android team toiled away on a software platform designed to work on any handset and packed with a full Internet browser and Google applications such as Maps and YouTube. The first hardware-maker to jump on board was Taiwan-based HTC, which had been offered cash and free access to Android to help build the phone. The original plan was to equip the device with a physical keyboard, but the iPhone so astonished Rubin[6] when it was unveiled in early 2007 that he decided to switch gears and focus on touchscreens.[7] Called the T-Mobile G1, the HTC device was set to hit stores in the latter part of 2008.

At first glance, Google's gambit did not appear to be threatening. Microsoft had offered its Windows Mobile and Pocket PC software to hardware-makers such as Palm and HTC without much success. The problem for earlier competitors was bandwidth. In the past, bandwidth was so limited that it was not possible to surf the Internet effectively on a smartphone. The other issue was a lack of standardization. Nearly every smartphone-maker, including RIM and Apple, controlled the hardware and software process from start to finish. Also known as a "walled-garden" approach, it made the writing of applications and programs that would work across a suite of phones impossible. With its open-source Android platform, Google was attempting to break down the walls of the garden at a time when bandwidth and processing power were increasing. It was truly an inflection point in the history of smartphones. Apple and RIM planned to stick with the walled-garden approach, but sales of the iPhone would become so enormous that it was able to buck the trend. RIM would not be so fortunate.[8]

* * *

The tension in the room was thick. Best-selling Canadian author Malcolm Gladwell had asked Balsillie for his impressions of the iPhone, but the RIM executive was being evasive. The University of Waterloo had brought the pair together in the fall of 2007 for a conference on the workplace of tomorrow. By a strange coincidence, Gladwell and Balsillie had lived in the same dormitory at the University of Toronto's Trinity College in the early 1980s. The pair had become close friends, jogging, attending classes, eating meals and studying together. At times, they would play backgammon up to ten times a day. Gladwell had gone on to become a staff writer of *The New Yorker* magazine and the author of such popular books as *The Tipping Point* and *Blink*. He had grown up in the town of Elmira, just north of Waterloo, and was often invited back to speak on his home turf. This time he had been tapped to interview old pal Balsillie for his thoughts on what the workplace would look like ten years down the road. Anticipation had been building for weeks about this meeting of the minds: two local heroes, one of whom had conquered the arts world and the other the business realm. Their conversation was the marquee event at the conference, called 2017: The Workplace.

After some chatter about his approach to business challenges and his chances of acquiring an NHL team in the near future — it's about 50-50, Balsillie said — Gladwell moved to the topic of competition. How was he handling the pressure of having a major new competitor like Apple in the game? Not a big concern, Balsillie replied. RIM will only benefit from the increased awareness brought to the mobile industry. More discussion followed about the impact of the iPhone. Each time Balsillie avoided naming the device or its creator. Spectators shifted in their seats or glanced uneasily at each other. The elephant in the room was growing larger with each attempt to ignore its existence. It was painfully obvious that the RIM exec dared not utter the words Apple or iPhone. Balsillie's reticence was curious. Months earlier, during a quarterly conference call with shareholders, he hadn't hesitated to slam Apple's new phone. "The phone of the year will earn its position at the top the old fashioned way, not because it is the most revolutionary gadget, but because it will probably be the best phone," he said, quoting from a review of the BlackBerry Curve by Mike Elgan of *Computerworld*. The iPhone was launching on one carrier in one country while "we're in about 100 countries on 300 carriers." RIM was not going to get caught in a game of who could come up with the funkiest "input mechanism," Balsillie told shareholders.[9] The same bravado seemed to be lacking at the UW event. Finally, Gladwell could take it no longer. "You're allowed to say it," he said of the word, iPhone. The RIM chieftain laughed awkwardly and quickly moved on to his next comment. Later in the interview, the words Apple and iPhone did indeed cross his lips as he mused about the adulation of Apple CEO Steve Jobs. "I would not want to keep up the culture of idolatry. It would exhaust me," said Balsillie, never one to avoid the spotlight himself.[10]

* * *

In the beginning, the critics loved it. They loved the clickable touchscreen on the BlackBerry Storm, the bold engineering behind it and the fact RIM didn't just copy the iPhone. "The term iPhone-killer is clumsily tossed around by bloggers and journos to describe almost any phone with a touchscreen, but by trying to actually innovate rather than imitate, RIM has conjured up the phone most deserving of the title yet," said Matt Buchanan of Gizmodo, a popular gadget website. "Yes, the screen is a giant button, one you have to punch for basically every action, even every letter you type, completely breaking the touchscreen paradigm. Surprisingly it works," he said.[11] "The true test of any touch-based phone is typing, and we won't hold any punches here: we're in love," gushed Paul Miller of Engadget, another tech website. "In fact, we like it enough to pit it against regular button-based keyboards, since it easily leaves traditional touchscreen typing in the dust."[12]

But gradually the detractors began to hold sway. The touchscreen featured one large spring-mounted sensor in the middle, which tended to work well in the centre of the display but not on the edges. As a result, clicking on the screen felt like typing on a seesaw. Not helping matters was the fact that many customers were not taking off the "screen cling," a transparent cover placed on the screen to protect it during shipping. Gibson picked up this problem during some of her focus groups. Images were printed on future screen clings so customers would know to remove them.[13] David Pogue, the influential tech critic of the *New York Times*, had praised the Pearl Flip and Bold smartphones released earlier in the year by RIM. But he was blunt in his criticism of the Storm. Typing on the device was like pounding on a manual typewriter, he said, and users had to contend with two different keyboards — a full one for horizontal views and a smaller one with two letters per key for vertical. Scrolling was exhausting, and freezes and reboots were common. "How did this thing ever reach the market? Was everyone involved just too terrified to pull the emergency brake on this train?"[14]

Despite the negative reviews, initial sales of the Storm were good thanks to RIM's reputation for making quality handsets. When the device went on sale in the US on November 21, 2008, customers lined up at many Verizon stores, and more new subscribers inked deals on that day than on any other day in RIM's history. In Britain, Vodafone sold a Storm every thirteen seconds on the first weekend of sales. Demand was so robust that RIM had trouble making Storms fast enough in the early weeks of the launch.[15] The company's reputation was enhanced by the news that newly elected US president Barack Obama was reluctant to give up his BlackBerry 8830 World Edition phone when he entered the White House. The Bold, a high-end BlackBerry with a physical keyboard, was also selling well thanks to a marketing campaign featuring US swimmer Michael Phelps, who had won eight gold medals that summer at the Beijing Olympics.

Alas, once customers had a chance to use the Storm, they were not impressed. Returns were massive. In the spring of 2009, Verizon demanded almost $500 million from RIM to cover the nearly 1 million Storms returned by disgruntled users. A shocked Balsillie was forced to fly to Verizon headquarters in New Jersey where he managed to talk the carrier down to $100 million in return for a free repair and upgrade program and a bunch of free BlackBerrys. RIM sales and marketing staff were used to attending glitzy promotional events staged by carriers such as T-Mobile and Verizon. After the disaster of Storm 1, that all stopped, said Gibson. "Everything became negative" from the carriers.[16] RIM was able to iron out many of the glitches in the second-generation Storm released in the fall of 2009. Instead of one sensor in the middle of the display on Storm 1, Storm 2 featured four sensors, one in each quadrant. Pogue of the *New York Times* was much more complimentary this time around, though he still didn't see the point of the clickable screen and found the web browser slow and buggy.[17] Sales of the Storm 2 failed to take off, and RIM finally gave up on the clickable touchscreen early in 2010 when AT&T requested a regular touchscreen device.[18]

* * *

While the battle for smartphone supremacy was heating up, two other companies in the Waterloo tech sector were generating plenty of drama as well, this time of the Hollywood kind. Dalsa was working on a digital-cinema camera that promised to revolutionize the motion picture industry, and Christie Digital was rolling out its new digital-cinema projectors in movie theatres across the continent. The two companies had both ends of the movie experience covered.

Dalsa's main line of business was image sensors and cameras used in fax machines, cheque-scanning equipment, machine-vision systems and medical and scientific imaging equipment. The company was started in 1980 by University of Waterloo professor Savvas Chamberlain. A native of Cyprus, he had developed an expertise in charge-coupled devices (CCD), a type of microchip with an amazing ability to capture images. Few engineers were designing CCD image sensors at the time and Chamberlain's skill attracted the attention of such major customers as IBM, Ford Aerospace and Bell Northern Research. Even so, growth didn't take off until the early 1990s when the cost of computing to process Dalsa's imaging data came down. In the meantime, Chamberlain kept plugging away until his products gained traction. He was driven by ambition and the desire to commercialize his technology for the good of the country. "We are as good as the Germans. We are as good as the Americans," he once said.[19] He took pride in the fact that many of his employees were former students of his and held shares in the company.

By 2005, the company that Chamberlain had started as a one-person consulting firm had grown to employ more than 1,000 people with global sales of $180 million a year. The firm owned a research and manufacturing plant in north Waterloo and semiconductor plants in Quebec and the Netherlands that manufactured silicon wafers used in its imaging equipment. Dalsa went public in 1996, raising $22.9 million on the Toronto Stock Exchange.

Its venture into digital cinema cameras began almost by accident. Dalsa had developed a sensor for use in an HDTV camera in Japan. Word spread to Hollywood where digital pioneers were looking for something to replace the reliable but cumbersome 35-mm film camera. They approached Dalsa. After several years of research, the Waterloo company fashioned a prototype that could produce images with four times the resolution and twice the speed of HDTV cameras.[20] In 2005, Dalsa opened a digital rental facility in a suburb of Los Angeles. At $300,000 to $400,000 each, its cinema cameras were too expensive to purchase so the company was letting potential customers use them for free. Rental charges would kick in once their appetites were whetted. Companies producing commercials and special-effects projects were showing interest. Alas, Dalsa would scrap the cinema project in 2008 amid rising costs and slow adoption by the movie industry. The camera was about ten years ahead of its time, Chamberlain said, and Dalsa could have kept the project going if it had remained a private company and not been accountable to the whims of impatient shareholders.[21]

In 2011, Chamberlain's world came crashing down. Now chair of Dalsa's board, he was forced to sell controlling interest in the company to California-based Teledyne Technologies for $337 million. In tears, he told employees he had no choice but to put the company on the block because three large, activist hedge-fund shareholders, whom he likened to "barbarians at the gate," wanted to cash in their holdings. They were going to "chop up the company and sell it in pieces." The buyers they had in mind would have shut down operations in Waterloo within two years. Instead, he took matters into his own hands and found a purchaser committed to keeping the company in Waterloo. One of his biggest mistakes was taking the company public in 1996, he admitted. Some stockholders wanted to cash in their shares. Investment capital was plentiful and "everybody was eager to dip their fingers in the honey." But the company didn't really need the money and could have avoided its eventual sale if it had remained private, he said.[22] Chamberlain's efforts to keep the company in Waterloo paid off. Teledyne-Dalsa continues to design and manufacture digital-imaging products in the city and has a global workforce of close to 1,000 employees.

The digital-cinema camera was a side project for Dalsa, but the same could not be said for Christie Digital's digital-cinema projector. It was a flagship product for the Kitchener-based company, formerly known as Electrohome. Once a dominant player in the production of radios and TVs, Electrohome was looking for new worlds to conquer after the Japanese took over the television market in the late 1970s. At this point, Electrohome engineered a clever pivot. It began to diversify into projection systems. Using its projectors, images as large as thirty feet by fifty feet could be displayed on a screen.

From there a shift into projectors for movie theatres was a natural one. The market possibilities were endless. Distributing and screening movies digitally using CDs and the Internet was much cheaper than shipping bulky and cumbersome film reels. Yet Electrohome couldn't afford the capital investment to fully develop the technology and was struggling to make money. At this point, Gerry Remers entered the picture. A Wilfrid Laurier University arts grad, he had started his career at Electrohome in the late 1980s, then spent seven years at Canadian telecom equipment giant Nortel. Returning to Electrohome in 1994, he was named director of marketing in the projection systems division. At the time, it was the company's fastest growing department. Remers was a savvy guy and it didn't take him long to start turning heads. Within two years he was running the entire division and three years later, in 1999, he was tapped by CEO John Pollock to find a partner to help finance the company's expansion into cinema projectors. An earlier attempt to sell the projection division had failed largely because the company used investment banks and other intermediaries to handle negotiations, which slowed down and complicated the process.

This time Remers took charge and successfully negotiated a deal with Christie Inc., a California-based manufacturer of mechanical projectors. Christie was anxious to get into digital projection but its technology was years behind Electrohome's. It didn't make sense to ship all this brainpower and equipment to California, so Christie decided to leave Electrohome's 170 employees in Kitchener with Remers in charge as president and chief operating officer.

By 2005, the company was ready to roll out its first digital-cinema projector for mass deployment in movie theatres across North America. The goal was to install projectors in 4,000 cinemas, roughly 10 per cent of the North American market, over the next year or so in the first stage of the rollout. At $75,000 to $100,000 a pop, the machines weren't cheap and the company faced the daunting task of persuading exhibitors to fork over the cash to install them. Instead of having theatre chains pony up the bucks, Remers and his crew engineered a solution as creative as the technology behind its projectors. Hollywood studios would pay a fee every time one of their films was screened on a new projector and the proceeds would cover the purchase costs for exhibitors. The fee would come from money saved by the studios through digital's lower distribution costs. "We had to take the initiative ourselves to launch digital cinema," Remers explained. Not only was Christie leading the way in digital technology, its financing arrangements "were miles ahead of our competitors," he declared.[23]

With a Kitchener workforce that would grow to 700 people, Christie went on to install 47,000 digital cinema projectors in movie theatres around the world over the next ten years, more than one-third of the total market, with Remers leading the deployment. In 2016, at the age of sixty, he stepped down as president and chief operating officer to serve as a special adviser to the company. As of 2019, the company had installed 100,000 projectors worldwide and continued to employ more than 600 people at its Kitchener plant.

* * *

David Yach was stressed out. After ten years as chief technology officer for software at RIM, he felt he could handle any kind of pressure. But lately the workload and product delays were driving him crazy. Normally RIM introduced one new electronic design and microchip a year and built different phones using that design. In 2008, it introduced four. The Storm, Bold, BlackBerry 8900 and a special RIM walkie-talkie all had their own microchips. RIM's production strategy didn't help either. BlackBerry models were kept waiting while teams in charge of software, electronics, graphics, keyboards and so on worked on one handset at a time, then moved on to the next one. To Yach, it would have made more sense if each device had a full crew so they could be assembled simultaneously. Making matters worse, the teams were working on tighter deadlines. Lazaridis didn't just squeeze the Storm deadline, he "sliced it half," said Yach. Lazaridis and Balsillie were like many successful CEOs. Early on they were realistic about deadlines, but "towards the end their expectations became unreasonable."

Yach had come to RIM in 1998 partly because he was tired of travelling to California once or twice a month to the head office of Sybase.

A UW grad in math and computer science, he had started his career at Watcom, the university's first software spinoff company, then found himself on a frequent-flyer treadmill when it was acquired by Sybase in 1995. After he met Balsillie socially, the RIM boss began recruiting him to join the BlackBerry-maker. The company was looking for someone to replace software chief Michael Barnstijn, who had taken a leave of absence, then did not come back. The affable and easy-going Yach, the son of a local police officer, seemed to have all the right skills. He had honed his management chops with an MBA at Wilfrid Laurier University, then risen to a senior level at Watcom and Sybase. RIM's head office was in Waterloo. "I figured life would be simpler if I went to RIM. By the third day, I knew I wasn't in Kansas any more," he said.

The first iteration of the Storm should never have made it out of R&D, Yach said. It tarnished the brand and undermined the public's reaction to Storm 2. He takes some of the blame for RIM's scramble to get the devices done. "My job was to build what Mike (Lazaridis) wanted to build, but also to anticipate what he wanted to build." RIM's reaction to the iPhone was a combination of "worry and dismissal," said the chief technology officer, who left the company in 2012. "There was constant discussion about it" in meetings. On the one hand, Apple had produced something groundbreaking and different. On the other, there had been ten BlackBerry-killers before it and all had failed. It was not obvious when the iPhone was first released that it would be a success. Battery life was terrible, the browser was unusable on cellular networks and it was expensive. "In the typical, very analytical BlackBerry way, we concluded it would not succeed. We were wrong," said Yach. The iPhone "changed the basis of competition." The old priorities were battery life, security, efficient use of the network, communication and a physical keyboard. The new priorities were a fast browser and sleek design. "We underestimated beauty," he said, pausing to emphasize those words. Yach knew RIM was in trouble when the company organized a focus group to rate browsers on the BlackBerry, the iPhone and several other devices. The iPhone browser was slower than the rest but got a higher rating because the web pages it produced were sharper. The other factor working in Apple's favour was robust support from its exclusive carrier in the US. AT&T "tortured themselves to support the iPhone," Yach said. The carrier spent billions to enhance its network to accommodate the iPhone. "It all snowballed in Apple's favour."[24]

The first Storm was a disaster, the iPhone was sexy, but what really damaged RIM was the release of the Motorola Droid. The first phone based on the Android operating system, the T-Mobile G1, had not sold well when released in the fall of 2008. Some of its touchscreen features had been removed at the request of an unlikely source — Steve Jobs. Apple and Google had an incestuous relationship at this point. A team of Google engineers had been brought in to help install Google search, maps and YouTube on the iPhone. Google CEO Eric Schmidt even sat on Apple's board of directors. In return for getting its apps on the iPhone, Google let Jobs see some of the features on the first Android phone. When the Apple CEO saw what Rubin was doing, especially with touchscreen gestures such as pinch and zoom and double tap, he screamed patent infringement. Google disagreed, arguing that Microsoft and Sun Microsystems had been experimenting with those touchscreen features back in the 1990s. When the Apple CEO threatened to sue, Rubin removed some of the touchscreen features, and even installed a slide-out keyboard on the G1. It looked clunky compared to the iPhone. The G1 launch was not helped when Page and Brin showed up at the New York unveiling on rollerblades. Sales tanked. But Jobs's power-play left a bad taste in the mouths at Google. They decided to hold nothing back on the second Android phone, called the Motorola Droid, and every Android phone after that. Landing in US stores in the fall of 2009, the same time as Storm 2, the Droid was an immediate success, surpassing sales of the original iPhone in the first three months.[25] Heavily promoted by Verizon on its carrier network, the touchscreen Droid, which also featured a physical keyboard that slid out horizontally, essentially destroyed any chance of RIM becoming a viable contender to the iPhone.[26]

* * *

Paul Lucier was riding a train into downtown Stockholm in 2010 when he noticed something alarming. Sitting nearby was a woman in her sixties. She was fiddling with her smartphone, but it wasn't just any phone. It was an iPhone. He looked around the train at some of the other passengers. Not far away sat a boy who looked about twelve years old. He too was playing with an iPhone. A sinking feeling came over Lucier. Sales of the iPhone were soaring across the globe but most of the buyers were young people in their twenties and thirties. RIM still had a lock on the more conservative demographic of older buyers and business customers. Now even seniors and children were using the iPhone. Worse, Swedes were famous for being design-leaders and trendsetters. The country was the home of IKEA, the innovative furniture giant. If children and seniors in Sweden were now using the iPhone, it was only a matter of time before the trend migrated to other countries. Appointed RIM's vice-president and managing director of sales for northern Europe and Russia in 2010, Lucier had moved to Stockholm with high hopes. "I thought we would blow the doors off Sweden," he said. Soon after arriving, he was contacted by the agent for hockey stars Mats Sundin and the Sedin brothers. "Anything we can do to help?" the agent wondered. Lucier's main priority in his new job was to open up the Russian market to sales of the BlackBerry. "It's not an easy place to do business." Even so, he was making some headway, arranging a meeting between Balsillie and Russian president Dmitry Medvedev. Lucier also talked up the benefits of BlackBerry with Arkady Dvorkovich, Medvedev's top assistant. It was exhilarating stuff for a guy from Elmira, Ontario. But soon after, RIM's market share started to plunge. The meetings with high-level Russian politicians ended. The calls from Swedish agents stopped. "We lost our leverage, our cachet."[27]

Chapter 12
THE FALL

The story was impossible to miss. Plastered across the top of the front page of the *Globe and Mail*, along with a large photo of Balsillie and Lazaridis wearing grim looks on their faces, was the news that the Ontario Securities Commission was seeking a record fine of close to $100 million from the two CEOs for RIM's stock-option violations dating back to 2007. It was the morning of January 22, 2009, and Balsillie was slated to receive an award that day from Wilfrid Laurier University in Waterloo. The university's school of business had selected him as the outstanding business leader of the year for 2008. The agenda called for him to address business students on campus, then attend a luncheon at the nearby Waterloo Inn where he would deliver a second speech to a huge gathering of local business and political leaders.

For Balsillie and the university, it was a public relations nightmare. On the very day the *Globe* had splashed an embarrassing story across its front page about RIM's stock-option transgressions, he would be out in the community making speeches, greeting students and schmoozing with local dignitaries. Not only that, he was receiving one of Laurier's most prestigious business awards, an honour that was handed out just once a year. The timing couldn't be worse. Members of the media were champing at the bit for comments about the stock-option story, which had been based on anonymous sources. There was nowhere to hide for the beleaguered RIM executive. But if there was no way to avoid public contact, Laurier would do the next best thing. All media, large and small, were told by university officials to stay away from him. Balsillie would not be taking any questions about stock options or any other issue for that matter. He would be moving in an imaginary protective bubble. "He was our guest at Laurier that day. He was getting one of our biggest awards," said Kevin Crowley, former business editor at the *Record* and now director of communications and public affairs at Laurier. "We wanted to get a good headline in the paper."[1]

Balsillie entered the large, second-floor conference room at Laurier's John Aird Centre and took a seat near the back. An anticipatory buzz swirled about the room as the chattering throng of business students eagerly awaited the remarks of the RIM kingpin. At the front stood Ginny Dybenko, the affable and effusive dean of the Laurier business school and a former executive at Bell Canada. She hushed the crowd. Smiling broadly, she spoke briefly about Laurier's business leader of the year award. Past winners included a who's who of local industry titans — Linda Hasenfratz, CEO of Guelph auto-parts giant Linamar; Klaus Woerner, founder of Cambridge factory-automation standout ATS; and Val O'Donovan, founder of satellite-equipment maker Com Dev. Dybenko then moved quickly to the main order of business. "I'm sure you all can't wait to hear from this year's winner," she said. Pausing dramatically, Dybenko looked towards Balsillie at the back of the room. "Jiiiiiiiiiim," she beckoned, drawing out his name in one, long exclamation. As professional introductions go, it bordered on the fawning. But stock-option fine be damned, Laurier was going to show its local hero some love. Like an Olympic medallist returning in triumph to his hometown, Balsillie slowly made his way up the middle aisle, nodding and smiling to the cheering students who had jumped to their feet. The room literally shook with excitement. The only thing missing was high-fives or a couple of the brawnier students hoisting him on their shoulders and carrying him to the front. Everyone wanted a piece of the RIM boss. If they couldn't reach out and touch him, at least they could bask in his aura. Past winners of the award surely had never been accorded a reception like this. The contrast between the adulation showered on the RIM boss and the turmoil swirling about the company outside the Waterloo bubble could not have been starker. Slipping off his suit coat and tossing it on a chair, Balsillie stepped to the podium.

Students lucky enough to get a seat were likely hoping to hear the stunning story of RIM's rise to world domination. Young techies talk a lot about wanting to change the world. It's mostly hype, but in this case RIM had actually pulled it off with Balsillie in the co-pilot's seat. Goodness knows, he had a million stories to tell. Like, how he risked nearly everything to buy his way into the co-CEO's job when he joined the company in 1992.[2] How he preferred smart, energetic recruits from university business schools to boring industry veterans to pitch the BlackBerry. How he had raised hundreds of millions of dollars through IPOs on the TSX and the NASDAQ when Canadians just didn't do that kind of thing. How he and Lazaridis nearly blew the most important sales pitch in the company's history when they left the foam prototype of the Pager 950 in that Atlanta taxi.[3] How RIM sales staff had done end-runs around skeptical IT departments by going right to the CEO's office to pitch the BlackBerry. How BlackBerrys designed in Waterloo — Waterloo! — were sold on every continent in the world. It would have been a kick to hear some of those stories.

It didn't happen. Balsillie threw a knuckleball when everyone was expecting heat. Speaking without notes but glancing occasionally at his BlackBerry, he proceeded to morph into a pop psychologist. He told students they needed to develop a personal narrative to shape their lives, something along the lines of former Prime Minister Jean Chretien's "little guy from Shawinigan." Balsillie's personal narrative? "The quant jock from Peterborough who doesn't quit." Puzzled looks crossed the faces of some in the audience. Did he say quad-jock or quant-jock? Was he a four-sport athlete or someone who guzzled large quantities

of vitamin drinks? Was he a jock who dabbled in quantum computing? Some students fumbled for their smartphones to look up the word.
Balsillie had definitely used the word "quant," Crowley explained afterwards. It means a numbers person, someone who is good at math and
accounting. As slogans go, it was unique, but many in the audience were
left scratching their heads. After the way he had handled the NTP case,
a more appropriate slogan might have been "the quant jock from Peterborough who doesn't know when to quit."

But Balsillie wasn't done with the pep talk. Bring a "joyful, compassion-
ate, and positive" attitude to your personal narrative, and make friends and
hang around with the brightest people you can find, he urged them. "Peer
groups really do matter." Balsillie was no slouch in that department. While
a student at the University of Toronto, he befriended future best-selling
author Malcolm Gladwell, and Nigel Wright, who later served as chief of
staff to former Prime Minister Stephen Harper.[4] It was good advice on one
level. Better to hang out with the dude who'd rather hit the books than
tuck into a case of beer. When asked during a question period if Apple
posed the biggest threat to RIM, he offered a puzzling analogy. The war
with Apple is like a battle between an alligator and a bear, he said. The bear
is good on land, the alligator in water. The fight will be fought on neutral
ground that keeps changing. In the end, the message he conveyed didn't
seem terribly original. One could imagine students in the audience being
confronted by eager colleagues afterwards. "So, how was it?" Well, he told
us to look on the bright side and hang around with smart people. Huh?
Yet, it didn't matter. Balsillie could have been reading his grocery list and
students would still have been hanging on every word.

Even so, the speech he delivered to Laurier business students was far
more entertaining than the dry lecture he dropped on a packed room
of chamber of commerce types shortly after at the Waterloo Inn luncheon. Once again here was an opportunity to regale the audience with
RIM's stirring story. If not that, then a reasoned analysis of how RIM
was going to prevail in the fiercely contested smartphone race. Instead,
Balsillie treated the local business community to a seminar on . . . inter-

national politics. His CIGI and other governance bodies would bring fresh thinking to global problems and keep borders open for business. That was the message in a nutshell. Well-intentioned, certainly, but more like a speech from the ambassador to the UN than the CEO of a Fortune 500 company fighting for its life in one of the most competitive markets on the planet. Following his talk, reprinted in full the next day in the *Record*, luncheon guests formed a long line to congratulate him on his award. Picture a receiving line at a wedding or a funeral — except almost everyone in the room was standing in that line. There must have been 300 people waiting to shake his hand. It took Balsillie about an hour to get through the whole group.[5] There was no press scrum afterwards, as might normally be expected in the wake of the stock-option story. Balsillie's don't-fuck-with-me reputation kept the media at bay.

Reaction to the *Globe* story, which turned out to be pretty close to the truth, was predictably hostile among business leaders attending the luncheon. People were pissed off. "He is our boy," said Joan Fisk, chief executive of the Greater Kitchener-Waterloo Chamber of Commerce. "In this crowd, Jim has tremendous credibility." Randall Howard, a local tech entrepreneur and angel investor, agreed that strict regulation of stock options was needed. "But it's an odd time to get righteous. . . . We need to find ways to create champions."[6] Howard's defence of Balsillie was ironic, for just over a year later he would sound an alarm about serious troubles with RIM's technology.

* * *

Though he hadn't run a company in years, Randall Howard wasn't just an armchair quarterback. He backed up the talk with on-the-field experience. A native of Listowel, a small town northwest of Waterloo, he studied math and computer science at UW in the 1970s, experimenting with early versions of email, then honed his skills on the Unix computer operating system at a UW research lab after graduating. This was followed by a stint at a Chicago software firm that created one of the first Unix systems for IBM PCs. In 1984, he returned to Waterloo to co-found a company specializing in software-development tools. By the time he left in 2001, MKS, formerly Mortice Kern Systems, had 400 employees and $45 million in annual sales. Thereafter Howard morphed into a local tech consultant and angel investor helping young startups to prosper and grow. "He knows a lot, but he also knows a lot of people," said business partner Ray Simonson. "If you're talking about something, he can dig up the name of some guy he met three years ago who's the world expert on that."[7] Bookish in appearance with short brown hair and matching goatee, Howard had his ear to the ground on local tech issues, and when he spoke, people listened. Writing was one of his many talents, and he occasionally enjoyed authoring a blog on the regional technology scene. On August 3, 2010, his blog landed like a bomb on the Waterloo tech community. After many years of use, he was now considering giving up his beloved BlackBerry for an iPhone. To underscore his message, he titled the blog post "How You Gonna Keep 'Em Down on the Farm," after the famous First World War song about soldiers who had little desire to return to rural life after seeing Paris. There was no mistaking his meaning. Paris was the iPhone and the farm was BlackBerry.

A tech junkie who had owned a RIM handset since the company released its first Inter@ctive Pager, Howard said he had taken to carrying two smartphones in recent years. The BlackBerry was his mission-critical device for email, contacts and calendar. On that score, RIM's solution was secure, seamless, reliable and fast. His second device was an iPhone, which he used for web browsing, social media, testing and using applications. While carrying two devices might have seemed strange, and no doubt drew snickers at social gatherings, it was actually fairly typical among tech aficionados, he said. But his current Black-Berry had recently broken down and he was reluctant to buy another because RIM had failed to deliver in three key areas: "a robust applications ecosystem, user-friendly multi-media interface and a secure, modern and scalable operating system." Not only did RIM offer fewer apps, downloading them made his BlackBerry slower and less reliable, and he ended up removing most of them anyway.

As for interface, "touchscreen technologies used in both the iPhone and Android seem to have won the race against competing keyboard-only or stylus-based alternatives," he wrote. And the operating system? All modern smartphones seem to be built around a Unix-Linux variant, including the iPhone and Android phones, Howard wrote. It offers a "proven, scalable and efficient platform for secure computing from mobiles to desktops to servers." But the BlackBerry OS was different. "It appears to be a victim of its long heritage, starting life less as a real operating system," and more like a stack of Internet communications protocols bundled with the Java computer programming language in a package that has "morphed over time." Into what, he didn't say, but his message was clear. It wasn't up to the task. In fairness to RIM, Nokia and Microsoft seem to have failed to adapt to the new mobile paradigm as well, Howard noted.

RIM's failure was not for a lack of resources or talent, he insisted. "I know from personal experience that RIM has some of the smartest and most innovative people in their various product design groups, not to mention having gazillions of dollars that could fund any development." Instead the blame lies squarely at the top levels of the company, he wrote. "I am baffled why they have taken so long to address the above strategic challenges, which have already rewritten the smartphone landscape," Howard said. Here, he did not mince words. "The lack of a strategic response, or the huge delays to do so, remains an astonishing misstep."[8] The blog was posted in the summer of 2010, but Howard had been having doubts much earlier. In fact, he had actually started writing it in 2008. The disruption caused by the iPhone and RIM's slow response was apparent even then. He wasn't happy with initial drafts and kept mulling over the content and hoping RIM would turn things around until finally deciding he couldn't remain silent any longer. After the blog was posted, negative feedback poured in. People would come up to him and say, "You just wrote the obituary for BlackBerry." Yet his real motivation was born out of tough love, Howard insisted. He wanted to fire "a shot across the bow" to get the company going in the right direction. The blog attracted many positive comments as well from "thought leaders" all over the world. From RIM? Silence.[9]

* * *

Howard's blog post was prescient. Behind the scenes, RIM was already taking steps to fix its aging software operating system. In the spring of 2010, it announced the acquisition of QNX Software Systems of Ottawa for $200 million. The aim was to get RIM software into automobile communication systems, which QNX specialized in, but also to use the QNX platform to build RIM's new tablet device called the PlayBook and to develop its next generation of smartphones. Better yet, QNX appeared to be a fail-safe technology. In addition to car applications, the company specialized in mission-critical software for Internet equipment suppliers, nuclear power plants and air traffic control systems. Customers bought QNX software when failure was not an option.

Like RIM, QNX had a Waterloo connection. Founder Dan Dodge earned an honours physics degree and a masters in computer science at the University of Waterloo. After graduating in 1981, he launched Quantum Software Systems. It was later shortened to QNX, the N and X standing for the Unix computer operating system used by the company. A geek of the first order, the Belleville, Ontario, native put together his first computer while living in residence at UW using parts scrounged from summer jobs at Bell Northern Research and Digital Equipment Corp. Over the next two decades, Dodge built QNX into a thriving software business with 200 employees and major customers in the automotive, Internet and nuclear industries, among others. By the early 2000s, it was hard to buy a car without QNX software in it. In 2004, the company was purchased by Harman International Industries, a Connecticut-based outfit specializing in connected-car systems, with Dodge staying on to run QNX. Five years later, Harman was looking to unload QNX, and Dodge targeted RIM as a potential buyer. He asked UW president David Johnston[10] to arrange a meeting with Lazaridis. The RIM chieftain was dazzled by what he saw. Here was the potential solution to all the software and platform problems plaguing recent iterations of the BlackBerry.[11] With QNX now in the fold, Dodge began to assume a pivotal role in RIM's future.

He also had some perceptive views on what was wrong with RIM's software. When the BlackBerry first came out in 1999, its operating system[12] was crafted to meet the needs and expectations of the time — sending and receiving email, Dodge said in a candid interview with the *Record* at a BlackBerry developers conference in San Jose, California, in 2012. Over the years, features were gradually added — contacts, calendar, voice, email attachments, a camera, music, gaming applications, Internet browsing and the like. But as mobile software became richer and more complex, in effect transforming smartphones into handheld computers, RIM's legacy operating system simply wasn't up to the task. "It was never designed as a mobile computing platform. The world had changed," explained Dodge, a round-faced man with straight, sandy-coloured hair. RIM tried its best to customize and upgrade its OS to handle this smorgasbord of new features. But over time, as it augmented, patched and modified the OS, it started to resemble a giant plate of spaghetti, Dodge said. Spaghetti code was a common term among developers for any software beset by this problem. RIM's operating system was so complicated and byzantine that few engineers understood how it functioned. The OS also became bug-prone and glitch-infested, and many of the original designers who understood this tangled network of pasta had departed. RIM's initial OS was never designed to serve as a mobile computer platform, said Dodge. "To try to take it there would have been too difficult, perhaps even impossible."

BlackBerry's OS had another fundamental problem, he continued. It was monolithic. Part of it could not be changed without impacting the whole platform. QNX's software was the opposite. It was based on "microkernel" architecture. Parts could be removed like pieces of Lego and replaced by other parts without undermining the whole platform. "That's what we brought to the table. We had that industrial-grade, high-performance, reliable operating system that could compete with the likes of iOS (Apple platform)," Dodge said.[13]

RIM faced another critical problem besides the nature of its software platform. Building a new mobile operating system from the ground up could not be accomplished overnight. In fact, it would take two to three years. The first phones based on the QNX platform, later renamed BlackBerry 10, would not hit stores until January 2013, nearly three years after RIM bought QNX. The Waterloo company's only alternative in the meantime was to continue patching up the original BlackBerry OS and hope customers still bought BlackBerrys until the new platform was ready. The strategy did not work. RIM lost so much market share and its stock took such a beating in the intervening years that calls grew more vociferous for Lazaridis and Balsillie to step down and clear the way for new leadership. 2011 was a particularly bad year. On a road show to promote the just-released PlayBook, Lazaridis lost his composure and abruptly ended an interview in London after a BBC reporter went off-script and asked about a dispute with India. The country wanted access to BlackBerry emails to root out terrorists. The outbursts continued back in Waterloo, with Lazaridis telling a *Globe and Mail* reporter that RIM might have been better off leaving Canada years ago.[14]

During its quarterly financial release in June, RIM announced major layoffs to its global workforce of 19,000 people, about half of whom worked in Waterloo Region. The company's head count had grown nearly sixfold since 2004, both organically and through acquisitions. The number of subscribers had pushed past 70 million worldwide and annual revenues were approaching $20 billion US, but sales had not kept up, particularly in the bell-weather US market. Two thousand employees would lose their jobs during the next quarter. RIM was locked in a "features and performance arms race" with Apple and the Android phones in the US, shareholders were told by Lazaridis, who joined the conference call for the first time in years. Just when it appeared things couldn't get any worse, an anonymous letter was published on a prominent American tech website blasting the company for a litany of issues including poor working conditions, late products, software delays and overall mismanagement. It was written by a high-level employee who insisted the goal was to see RIM regain its lost prestige.[15]

The reaction in Waterloo Region to RIM's dire situation ran through the classic stages of grief. "I think people here just see this as a blip that will go away as RIM seizes opportunities globally to continue to sell the product," said John Jung, head of Canada's Technology Triangle, a local government agency aimed at attracting foreign investment. "We're not a one-horse town. It's a really balanced economy," added Waterloo Region chair Ken Seiling, the highest-ranking local politician. "A train-wreck in slow motion," was the sober assessment of tech investor Randall Howard. RIM isn't being treated fairly, charged UW economics professor Larry Smith, who blamed stock analysts and the media. It had 70 million sub-scribers and $3 billion US in reserves, yet it was being called "desperate." Critics, especially in the US, just couldn't fathom how a Canadian com-pany could become a global technology leader, Smith said.[16]

Naturally everyone looked to Iain Klugman, CEO of Communitech, to rally the troops in the face of this unprecedented assault on RIM. And Klugman did not disappoint. Behind the scenes, Communitech prepared a series of "talking points" so community leaders would be speaking from the same page when reporters called. RIM was no longer to be referred to as the "epicentre" of the local sector, but just a part of the sector. The company was still the "tallest tree" in the forest, but there were 1,000 other trees as well growing and thriving independently, said the talking points, later leaked to the media. Waterloo Region is not a car-manufacturing town with an ecosystem of local suppliers that gets sucked under once the automaker starts to sink, Klugman added. On the contrary, much of RIM's "value chain resides outside Canada." The company's decline is often compared to that of Nortel Networks, but the only similarity is that both were leaders of Canada's tech industry. "As Canadians, we're proud of our tech success stories and we count on their leadership. So when there's a setback, we look at it under the microscope for fear it's indicative of Canada's competitive position slipping, and we put extreme pressure on the company to turn things around and restore collective confidence."[17]

Despite the vote of confidence from some local leaders, the bad news just kept on coming. Mike Abramsky, an influential stock analyst from RBC Capital Markets and long-time RIM supporter, painted a bleak picture in a September 2011 research note. With 70 million subscribers and continued growth in international sales, the company still had a "turnaround window," he wrote. On the downside, products and software were uncompetitive, often shipped late and unfinished, financial guidance was unreliable and the company's board of directors was weak, Abramsky noted. Most tellingly, he wrote, "Four years after the iPhone launched, RIM still hasn't launched competitive smartphone innovations or addressed its app gap."[18] The technology stumbles were reflected in RIM's share price. Late in the year it had fallen to $17 on the TSX, down from $63 a year earlier.

In December 2011, RIM announced a shocking $485 million US writedown of its PlayBook tablet inventory. Most of its PlayBook stock would have to be sold off at bargain-basement prices or written off as junk. Moreover, sales of its new suite of BlackBerry 7 phones, based on the old RIM operating system, had not gone as well as expected and earnings would have to be downgraded for the third time in the fiscal year.[19] Later that month, during RIM's quarterly release, Lazaridis announced that the new BlackBerry 10 devices, considered RIM's last hope for survival in the smartphone race, would be delayed until late 2012.[20]

When the inevitable happened in January 2012, it was still a shocker. The two men who had built RIM into a mobile juggernaut, who had turned the BlackBerry into a household name, who had put Waterloo on the global technology map, were stepping aside as CEOs. "The men who changed the way the world communicates and built Research In Motion into a Canadian technology giant have stepped down," read the headline on the front page of the *Globe and Mail*.[21] "In every successful company that's developed by founders," Lazaridis told the *New York*

Times, "there comes a time when it enters a new phase of growth and it's time for the founders to pass the torch."[22] Despite RIM's struggles over the past year, the news still caught Randall Howard by surprise. The company had a shot at turning things around, he said, adding that it was important to remember what Lazaridis and Balsillie had accomplished. "People can sit on the sidelines and snipe, but what they have done is phenomenal."[23] In an interview several days later with the *Record*, Lazaridis admitted the decision was hard. "Stepping aside as a founder after 27 years, I would be lying if I said that wasn't emotional for me and for my whole family."[24]

Lazaridis and Balsillie were replaced by Thorsten Heins, a former executive of Siemens in Germany who had joined the company in 2007 and risen to chief operating officer for product and sales. He denied more staff cuts were coming. "Right now I think we are at a good size." Five months later, Heins would slash 5,000 jobs from RIM's payroll.[25]

What of the other trees in the local technology forest? In 2012, there were still the sturdy oaks such as Open Text, Sandvine, Dalsa, Christie Digital, Descartes, SAP (formerly Sybase), Maplesoft, Com Dev and MKS. A few seedlings had grown into young hardwoods such as online education firm Desire2Learn, real estate software company Lone Wolf, intranet specialist Igloo and e-commerce firm Well.ca. But the vast majority were young saplings with fewer than fifty employees. "We've done a helluva good job to promote starting stuff, but we've done very little to finish stuff," Yvan Couture, chief executive of Primal, a startup in custom web-searching, observed in 2012.[26] Yet there was enough critical mass of small tech enterprises, abetted by a steady supply of talented students emerging from local universities, to attract at least one high-tech giant from outside the country.

* * *

Google's entrance into Waterloo in 2005 started inconspicuously. The search-engine company had its eye on a Waterloo startup whose software could open email images, attachments and web pages on wireless devices. That Reqwireless was located in Waterloo was merely a coincidence, a Google spokesperson said. Launched by UW grad Roger Skubowius four years earlier, Reqwireless had barely a dozen employees wedged into a small unit in a bland strip mall overlooking the city's main expressway. News of Google's acquisition only dribbled out when it held a job fair at the University of Waterloo. Eight hundred people showed up. But if Google's arrival was accidental, there may have been some intent behind it as well. Two years later, it moved into larger offices at the UW research park so it could be closer to the university. At the opening, Stuart Feldman, a Google vice-president from New York City, gushed about using the Watfor compiler during his student days at Princeton and the Massachusetts Institute of Technology, and Maple software, another UW spinoff product, in his work. "I have known about computing at this university for a long time."[27]

From there, it has been nothing but galloping growth. With its workforce pushing past seventy employees, Google moved in 2010 into more spacious quarters in the renovated Tannery in downtown Kitchener, the same building occupied by Communitech. Over the next six years, its payroll quadrupled, sparking another move in 2016 into the nearby Breithaupt Block, a renovated glass-and-brick structure originally built in 1902 for one of the city's rubber companies. Today the search-engine titan occupies one of the showpiece office spaces in downtown Kitchener where it employs more than 500 people. It is considered Google's most important engineering office outside the US. The irony is thick. As BlackBerry went down, the company that played a major role in its demise as a smartphone-maker rose up. And in BlackBerry's hometown. The other irony is that the architect of Google's expansion in Waterloo Region was once vilified as a major contributor to the brain-drain from Waterloo to Silicon Valley.

Steven Woods kept trying to leave Waterloo, yet something always brought him back. "They say you don't appreciate a place until you leave," he said. Born in 1965, he grew up in the small town of Melfort,

Saskatchewan, about 170 kilometres northeast of Saskatoon. Encouraged by his parents, he started fooling around with computers in his early teens, teaching himself to write software code on an old Commodore VIC-20. "I realized computers are fun," he said. After earning his degree in computer science at the University of Saskatchewan in 1987, Woods wasn't sure what to do next. One of his professors suggested the master's program at the University of Waterloo. The idea struck him as strange. He had never heard of UW and besides, young people from Saskatchewan just didn't move to Ontario. They either stayed in the province or moved west to Alberta or B.C. Needing an income, he took a job as a software developer at SaskTel. "It was a horrible experience," he recalls. The software developers were weak and so were the managers. Desperate to leave, he remembered his prof's advice about UW. A few weeks after arriving, he knew he'd made the right move. "It was the best out-of-the-box experience I've ever had," said Woods, who has short dark hair and prefers the casual dress of a software geek. Not only did the faculty and students work at a high level, he learned how to collaborate with others on research.

After graduation, he spent several years working in government research labs in Australia and Quebec, then returned to Waterloo in 1993 for his PhD in computer software. Three years later, he was off to the University of Hawai'i for post-doctoral work and to co-write a book on his PhD research. He was in paradise, but being so far from the high-tech centres of power "didn't feel right," so the globe-trotting Woods moved to Carnegie Mellon University in Pittsburgh to work at the Software Engineering Institute. It was there that Woods started meeting co-op and grad students from Waterloo. It seems the two universities had a working relationship of sorts. Some of these students "were absolutely unbelievable," he said. "They could write software a lot faster than me." Out of boredom, they started a company on the side called Quack.com. Their flagship product would be the world's first interactive voice portal allowing users to access the Internet over the telephone. Trying to make a computer understand speech "was hard, very hard. But a lot of fun. We eventually made something that sounded even more broken than Siri," Woods quipped, referring to the Apple voice app.[28]

In the fall of 1998, they moved the company to Silicon Valley and began recruiting more students from UW. "It was all about the Waterloo magic, the shared understanding of how to write software," said Woods. Quack lured so many students to California that it was criticized in the media for contributing to the brain-drain from Canada. "Some bad things were written about me," Woods admits.[29] Many were co-op students who just wanted to see what it was like to work in the Valley. The connection ran so deep that Quack opened a research office in Waterloo. In 2000, Quack was acquired by America Online (AOL) for $200 million. Flush with cash, Woods stayed on at AOL for several years, then co-founded a second company called NeoEdge Networks to help gaming and entertainment companies monetize their content. He kept recruiting from UW and estimates that over his time in California he brought 100 people to the Valley from Waterloo. But many graduates wouldn't leave UW, making him think he was missing something back on his old turf. "Waterloo and the Valley were different . . . sufficiently different to matter and maybe to make all the difference," Woods said. When Google came calling in 2008, looking for someone to run its Waterloo office, he jumped.[30]

The local Google office hasn't grown just because the company likes Kitchener. It has had to earn it. Each Google site is expected to come up with new ideas, deliver when called upon and compete with other company sites and the best minds at competitors such as Apple and Microsoft. Woods likens his job to being the general manager of a major-league sports team. Finish near the bottom and you are fired. Project managers are like playing coaches. If their team needs help, they jump in and start working. "I only hire people who can build software," said Woods.[31] The list of projects worked on in Kitchener is long and impressive: mobile Gmail, the Chrome web browser, the OnHub WiFi router, Google Ads, Google Fiber and tablets and laptops for the Pixel. The mobile Gmail app was developed solely in Kitchener and the

Chrome browser was largely developed there as well.[32] Around 2010, the local office came up with an application called conversion optimizer that generated more than $1 billion in online ads. Roughly 60 per cent of the software engineers working at the local Google office are UW grads. Outsiders often ask Woods how they can make their cities like Waterloo. His answer is, "You can't," followed by "find your own magic." UW has a formula for turning out "tremendously grounded" graduates with "enormous individual capacity that has absolutely set this university at the forefront of computer science in the world."[33]

Chapter 13
SILVER LINING

Released early in 2013, the BlackBerry 10 smartphones were solid, reliable devices. The QNX operating system appeared up to the task. Browsing the web was quick and fluid. Mobile apps were rendered crisply and efficiently. The new phones were communication powerhouses, gathering emails, texting, Facebook messages, calls and every kind of message in one place called the BlackBerry Hub. Reviews were positive. "It's lovely, fast and efficient, bristling with fresh useful ideas. And here's the shocker — it's complete," said David Pogue in the *New York Times*.[1] To coincide with the launch, Heins ditched the name Research In Motion. From now on, the company would be known simply as BlackBerry, after its flagship device. But the BB10 devices failed to revive the company's fortunes. Sales were tepid. Its market share continued to slide. They were classic "me-too" handsets, similar to the iPhone and Android devices, but not a leap forward and four years too late. There was no compelling reason for an iPhone or Android user to switch to the BlackBerry platform. Worse, the company's declining market share drove away most apps developers. They were reluctant to hitch their fortunes to a broken-down wagon. After the BB10 phones failed to gain much traction in the market, Heins was fired as CEO in November 2013 and left with a boatload of cash. He was replaced by a tech executive from Silicon Valley named John Chen.[2] Known as a turnaround specialist, Chen had orchestrated a revival at Sybase, the same California-based enterprise services company that had purchased Watcom back in the 1990s and opened an office in Waterloo.

Prior to Sybase, Chen helped rescue Pyramid Technology Corp., a California computer-maker. "Pyramid was the most interesting turnaround. We were one quarter away from not making payroll," he told the Greater Kitchener-Waterloo Chamber of Commerce in a 2015 interview. When he joined BlackBerry, the company lost $1.2 billion US in one quarter alone. "We were bleeding hard." A Hong Kong native who came to the US to attend university and stayed, Chen said BlackBerry refused to believe "there was a sea change, and we reacted too slow." His vision was to take the company beyond the world of smartphones. One billion cellphones are in use today across the globe, but there are ten times as many endpoints, he noted, including cars, TVs, washing machines and fridges. Every company has its ups and downs, even large ones such as Apple, IBM, GM and Intel, said Chen, who spoke in a relaxed but confident manner. "The fact that you're down doesn't mean you're out." Every turnaround is different, he noted. "There is no one game plan."[3]

All the same, the turnaround he executed at BlackBerry was like a train travelling 100 kilometres down the track, turning around and travelling just ten kilometres back. Some derided it as the turnaround that never ended. One of his first steps was outsourcing phone production to the Foxconn Group of Taiwan, the same manufacturing company used by Apple. BlackBerry would still design the phones, but would no longer manufacture them.[4]

A battery of new smartphones was launched under Chen's watch including the Z30, the Passport, the Classic and BlackBerry's first Android device, called the Priv. Some were quite innovative. The Passport was shaped like an actual passport with square corners and three rows of hardware keys at the bottom. None gained a significant foothold in the market. In the fall of 2016, Chen finally pulled the plug on hardware design. Going forward, the company would license other firms to design and build BlackBerrys. "It's really more about the smart of a smartphone, not about the phone of a smartphone," he told analysts.[5] BlackBerry would now be known as a software and services company, offering solutions in security, auto connectivity and the Internet of Things. Meanwhile, the payroll cuts and real estate sell-off continued in Waterloo. Once a vast realm of more than thirty buildings in Waterloo Region, BlackBerry was reduced to a cluster of three office buildings in the northeast corner of Waterloo. By the end of its 2018 fiscal year, the company's workforce had fallen to about 3,200 employees — about half in Waterloo — and annual revenue to less than $1 billion US, a far cry from the days when it employed nearly 20,000 and sales approached $20 billion a year.[6] The BlackBerry operating system's share of the global smartphone market had shrunk below 0.001 per cent. Chen, who was the highest paid CEO in Canada in 2014, earning $341,000 in base salary and $88 million in BlackBerry stock,[7] ran the company from his office near San Francisco though the head office remained in Waterloo.

And yet there were hopeful signs. By late 2018, the bleeding in revenues had stopped and the company was actually showing signs of growth, particularly in its automobile software division. Annual revenues were about $930 million US, down from $1.3 billion US in fiscal 2017, but sales had held steady for four straight quarters. In the fall of 2018, BlackBerry made its biggest acquisition in company history, purchasing the California artificial intelligence firm Cylance for $1.4 billion US. The funds came from the company's cash reserve of $1.7 billion. "I always said I would be patient for the right asset," Chen said.[8] And early in 2019, BlackBerry announced an investment of $310 million, including $40 million from the federal government, to expand its technology in self-driving cars and other automotive applications. Eight hundred jobs would be added over the next decade, mostly to the QNX division in Kanata, near Ottawa. QNX could be the Microsoft Office of the automotive sector, said analyst Gus Papageorgiou of Macquarie Research. "It has a chance of being the core operating system of the connected car."[9]

* * *

BlackBerry axed about 5,000 to 6,000 employees in Waterloo Region from 2011 to 2014. Many of them left the area, but a lot stayed. Communitech tried to keep as many as possible in Waterloo Region. "The fear was that this world-class talent would scatter to the winds," said Anthony Reinhart, director of editorial strategy at Communitech. Backed by $1.2 million in funding from the province, the association set up a job-action centre and ran job fairs specifically for laid-off Black-Berry workers. More than 2,000 people used the program, called Tech Jobs Connex, in some way during its three-year run, with about 1,400 finding other jobs in the area or going back to school, Iain Klugman estimated.[10] Former BlackBerry employees even staffed the program. "The release of talent as BlackBerry downsized was a bonanza for other companies in town," said Reinhart.[11] The numbers and variety were remarkable. Local startups specializing in IT network management, property and casualty insurance, the Internet of Things, product-testing, text-messaging, drones, legal software, health-monitoring, talent recruitment and even horse-monitoring and baseball analytics were all launched or assisted by former BlackBerry employees. One ex-RIM worker found an unusual avenue for employment. Dave Jaworsky, a twelve-year RIM executive, was elected mayor of Waterloo in 2014 and was re-elected to another four-year term in 2018.

It's no surprise that some of the most successful enterprises focused on wireless security and encryption, two of BlackBerry's core strengths. Magnet Forensics, helps police retrieve incriminating data on computers. Its CEO is Adam Belsher, a former vice-president of BlackBerry's Verizon business unit, and its executive team is stocked with former RIM employees. TrustPoint Innovation, acquired by a German company in 2017, specializes in anti-counterfeit software and machine-to-machine security, and Cognitive Systems detects unwanted wireless signals in the home. Cognitive was among the first startups funded by Quantum Valley Investments, the venture-capital firm launched by Lazaridis and

Doug Fregin, RIM's co-founders. Also financed by Quantum Valley was Isara Corp., a firm specializing in quantum cryptography started by several former BlackBerry employees including Mark Pecen.

Some departed staffers even found themselves back in old Black-Berry buildings, this time working for other companies. David Yach has worked in not one but three former BlackBerry buildings for Auvik Networks, the company he co-founded in 2012 after leaving RIM. Some of the other buildings Auvik occupied still had BlackBerry furniture. "This one is not as spooky," he said of their current office, located in RIM's former manufacturing plant at 451 Phillip Street in Waterloo. It has been redeveloped into chic office space with an interior courtyard, large windows and numerous skylights. Auvik manages networks for Internet service providers. Its technology "allows a mere mortal to keep a network up and running," quipped Yach. Growth in business and staff prompted the frequent moves. Late in 2018, it employed 135 people. "We're in the teenager stage" of maturity, Yach said. "We're not big, but we're not small." Many of its employees are former RIM workers, some long-term, others just there briefly. Auvik manages 20,000 Internet networks, mostly in the US.[12] The fact that Auvik moved into three different BlackBerry buildings as it grew is not as unusual as it sounds. As it downsized, BlackBerry dumped a lot of real estate on the market at the same time.

* * *

John Whitney pulls out a chart filled with multicoloured boxes and arrows. It shows BlackBerry's real estate holdings from 2014, when the giant sell-off began, through to 2018. The company put its entire real estate portfolio — 2.8 million square feet of space — on the market with an enormous thud. A concrete-and-glass fire sale of monumental proportions. When it happened, he and other commercial real estate agents in the area were worried. BlackBerry planned to lease back what it needed, but a huge glut of space might sit empty. The office district around UW would look like a ghost town. Lease prices would drop and not recover for years. New construction would halt. Surely, the market couldn't take shocks like this. Whitney felt the pain more than most. As RIM's real estate agent during the company's rise, he had engineered the purchase of many of these buildings. Their pictures loomed over him as he bent over his desk in north Waterloo. Bad enough that the company was getting pounded in the marketplace and thousands were losing their jobs. Now BlackBerry offices were on the block and might remain vacant for months, even years. When he thinks back to that time, Whitney shakes his head and smiles. Within twenty-six months, most of that empty space vanished. Just like that 2.3 million square feet was snapped up by large investors and leased to tech companies and other firms in the area. "I never thought in two years all that space would be gone," said the veteran agent. "It was incredible."

When Blackberry put its land and buildings on the market in 2014, the big real estate investors in Toronto yawned. There wasn't much interest. But a private-equity firm in San Francisco sat up and took notice. Spear Street Capital liked to invest in tech clusters across the US that were going through transitions. Silicon Valley, Seattle, Pittsburgh and Austin, Texas, all had struggled with swoons in their tech sectors, leaving plenty of real estate on the open market. Spear Street swooped in, scooped up properties, renovated them and re-sold or leased them to the next generation of tech startups. But the company, founded in 2001, had never invested in Canada. It didn't take long to shed its fears of venturing north of the border. BlackBerry listed 2.8 million square feet of real estate in January 2014. Five months later, Spear Street bought 2.3 million square feet in Waterloo, Cambridge, Mississauga and Ottawa for $305 million. "It is a hotbed of engineering talent," John Grassi, founder and president of Spear Street, said of Waterloo, where most of the BlackBerry land was located.[13] Waterloo reminded him of Pittsburgh. Both have highly regarded tech universities; Pittsburgh has Carnegie Mellon and Waterloo has UW. And both have attracted major tech companies such as Google. Spear Street also liked the fact that

BlackBerry packaged its real estate in bulk, and the region was putting the finishing touches on a light-rail transit line that would run right by many of the BlackBerry properties.[14]

Spear Street didn't sit on its acquisition for long. Within a year it sold five buildings in Waterloo to Michael Wekerle, a flamboyant Toronto investment banker and star of *Dragon's Den*, a TV show where entrepreneurs pitched ideas to investors. Wekerle had already purchased a BlackBerry building directly from the company, and planned to stock his new properties with tech companies in the area. He had been lured to the region by Tim Ellis, a former CEO of the Accelerator Centre, UW's tech incubator. Ellis had seen too many startups run into difficulty raising capital locally, then leave for Silicon Valley.[15] To prime the pump, the colourful Wekerle planned to launch a venture-capital firm to invest in startups in the area. His cluster of tech buildings would be called the Waterloo Innovation Network. "Out of what many people saw as a negative, I saw as a positive," he said of BlackBerry's decline. Wekerle had another BlackBerry connection. As a senior trader at GMP Securities in the late 1990s, he had helped RIM raise $125 million when it went public.[16]

Spear Street kept four BlackBerry buildings, three of which it leased back to the company, and sold another four to a Toronto real estate investment company called CanFirst Capital over the 2015–17 period. Three of those buildings, located on Phillip Street just north of the campus, have been renovated into upscale office space that Waterloo is calling the Idea Quarter. BlackBerry also sold five buildings to the University of Waterloo early in the sale process. Much of the credit for the interest in BlackBerry real estate should go to Spear Street, said Whitney. "That vote of confidence, and Phillip Street's proximity to the University of Waterloo, ensured the area would continue to prosper," he noted.[17]

Among all the purchasers of BlackBerry buildings, one stood out more than any other. Early in 2014, RIM's co-founders Mike Lazaridis and Doug Fregin purchased a handsome stone-and-glass structure near a wooded area on the west side of Waterloo, the same building erected to house the company's research division headed by Mark Pecen. Lazaridis and Fregin needed a home for their new venture-capital firm, Quantum Valley Investments. Armed with a war chest of $100 million, they were looking to invest in what they considered the next big thing, something even bigger than the smartphone — the quantum computer.

* * *

Mike Lazaridis had worked himself up into full professorial mode. Striding back and forth across the stage at the University of Waterloo's Humanities Theatre, clicking the remote on his PowerPoint presentation, he kept repeating the phrase "bending the curve of history."

For thousands of years, the curve barely moved, he stated, flashing a graph up on the screen under the title Engines of History. Then, in the late 1700s, something remarkable happened — James Watt invented a new kind of steam engine. As he spoke, the audience of academics, entrepreneurs, CEOs and business leaders gave him their full attention. The 720-seat theatre, filled almost to capacity, was small and intimate so everyone had a good view of the inventor of the once-indispensable BlackBerry smartphone.

They had gathered on this balmy September morning in 2017 at a conference called Hacking the Future: The Waterloo Innovation Summit to hear Lazaridis and other industry titans talk about the latest disruptions in technology.

Prior to Watt's discovery, steam engines were even less useful than horses or humans, Lazaridis continued. Ninety-nine per cent of the heat generated by burning wood or coal was dissipated or lost. With Watt's invention, steam engines became marginally more efficient, but a door was opened and their effectiveness gradually took off, ushering in the Industrial Revolution, he said.

Yet it wasn't the mechanics of Watt's engine that enabled the breakthrough. Something deeper and more fundamental was at work, Lazaridis said. And that something was thermodynamics, also known as theoretical physics. Through a basic understanding of thermodynamics,

Watt realized he could dissipate some of that heat through an external condenser. That was the beginning of the modern steam engine, Lazaridis said, slowing to emphasize his words. "But we didn't stop there."

One by one, he began ticking off other inventors who bent the curve of history. Michael Faraday discovered electro-magnetism. James Maxwell came up with mathematical formulas describing the relationship between electricity and magnetism that led to the creation of radio waves. Heinrich Hertz detected the first radio waves and Guglielmo Marconi transformed that discovery into radio. Standing on their shoulders, Nikola Tesla and George Westinghouse started building electric motors, generators and transmission lines to transmit energy more reliably and efficiently.

The curve of history moved higher.

And then in the early 1900s, theoretical physicists discovered quantum mechanics and relativity. Our eyes were opened to how energy worked at the atomic level and how to make things smaller, Lazaridis said. Inventions such as the transistor in 1947 and integrated circuits in the 1950s and '60s followed, leading to the creation of lasers and computers, and "everything was transformed."

This marked the first quantum revolution, he noted.

And now we stand on the precipice of something as ground-shaking as those discoveries, something that will bend the curve of history once again, Lazaridis said almost breathlessly.

As speeches go, it was not filled with fire and brimstone. Now in his mid-fifties, dressed in a light grey sports jacket and open-necked shirt, the smartphone pioneer spoke in a slow, quiet, methodical manner, as if he were entertaining a social gathering in his living-room. We stand on the precipice, he intoned dramatically — you almost expected a drumroll or a blast of trumpets — we stand on the precipice . . . of the second quantum revolution.

Quantum mechanics has the power to create computers that will leave today's machines in the dust, he continued. Thanks to the miracle of quantum computers, a series of breakthroughs will be possible in almost every field you can imagine, from medicine, cybersecurity, transportation and finance to defence, mining, agriculture and even artificial intelligence.

Quantum sensors, to cite one example, could detect biological processes down to the level of single photons, offering far higher resolution than today's diagnostic tools, Lazaridis said. And quantum simulators completely blow away today's technology, called computational fluid dynamics, used to design and test airplanes, boats, cars and wind turbines.

And Waterloo Region was poised to capitalize on this second quantum revolution thanks to the millions of dollars he and others had poured into Perimeter Institute for Theoretical Physics, the Institute for Quantum Computing, Quantum Valley Investments and the Lazaridis School of Business and Economics, investments that were topped up by government assistance, he was careful to add.

By starting early and investing more than $1.5 billion in private and public money in Waterloo, Canada now sits among the top five countries in the world in the quantum field, Lazaridis noted, and has a head start on tech icons such as Google, IBM, Intel and Microsoft, all of which are racing to build their own quantum computers.

The goal was to "intercept the second quantum revolution" by recruiting and retaining the best quantum experts from around the world, giving them the resources and capital to do their work and train new students so that a critical density could be reached. Only by doing all that do those "spontaneous events of entrepreneurship" happen, leading to new companies and jobs in the quantum field, he noted. He didn't say it, but he was obviously referring to companies like Research In Motion, which had benefited from such a critical mass twenty years earlier.

"Not only will the second quantum revolution impact all technology in all industries, it will transform our lives. It will give us the basic insights of how nature works. And every time man has figured out how nature works at that level, he's bent the curve of history."

One couldn't help but marvel at the huge shot of energy, determination and money Lazaridis was injecting into this new holy grail. More than five years after he had resigned as co-chief executive officer of RIM, the tech pioneer was back with a new cause to champion. Once known as Canada's Steve Jobs, was he now bidding to become Canada's Elon Musk, creator of game-changing products in several different fields?

The university had lined up a stellar cast of presenters for the two-day summit. Among the speakers was Jared Cohen, a Google expert on cybersecurity; J.B. Straubel, chief technical officer at Tesla; and Mary-Ellen Anderson, vice-president of customer success at Microsoft. The fact that Lazaridis was a headliner at the two-day conference was clear evidence that, despite the decline of the BlackBerry, he was still viewed as a tech giant in Waterloo Region and across Canada. Just a month later he would be featured on the cover of the *Globe and Mail*'s "Report on Business" magazine in an article on the race between Waterloo and a B.C. firm for Canadian leadership in the quantum-computing field.

Author and broadcaster Amanda Lang, star of her own show on Bloomberg TV Canada and veteran of other high-profile media gigs including the CBC and *Globe and Mail*, had been recruited to co-chair the conference and lend some glitz to the proceedings. She couldn't hide her excitement at sharing the stage with the august Lazaridis, noting that he had asked her backstage if there would be one of those "clicker things" at the podium to run his PowerPoint presentation. If even he doesn't know what it's called, there's hope for us all, she joked before welcoming him to the stage.

In a question and answer session after Lazaridis finished his thirty-minute speech, Lang didn't waste much time getting to the heart of the matter. For the longest time, she had thought of the quantum computer as Snuffleupagus, the Sesame Street character portrayed for many years as a figment of Big Bird's imagination. "Is it real? Is there a quantum computer?" she wondered.

Lazaridis had first become aware of quantum theory while studying physics at UW in the early 1980s. Professor Lynn Watt had opened his eyes to the work of physicists Alain Aspect of France and Richard Feynman of the US. Drawing from a branch of physics known as quantum mechanics, their research suggested that tiny particles of matter such as atoms or photons — also known as quanta — could be in two places at the same time. This quality is known as "superposition" or "entanglement." Particles that are entangled can instantly coordinate their properties regardless of their distance in space and time. If this idea were applied to computers, the possibilities would be enormous, Feynman suggested.

Another milestone came in 1985 when an Oxford University professor named David Deutsch published a paper on the possibility of building a quantum computer and an algorithm that would run on it. In a classical computer, a processor represents information as ones and zeros by turning the many transistors in a microchip on and off. Each one and zero is known as a bit. Quantum computers don't use transistors or bits. Instead they use quantum bits or "qubits." Thanks to the magic of superposition, qubits can stand for one and zero at the same time. This means a quantum computer can do an enormous number of calculations at the same time. An analogy might be a locksmith trying to open a lock with dozens of keys. With a regular computer, he would use one key at a time. With a quantum computer, he could use all the keys at once. "The quantum computer isn't just 10 times faster than a Pentium," Lazaridis said in a 2013 interview in *Fast Company* magazine. "It's a whole different scale."

A good example of what a quantum computer could do is in the area of factorization. It's easy for any computer to multiply two large numbers. The reverse process, called factoring, is much more difficult. Finding the prime factors in a 400-digit number would take many years for today's most powerful computers. Much of current cryptography is based on the difficulty in solving factorization. But with a quantum computer, a 400-digit number could be factored in minutes using the superposition and entanglement of qubits.

Quantum computing also solves the problem of the shrinking processor. Since the 1960s, computer chip manufacturers have been able to double the speed of processors every eighteen to twenty-four months by packing more transistors onto each chip. This phenomenon is called Moore's Law, after the Intel Corp. executive who first noticed it. Yet in order for Moore's Law to continue into the 2020s, transistors would have to shrink to the size of atoms. Employing quantum theory, tech companies could continue to make computers faster by using atoms to make calculations. By harnessing quantum computers, scientists and researchers could gain new insights into the smallest features of the universe. Potential applications are immense, from dramatic new encryption systems, quicker searches of vast databases and new ways to design microchips to the discovery of new drugs, methods to detect cancer and optimizing geological exploration.[18]

Lazaridis was betting big money that the quantum computer was real, that it wasn't just another Snuffleupagus.

After founding Perimeter Institute in 2000 with a $100 million personal donation, one that later grew to $170 million, Lazaridis found further evidence of quantum computers by talking to physicists hired there. That led him to launch the Institute for Quantum Computing at UW in 2002 with personal donations that eventually mushroomed to $101 million. To ensure that startups in the quantum field would have venture capital to finance their ideas, he kicked in another $100 million with RIM co-founder Doug Fregin to launch Quantum Valley Investments in 2013. Finally, to ensure these quantum startups received the advice they needed to grow into large enterprises, he put up $20 million to start the Lazaridis Institute for Management of Technology Enterprises at Wilfrid Laurier University in 2015, a donation that spurred the university to name its business school after him.

In all, Lazaridis has contributed nearly $400 million of his own money to pursue this quantum dream. The feds and Ontario have contributed as much or more to the same dream. When all is said and done, close to $1.5 billion in public and private money has been poured into Waterloo to chase this quantum goal. Lazaridis calls it the most successful public-private partnership in Canadian history. It's an astonishing sum, largely made possible by one person.

And yet the world is still waiting for the first commercially viable quantum computers, not expected anytime soon.

Lazaridis preached patience.

Other technological breakthroughs took ages to come to fruition, he told Lang. The transistor was invented in 1947, yet it wasn't until the 1960s and 70s that we had the first commercially viable computers. The Institute for Quantum Computing has built a quantum computer, and he's seen one in operation in the US, Lazaridis said.

"We have built quantum computers. We know they work. We've factored prime numbers on them."

* * *

Since leaving RIM in 2012, Lazaridis and Balsillie have gone in different directions, but the paths they have chosen largely reflect the roles they played within the company. Lazaridis is following his passion for new technology, this time quantum computing instead of wireless pagers and smartphones. Balsillie, meanwhile, has reinvented himself as a government lobbyist and policy wonk whose goal is to pave the way for Canadian tech companies to scale into large enterprises and compete on the world stage. Hardware and software development were never his thing at RIM. An accountant and dealmaker by trade, his job was to create the best environment possible to enable the company to grow and sell BlackBerrys across the globe. In a sense, he is now doing the same thing for the tech industry. In 2015, he created the Council of Canadian Innovators, a business group with the aim of assisting Canadian tech firms to leap across the chasm into true global enterprises and to ensure that Canadian technology leaders and public policy-makers are working together to make that happen. Nearly 100 CEOs from Canadian tech firms are members of the council, including a solid contingent from Waterloo. Balsillie chairs the council and John Ruffalo, former CEO of OMERS Ventures, the venture capital arm of one of Canada's largest public pension funds, serves as vice-chair.

In speeches, interviews and presentations before government committees, Balsillie has not been afraid to take on the Canadian technology establishment. The years have not dulled his pugnacity. Canada has had an innovation problem that goes back thirty years and one of the reasons is that too much policy and government legislation is being made by people who have never walked the talk, who have never built a tech company into a significant enterprise, he believes. "Retired bankers, retired civil servants, retired journalists, current and retired university administrators, along with the incubator administrators who run our incubator-accelerator industrial complex, have together proliferated opinions that are outdated, misguided and often just made up," Balsillie told the CanTech Investment Conference in Toronto early in 2019. "In the process they have systemically pushed aside the input from our most successful high-growth entrepreneurs." Calling his approach a "dissident brand of advocacy," he urged Canadian entrepreneurs to "take back the podium."

Another theme he is pushing is the need to boost protection of intellectual property — the technology, inventions and innovation created by Canadian companies. You cannot commercialize technology and derive rent from it unless you own it, he suggested, and yet Canadian companies file far fewer patents than firms in other countries, according to figures from the Patent Co-operation Treaty. Microsoft, to cite one example, owns more than a thousand machine-learning patents, while Canadian firms own just forty-eight in total, Balsillie said. The wealth of the most valuable companies in the world, firms such as Apple, Amazon and Alphabet (Google's parent company), overwhelmingly resides in their data and IP, not in bricks, mortar and machines, Balsillie went on. Over the past few years he has spoken up about the need for stronger protection of Canadian intellectual property in trade deals such as the Trans-Pacific Partnership and the North American Free Trade Agreement. "Countries that generate and control IP and data assets are the winners in today's economy," Balsillie told the CanTech Conference.[19]

Balsillie's council also believes government investment should be directed towards winners, corporations with the best chance of achieving global success. It's similar to the Canadian Olympic Committee's "own the podium" strategy where the majority of resources go to the athletes with the best chance of winning a medal. The highest returns to national economies accrue from companies with annual revenues of $100 million to $1 billion, yet government policies are mostly geared towards helping startups, the council's executive-director Benjamin Bergen wrote in a 2019 article in the National Post. For example, Ottawa's Industrial Research Assistance Program provides matching grants of up to $10 million for companies that invest in research and development, but applicants must have fewer than 500 employees to qualify, he noted.

Among his other business activities, Balsillie was appointed in 2013 to chair Sustainable Development Technology Canada, a federal agency charged with helping small- and medium-sized enterprises bring green technologies to market. Chairing CIGI occupies some of his time, along with another think tank he founded in 2008 with American businessman George Soros and William Janeway called the Institute for New Economic Thinking. Based in New York, it is dedicated to learning from past mistakes such as the financial collapse of 2008. In the early days following his departure from BlackBerry, Balsillie also spent time counselling Waterloo startups on how to scale their businesses. Magnet Forensics, which specializes in forensic software for law enforcement and is headed by former BlackBerry executive Adam Belsher, is among the startups Balsillie worked with most closely. He has also made news outside the business world. After hearing about failed attempts to find two ships lost in the historic Franklin expedition to the Arctic in 1845, Balsillie and a friend personally financed the retrofitting of a fishing trawler to assist with the search. When one of the ships was found in 2014, the former RIM boss felt like he had won the Stanley Cup.[20]

Though Balsillie feels Canada has an innovation problem, the next generation of Waterloo tech companies is working hard to prove him wrong.

Chapter 14

SWINGING FOR THE FENCES

Matt Rendall couldn't believe it, but there it was spelled out in black and white. The University of Waterloo had rejected his application for admission to the mechatronics engineering program. It was the spring of 2003 and the Toronto native was about to graduate from high school. He had applied to twenty universities across the country. The only one to send back a rejection slip was UW. It was an unusual year, Rendall told himself. The province had eliminated Grade 13, and a double cohort of students was graduating in the same year. It meant twice as many students were seeking admission to universities across the province. Still, his marks should have been good enough to qualify for Waterloo. Rendall could have just enrolled at one of the universities where he had been accepted. Some reputable names were on the list, including his hometown University of Toronto. But something intrigued him about Waterloo. Whatever it was, he wanted a piece of it. Mechatronics engineering in particular caught his eye. In the program, students learned how to design computer-controlled robots, automation systems, tiny devices called micro-electromechanical systems and even prosthetic limbs. It sounded like a dream program for anyone with aspirations of being an engineer. "I made it my mission to get in." Rendall started making phone calls. He visited Waterloo and met with faculty. They told him he met all the requirements except for one — he had failed to submit a "qualitative assessment" of his skills. Rendall told them he had been accepted at the University of Toronto. "I played the competitive card." Rendall is not a loud person. Dark-haired with a five o'clock shadow on his cheeks, he talks with quiet intensity. His perseverance and determination paid off. When classes started in the fall of 2003, he was among the new recruits.

One day in his second year, Rendall agreed to help a classmate with his entry in a robotics competition. They gutted a small, remote-controlled race car, installed a microcontroller, sensors and cameras, and wrote some software so the car could be guided around a race course. It won first place over seven other entries. More important than the trophy was something that stirred inside Rendall. "I caught the robotics bug," he said. He joined the UW robotics team. It built everything from miniature tanks that could navigate obstacle courses to heavy all-terrain vehicles. He found himself spending more and more time with three members in particular, each of whom was in mechatronics engineering. Their passion for robotics ran deep. The notion that machines could be manipulated using software was fascinating. "We thought, wouldn't it be cool if we could do this for a living?"[1]

The quartet went on to start a company called Clearpath Robotics after graduation in 2009. They couldn't have picked a worse time. The world was reeling from the subprime mortgage crisis and credit freeze. Companies were cutting back everywhere. Software firms had a shot at making it in this environment, but hardware was a tough sell, and Clearpath was in the hardware category. They couldn't have survived without the Accelerator Centre, a business incubator at the University of Waterloo, said Rendall. It gave them office space and put them in front of mentors and potential investors. Money was so tight Rendell would make a huge batch of spaghetti every Sunday night and eat it at work for the rest of the week. The pace was punishing, but Rendall had learned how to handle it. Mechatronics engineering was no different. "They drill the work ethic into you." A novice at running a company, he learned about marketing, accounting, raising capital and the like during a one-year master's program at UW after finishing mechatronics engineering. His thesis was launching a robotics business.

Clearpath's first market was the education sector. Despite offering a robotics program, UW and other universities had trouble finding robots to use as prototypes in classrooms. Clearpath started making them, charging $5,000 to $10,000 for the finished product. UW was their first customer and others followed in Canada and the US. But the education market was small, so they moved into robots for marine and industrial purposes. Business was good. By 2014, the company had sold a thousand robots and was up to thirty-eight employees. Their machines were built to handle the "dull, dirty and dangerous jobs." But Clearpath had its eye on a more lucrative market — self-driving robots. Up until then, its robots were remote-controlled and could perform specific tasks. The new frontier was a marriage of machinery and artificial intelligence. To get there, the company had to raise capital. "We needed to pour some rocket fuel on the business," said Rendall, the company's CEO.[2] Clearpath started testing the waters, looking for venture-capital firms that had invested in hardware and software. Rendall talked to other tech startups in the area that had already raised funds. In the meantime, Clearpath moved into stealth mode, working on its first self-driving robot. The due diligence paid off. The company raised $41 million US in venture capital over two rounds in 2015–16. The money came from VC firms on both sides of the border. The timing was critical, said Rendall. A year earlier and the market wasn't ready. A year later and they would be playing catch-up.

The VC funding changed the trajectory of the company. Growth in the materials-handling field, where self-driving robots do the work, took off. So did Clearpath's workforce. By early 2019, it employed 180 people and boasted more than 500 customers in 40 countries for both its conventional and self-driving machines. Clients include such familiar names as Toyota, Caterpillar, General Electric and John Deere. Today, you can press a location on a factory map and a Clearpath robot, using sensors, cameras and software, will figure out how to get there and perform certain tasks, said Rendall. Large industrial buildings are like cities with aisles instead of streets. A Clearpath robot has much of the same technology as a self-driving car except for GPS. At its plant, in the south end of Kitchener where robots are assembled, a flat-topped machine about one foot high with wheels underneath moves items around a warehouse floor. A bigger and taller flat-topped robot, about the size of a small table, performs similar tasks. Four employees sit nearby, staring into computer screens. Rendall points to a self-driving forklift parked to one side. "We've been working on it for two years." Clearpath has come a long way from four founders in a shoebox-office in Waterloo ten years ago, but Rendall and his team aren't ready to relax. "We would love to be one of Canada's big employers."[3]

The fact that Clearpath was able to raise $41 million US to finance its expansion is not unusual these days in the Waterloo tech sector. The 1990s decade was the era of initial public offerings, of companies going public and raising money on the stock markets. But reporting to shareholders every three months sucked up company resources and energy, not to mention the flack executives took if financial targets weren't met and share prices fell. It was like "pulling your pants down every three months," said Klugman. The trend wasn't just restricted to Waterloo. IPOs were down everywhere in the tech sector. Raising money through venture-capital firms and angel investors was up. For a while, funding rounds of $10 million to $40 million seemed to be happening every few months in Waterloo. Though the money came with strings attached, including seats on the board and an eventual exit for investors, local tech firms were only too happy to step up to the trough. Vidyard, a video-marketing startup, raised more than $50 million US over a five-year period ending in 2016. Investors poured $45 million CA into Miovision, whose technology monitors traffic on city streets. Desire2Learn was founded by UW grad John Baker in 1999. Operating in the online education space, it raised $165 million CA over two rounds, helping it to grow to more than 700 employees. A group of UW students led by Ted Livingston launched Kik in 2009 when they noticed there was no messaging app that would work across mobile platforms such as BlackBerry, Apple and Android. Attracting millions of young users, it has raised $120 million CA in financing and has more than 200 employees. There were too many funding events to mention.

Among the most interesting was Thalmic Labs, a Waterloo startup launched in 2012 to make wearable technology. Thalmic had bold ambitions right out of the gate. Co-founder and Toronto native Stephen Lake, another graduate of UW's mechatronics engineering program, said his goal was to build a company as large as RIM at its peak.[4] Thalmic's first product was an armband that enabled users to operate computers and videogames with waves and gestures. In 2014, it moved into stealth mode on its next big project — computerized eyeglasses that could receive messages, alerts and other wireless data. It was a risky venture. Even Google and Intel had failed at this formidable challenge. In 2016 Thalmic raised a whopping $120 million US from American investors, including Intel and Amazon, and opened a manufacturing plant in Waterloo.[5] Two years later, it took the wraps off its Focals smart glasses and rebranded its corporate name to North. The glasses were feats of software and hardware engineering. A tiny projector in one of the arms beams a signal to a piece of holographic film on the lens. The signal bounces off the film and into the retina. Customers could be fitted for the spectacles, costing $999 US, at showrooms in Toronto and Brooklyn. At the same time, it abandoned the armband after it failed to gain widespread adoption.[6] Sales of Focals have been modest so far and North was forced to lay off 150 employees, one-third of its workforce, early in 2019 and cut the price of its smart glasses to $599 US.[7]

* * *

One of the early investors in North was another Waterloo entrepreneur who had launched his own firm focusing on video marketing and analytics. The smart-glasses venture was the kind of gutsy, swing-for-the-fences move that the local tech sector needs more of, said Michael Litt, co-founder of Vidyard. Dennis Kavelman, an early Vidyard investor and former chief financial officer at RIM, wore a pair of Focals to a Vidyard board meeting in San Francisco and other directors were blown away, Litt noted. Litt is an appropriate name for this high-tech renaissance man, who has lit up the region since bursting on the tech scene in 2011. Entrepreneurship is not his only talent. He's a venture capitalist, urban-renewal advocate, writer and community activist with the kind of rugged good looks that could easily find a home in a men's fashion magazine. Video started to intrigue him as a child when his uncle recorded family gatherings on a rented camcorder. His father made videos while working as an electrician at Kitchener-Wilmot Hydro. Video soon found a place in Litt's school projects and ski outings. At UW, in the systems-design engineering program, he included a film component in all of his projects. "It's easier to communicate complex ideas using video," Litt said. Systems-design engineering was the ideal program for Litt. It gave students a basic grounding in engineering but allowed them to explore topics outside the norm. Another student in the program, Devon Galloway, shared Litt's love of video. Between classes, they began making short videos for local businesses to post on their websites and advertise on YouTube. They then figured out a way to monitor how often customers watched the videos and for how long. The idea for the business came to Litt during his co-op work terms. He noticed that video was not a strong component of corporate marketing programs at the time. Another idea also occurred to Litt during those terms. He wanted to be his own boss. In 2010, Litt and Galloway launched Vidyard.

The next step was attending a tech incubator to learn the ropes of starting a company and perhaps attract some investors. But Litt didn't want to go to just any incubator. Y Combinator in Silicon Valley has a reputation for launching world-class startups, including Dropbox and Reddit. Its co-founder Paul Graham was considered a startup guru. Only 2 per cent of applicants gained admission. Even better, Y Combinator put founders in front of potential investors, as many as 300 on its nerve-wracking "demo day" held at the end of the term. Silicon Valley is like a ladder with no rungs at the bottom, explained Litt. "Y Combinator helps you to get to the bottom rung." Going to California was not a stretch for Litt. He had already done a co-op work term at Cypress Semiconductor in the Valley. Other UW students had done co-op terms at Cypress as well, including Kurtis McBride, founder and CEO of Miovision. "Every student at UW in engineering co-op has a California dream," said Litt. As part of their application to Y Combinator, Litt and Galloway included a video about Vidyard. Before leaving for California, the pair were able to monitor how the video was watched at the incubator. Judges were surprised when Litt and Galloway provided the data at the interview. "They had never seen anything like that before," said Litt.[8] The partners were among the first from Waterloo to gain admittance to Y Combinator. For Galloway, the California dream was not all sunshine and surfboards. He spent long hours writing software code, and Vidyard's product wasn't finished until the day before demo day. In the end, they were able to raise about $1.6 million US in seed financing, most of it coming from California investors.

Litt is not a conventional CEO. To recruit software talent from UW, he held pub nights every semester at a Waterloo bar. When the company ran out of space at Communitech's Velocity incubator in downtown Kitchener, it bought an old house nearby and moved employees there, calling it Vidyard House. A few years later it moved into a renovated building in downtown Kitchener that once housed the venerable Goudies department store, a popular destination for shoppers in the 1950s and '60s. Where visitors once sipped tea in the famous Grill Room, developers now pound keyboards. Vidyard's office is decorated in historical chic. Visitors wait for appointments on a swinging wooden bench suspended from the ceiling on chains while gazing at a colourful psychedelic mural by Kitchener artist Stephanie Scott. Employees regularly serve meals at a local hostel, put in extensive volunteer hours and enter a float in the annual Oktoberfest Parade.

Litt is not afraid to speak out when he feels something needs attention. Waterloo Region is great at producing engineering talent, but woefully inadequate at imparting sales and business-development skills, he told a local tech conference in 2016. Vidyard's chief operating officer commutes from Portland, ME, and its vice-president of sales flies in from Seattle, Litt said.[9] Unhappy with the region's art scene, restaurants, health care, transit to and from Toronto and high-school rankings, he wrote an op-ed piece in the *Globe and Mail* in 2018 airing his grievances, earning criticism in the local media. A lot of people think "I'm an arrogant blow bag," he admitted, but he makes no apologies for his opinions. "These lifestyle factors hamper our ability to attract the best and the brightest people, as well as to cultivate and retain talent in our own backyard," he said in the *Globe* piece.[10]

While this rhetoric might seem like a distraction for Captain Video, he has kept his eye on the business. Vidyard kept upgrading its video platform with features such as social-media integration and search-engine optimization. By 2014, its customers included Honeywell, IBM, Square and Deltek. Two years later when Vidyard raised $35 million in venture capital, more than 500 businesses were using its video analytics software, including LinkedIn, Citibank and Lenovo. Customers make their own videos and host them on the Vidyard platform for tracking and management, or they can use Vidyard software to shoot the videos. Despite all the successes and a workforce of more than 200 people, Vidyard is not profitable yet. The company is still in the "land-grab" stage. "Is Salesforce profitable?" Litt remarks, referring to the American software giant when asked about Vidyard's balance sheet. If the demand is there and the company can execute, "we will build a global corporation that could employ thousands," said Litt.[11]

When Litt and Galloway launched Vidyard, they went to Silicon Valley to attract investors. The partners didn't want other local founders to face the same problem. In 2013, they started their own venture-capital firm with a third entrepreneur, Mike McCauley, who had sold his local parcel-delivery startup to Google. Armed with a pool of $1 million, they started writing cheques of $25,000 to $50,000 for early-stage firms. With the help of other local investors and a federal venture-capital program, the fund has moved into its third round of investments with a pool of $30 million to invest. Called Garage Capital, it has invested in more than sixty startups in the Toronto-Waterloo tech corridor. Silicon Valley was largely started when Fairchild Semiconductor declined in the 1960s. Employees took their money and launched new companies or invested in new startups, said Litt.[12] He is not the only Waterloo tech founder with a desire to help other local entrepreneurs.

* * *

Kurtis McBride faced a problem most other tech CEOs would love to have. His company, Miovision, had outgrown its office in an industrial area of south Kitchener. Founded in 2005, the firm uses cameras mounted at intersections to monitor and analyze city traffic. A Toronto native, McBride had spent summers in high school manually counting cars for his father, who worked as a traffic-engineering consultant. He enrolled in the systems-design engineering program at Waterloo, then did a master's degree in computer vision. Halfway through that year, he launched Miovision with two fellow engineering students. Getting his first customer was like scaling a mountain. He called the Traffic Group, a Baltimore consulting firm, three times a day for weeks. None of his calls were returned. One day he came into work at 6:30 a.m. and left a voicemail message with the company to show how early he started his day. The company called back that day and hired him. The contract was worth $8,200, "an order I would be embarrassed to take today," McBride said. "Sometimes the smallest amount raised is the hardest." The sweat and toil eventually paid off. By 2016, Miovision had 120 employees and customers in fifty countries. Its technology was used in numerous cities across North America. Detroit is a major customer. Two hundred sets of traffic lights there are equipped with Miovision technology to gather data and move traffic more efficiently.[13] With more growth on the way, McBride knew he had to find a larger facility.

Employees were eager to move closer to downtown Kitchener to be near the growing tech cluster anchored by the Communitech Hub. McBride approached local developer Frank Voisin, who showed him an old department store recently renovated by his company in the heart of downtown, the same building eventually occupied by Vidyard. It was too small, so Voisin began searching for a larger building nearby. A few blocks away sat a massive remnant from the city's rubber-making past. Erected by Dominion Tire in 1956 to store tires made at its factory next door, the sprawling warehouse at 137 Glasgow Street had later been used to store boots and shoes when it was taken over by Kaufman Footwear. By the time McBride and Voisin looked at it, the building had sat empty for four years. The problem was size. At 475,000 square feet it was large enough to accommodate three Walmarts and too big for just one tenant. While strolling through the facility, McBride had an epiphany. Much sophisticated software goes into Miovision cameras but at its heart, the company is a hardware business. Parts are manufactured elsewhere but tested and assembled at Miovision headquarters. The company has half-a-dozen thermal chambers to test circuit boards and other parts at different temperatures. For this reason, hardware firms need more space than software firms. If more tenants like Miovision could be found, the building might work as a hardware innovation hub, McBride thought. To test the waters, he and Voisin set up a meeting at the Tannery where Communitech is based. They were hoping to get fifty people. "Well, 260 showed up and the feedback was unbelievable," said Voisin.[14]

Miovision and Voisin teamed up to purchase the building, then enlisted the help of the real estate firm responsible for spearheading the retail revival of Toronto's historic Union Station. After $34 million in renovations, the transformation of the old warehouse was jaw-dropping. Named Catalyst 137 after its postal address, the complex features a clean, open-concept look with wide hallways and a mixture of units for large and small tenants. A spacious foyer near the front can host public events, and a restaurant and coffee shop ensure that tenants don't have to leave the premises to eat. Miovision occupies 130,000 square feet, about one-quarter of the building. By early 2019, Catalyst 137 was 80 percent leased with a mix of small to large tenants. McBride was moved to catalyze Catalyst 137 by the region's barn-raiser spirit. The area was heavily populated by Old Order Mennonites from Pennsylvania in the early 1800s and then Russia in the 1920s. Black, horse-drawn buggies are a common sight on the roads north of Waterloo. When a barn is destroyed by fire, Mennonites from the area arrive in droves to build a new one, often in one or two days. McBride stressed that he is not a property developer. "This is the only one I've done and the only one I will do."[15]

* * *

With young guns like Miovision, Clearpath Robotics and Vidyard hitting their stride, the Waterloo tech sector appears to have a bright future. But can it achieve the same lofty heights it once did with RIM on top of the world? For many years, RIM's success created a "halo effect" over the local tech community and the entire country, said Gary Will, the Waterloo blogger and startup consultant. There was a perception that Waterloo had the magic touch, that something special was going on that would rub off on other companies. Startups and established firms were pulled along in RIM's slipstream. BlackBerry is still pulling in nearly a billion dollars a year in revenue and remains one of the largest tech companies in Waterloo Region. Yet the BlackBerry name doesn't have the cachet it used to have. The halo effect has faded. In the early years after the company declined, anxiety about finding another BlackBerry ran strong. In many ways it was a foolish fantasy, Will believes, like Liverpool trying to replace Beatles. That dream has largely faded. Will there ever be another RIM in Waterloo? Not likely, said Will. "It was a huge outlier. At one point it was the most valuable company in Canada. It was insane." As for the Waterloo tech sector itself, it's small, it's not Toronto, but "for its size it's as good as anywhere in Canada, and it's up there with the best in the world." And the economy of Waterloo Region is doing just fine with a smaller BlackBerry, in his view. "RIM was a product of Waterloo, not vice-versa." With the office sector bouncing back and a forest of condos and high-rises going up in downtown Kitchener and near UW, if anything the problem is gentrification, said Will. Some thought Waterloo might end up like Detroit. Instead it's more like San Francisco, he suggested. In 2010, Will moved 100 kilometres west to London, Ontario, to accept a job leading an innovation centre there. But it wasn't the same as Waterloo. To build an outstanding tech sector, "You need people with ambition and vision," people like former UW president Doug Wright and Communitech CEO Iain Klugman, he said, dropping a few names. "You don't need a lot, but you need a few people to be the catalyst."[16]

If RIM was the tech equivalent of the Beatles, going forward, Waterloo may have to settle for Gerry and the Pacemakers, multiplied a number of times. For the moment, the mantle has been passed to Open Text, Canada's largest software company. In recent years it has made a number of major acquisitions, pushing its workforce to 12,200 people at headquarters in Waterloo and offices around the world. Its annual revenues in fiscal 2018 were nearly $3 billion US and its business software is used in every sector of the economy from retail and automotive to government and energy. And yet the average person in Canada has no idea what Open Text does, said Will. As a business-to-business enterprise, its products don't touch retail consumers. When Open Text exited the public search-engine market in the late 1990s, sending its stock into a nosedive, it opted for the less glamorous but more stable private intranet market. The company has been called the anti-BlackBerry for keeping its focus on the business market rather than trying to expand into more visible sectors. Open Text's goal is to be the Switzerland of software, able to work with all operators in the market, John Shackleton, the company's CEO at the time, told the *National Post* in 2007.[17] "Slow and steady wins the race," said the headline in the *Globe and Mail* in 2017 as Open Text grew into Canada's third-most valuable publicly traded firm.[18] Even so, the company has been on an acquisition tear in recent years. At one point, it bought seven companies in fourteen months. The largest was the enterprise content management division of Dell Computers for $1.6 billion US in 2016. The buying spree prompted the *Globe* to call Open Text "Canada's tech acquisition machine."[19]

It doesn't bother Tom Jenkins that Open Text has a low profile compared to RIM at its zenith or that its current CEO Mark Barrenechea is not featured on the cover of *Maclean's* magazine or starring in TV commercials for American Express as Lazaridis once did. Nor does Jenkins think Open Text should try to be something that it isn't. That's like saying Citibank should be like Coke or that "you should only do things that make Hollywood movies," said the former CEO, now chair of Open Text's board of directors. To him, the premise doesn't make sense. "You don't set out to make things that everyone will recognize." The company has been criticized in the media for only growing through acquisition instead of developing new products in-house, but Jenkins rejects that argument as well. "That implies there is some definitive road map for how to achieve something." Should GM have not acquired Oldsmobile? There have been long periods when Open Text made no acquisitions, he noted. "You have to choose all the means at your disposal. You're competing in a volatile situation." Open Text is not better known in Canada because 95 per cent of its customers are located outside the country, he suggested. "We're not Bell. We're not Rogers." "We're quite happy with what we're doing."[20]

* * *

Iain Klugman is not worried that another tech superstar like RIM has yet to emerge from the Waterloo area. He would rather have ten $1-billion companies than one $10-billion company. A strong tech cluster is a diverse cluster with the risk spread out over a number of enterprises, said the CEO of Communitech. If one tree grows too tall, the other trees and bushes can't get any sunlight. "I like shrubbery." A few years ago he toured tech sectors in mid-sized cities such as Nashville, Austin, Raleigh, Boulder and Ann Arbor to see how they compared to Waterloo. In particular, he was struck by the similarities between Austin and Waterloo. The Texas capital was hit hard by the decline of Dell. The computer-maker went through a massive downsizing as the PC market reached maturity in the mid-2000s and cheaper Asian manufacturers moved in. Though Dell's downturn wasn't as bad as RIM's, the impact on the surrounding community was significant. Since then, however, the startup community in Austin has re-ignited and the tech sector is "on fire," Klugman said. Sometimes "cities can be too small to sustain a major player." Waterloo has survived the decline of RIM and come back even stronger, Klugman contends. It may not have the marquee value of BlackBerry but it has a solid mix of 1,400 companies "from startups to scale-ups to large global players," according to figures on Communitech's website. Klugman ranks Waterloo Region as the third-most important tech sector in Canada behind Toronto and Montreal.

A 2018 study of the Canadian tech sector by the commercial real estate giant CBRE ranked Waterloo Region as the fifth-most attractive tech market in the country behind Toronto, Ottawa, Montreal and Vancouver, in that order. The rankings were based on thirteen metrics including talent, educational institutions, density of tech firms and cost of living. With 20,400 tech workers, or 8.2 per cent of the total labour force, Waterloo had the third-highest concentration of tech workers in the country and the highest concentration among mid-market cities. Waterloo Region also employed 22,300 people in the tech sector in non-tech occupations such as sales, administrative support and finance. Toronto led the country with 241,400 tech workers or 8.9 per cent of the total work force, followed by Montreal with 127,300 or 6.8 per cent of the work force. Waterloo Region was fourth in venture-capital activity with forty-seven deals completed, worth $291 million, over an eighteen-month period ending in June 2018. Toronto led with 235 deals worth $1.7 billion. Though a healthy tech cluster contains a mix of large, medium and small companies, the biggest and most successful clusters tend to have a few large anchor companies that boost the area's brand value and lure smaller companies and workers to the area, the study noted. Apple and Amazon are two prime examples. "The success of these companies attracted many others, which went a long way in establishing Silicon Valley and Seattle as tech superclusters in the U.S." Canada needs to do a better job of developing tech superclusters to compete on the global stage, the CBRE study concluded.[21]

The federal government agreed and in 2018 launched a $950-million program over five years to develop five innovation superclusters across the country. Southern Ontario was selected as the advanced manufacturing supercluster, Quebec as the artificial intelligence and robotics supercluster and B.C. as the digital technology supercluster. More details of the program, which required matching funds from private companies, have not been announced and the initiative could change or even be shelved in the wake of the 2019 federal election. Nonetheless, Waterloo Region was already taking steps to forge closer links with Toronto to create a supercluster in the corridor between the two cities. Waterloo had pushed for better rail service over the 100 kilometres between the two cities, including all-day, two-way train service so tech workers and executives could move back and forth more quickly instead of driving on the congested Highway 401. Nick Waddell, editor of *Cantech Letter*, an online magazine focusing on Canadian technology, considers Waterloo "the crown jewel of a Greater Toronto tech corridor that could rival the world's greatest tech hubs." A high-speed rail network between the two communities and extending all the way to Windsor and Quebec City, with a branch to Ottawa, should have been built years ago, he said.[22]

The rest of the world is starting to look at the Toronto-Waterloo tech corridor as one entity. It was ranked among the top twenty technology sectors in the world — the only one in Canada to make the list — in a 2018 report by Startup Genome, a respected California research organization. Klugman has been pushing for more collaboration between the two communities for a number of years. "Not only can we not do it on our own, but we have a huge opportunity if we can connect what is happening here with what is going on in Toronto," he said in a 2018 interview with the *Record*.[23] A 2016 report financed by tech leaders in the corridor recommended the creation of an agency to promote collaboration and marketing of the Toronto-Waterloo brand. The corridor, which includes Hamilton, Mississauga and Guelph, is home to a wealth of startup incubators including Communitech, the Accelerator Centre and Velocity in Waterloo Region, the MaRS Discovery District and Next Canada in Toronto, the DMZ at Ryerson University and the Creative Destruction Lab at the University of Toronto, said the report, called *Tech North*. Prepared by the management consulting firm McKinsey and Co., the study also urged a focus on two sectors where the corridor leads: artificial intelligence and quantum computing.[24]

* * *

One outsider who believes in the value of the Waterloo tech sector is Tobias Lutke, the co-founder and chief executive officer of Shopify, one of Canada's new tech superstars. Shopify was founded in Ottawa in 2004 by Lutke and two friends after they tried to open an online store to sell snowboarding equipment. Unhappy with the software tools available to make this happen, Lutke built his own, then turned it into a platform other small businesses could use. Since then the company has exploded into a global firm with 800,000 customers in 175 countries and annual revenues of more than $1 billion US. A native of Germany, Lutke moved to Canada in his early twenties after meeting his girlfriend, now his wife, on a ski trip to B.C. His original ambition was to move to the US but he found that he liked Canada. "Canada is America for Europeans," he told himself. He first heard of UW on a trip to Silicon Valley to find investors for Shopify. It must be great to be from Canada because that's where Waterloo is, he was told. "I didn't know what Waterloo was. I had to look it up," said Lutke, a slim, soft-spoken man who is rarely seen in public without a flat cap on his head.[25]

He began hiring co-op students from UW and was so impressed, he decided to open an office in the city. "This is an amazing place. There is so much depth here in math, hackers, entrepreneurs," Lutke said during a visit in 2015 when the company announced it was opening a major office in Waterloo with 300 workers.[26] It would be located in the Seagram Museum, the former home of the Centre for International Governance Innovation, which had moved into a new building next door. Two years later Shopify doubled its workforce in Waterloo while leasing office space in a new building going up nearby.

The irony is that a few years ago Waterloo was better known in Silicon Valley than it was in the rest of Canada, said Anthony Reinhart, director of editorial strategy at Communitech. In his view that is no longer the case. He names off a bunch of Waterloo's most successful startups: Vidyard, North, Clearpath Robotics, Aeryon Labs, Kik, Miovision, Magnet Forensics, Auvik Networks, Axonify, Ssimwave, eSentire. There are more but the names escape him for the moment. None of them existed ten to fifteen years ago, said Reinhart. Most startups fail, many don't grow to a significant size, but these companies have not only survived, they have blossomed into enterprises that employ hundreds of people with customers all over the world. Reinhart and others in the tech industry have a name for these firms: scale-ups. They are moving into the big leagues and inspiring new founders in the process. To him, they are tangible evidence that the Waterloo tech sector has rebounded from the fall of BlackBerry. "We are on the map across Canada and globally," said Reinhart, a former journalist at the Record and the Globe and Mail who was hired in 2011 by Klugman to write about companies in the local tech sector. In his mind, despite RIM's troubles, the company's stunning success will always serve as a beacon for every young entrepreneur with a dream, for every kid who's ever tinkered with code or tried to build a home computer or robot. "There's that sense of possibility. If they can do it, we can do it too."[27]

CONCLUSION

The implosion of BlackBerry-RIM has taken its place among the biggest disasters in Canadian corporate history, alongside the Avro Arrow, Eaton's, Nortel Networks and others. BlackBerry's place in this dubious hall of fame is assured, and the reasons behind its decline will be studied in university business schools for years to come. Though the company remains a viable enterprise, it is a far smaller and different operation than when it ruled the smartphone market, and its precipitous fall has given new meaning to Waterloo as a name synonymous with failure. And yet, if you drive into Waterloo Region today, you would never guess that the community of 600,000, Canada's tenth-largest urban area, had ever played host to such a spectacular business debacle. Downtown Kitchener is in the midst of a building boom. High-rise condos and construction cranes dot the landscape, fuelled in large part by the tech startups and scale-ups that have set up shop in the renovated factories and buildings in the urban core. High-tech names such as Google, Igloo software, Desire2Learn, Miovision and Kik festoon many of the structures. The growth in central Kitchener has been so dramatic it has engendered a backlash among residents of older single-family homes, fearing a loss of their neighbourhood ambience.

Farther north in Waterloo, the area around the city's two universities resembles mini-Manhattan. King Street North, the city's main strip, is lined with high-rise apartments and student residences. Enrolment seems stronger than ever as Canadian and international students clamour for spots in UW's booming engineering or computer science programs, to name a few, or WLU's business program, housed in a sparkling new building named after Mike Lazaridis. Not far away in UW's David Johnston Research and Technology Park, named after the university's erstwhile president and Canada's former governor-general, corporate names such as Open Text, SAP, Agfa Healthcare, Ssimwave and Text Now glow on the landscape. Bordering the east side of the park is RIM's former corporate campus, now filled with smaller tech businesses, many employing or started by people who once worked on the groundbreaking BlackBerry. On the UW campus itself, students can stroll across an elevated walkway to reach the university's newest engineering building, dubbed Engineering 7. Seven! Let that number sink in for a minute. If there was ever any doubt of the university's dominant position in post-secondary engineering curriculum, this building has erased it. A short distance away, on the west side of the campus, the honeycomb facade of the Mike and Ophelia Lazaridis Quantum-Nano Centre looms on the horizon, its hexagonal panels designed to symbolize the cutting-edge research going on inside.

Not to be forgotten are the two think tanks in uptown Waterloo. Perimeter Institute for Theoretical Physics and the Centre for International Governance Innovation, sitting cheek by jowl just west of uptown, create an almost seamless link between the technology hubs in downtown Kitchener and the university district of north Waterloo. Even Cambridge, to the south of Highway 401, has been scrambling for a piece of the high-tech action. The Gaslight district, featuring condo towers, shops and a high-tech incubator launched in partnership with Conestoga College, is taking shape in a sprawling old warehouse on the southwest side of the Grand River in the old Galt section of the city. The project draws heavily from the playbook used to create the Communitech Hub in the old Tannery building in downtown Kitchener.

The empirical evidence is rock-solid. Six years after it became clear there would be no comeback for BlackBerry in the smartphone space, that the halo effect of RIM's glorious achievements had faded, the Waterloo tech sector has survived and even thrived. According to the 2018 study by CBRE, the region's tech labour force didn't shrink after BlackBerry shed all those jobs. It actually grew by 22 per cent in the 2012–17 period and now stands at more than 20,000, the third-highest concentration of tech workers in the country, behind only Ottawa and Toronto. Those 20,000 tech workers are spread throughout more than 1,000 tech enterprises — from small to big, young to old. Waterloo is firmly on the map as arguably the most vibrant and robust tech market among medium-sized urban areas in Canada.

The rebound didn't happen by accident. The foundation laid by educational pioneers such as Gerald Hagey, Wes Graham and Doug Wright and industry leaders such as the Pollock family, Tom Jenkins, Savvas Chamberlain, Val O'Donovan, Iain Klugman and others established a tradition of innovation, excellence and a steady stream of young entrepreneurs to carry the torch. Not to be left out in the comeback story is the role played by BlackBerry itself. Numerous enterprises have been created or strengthened by former RIM employees, and the company itself, despite taking a major cut in size, appears to have stopped the bleeding and remains one of the largest employers in Waterloo Region. Major contributions have come from RIM's two former CEOs. Jim Balsillie counselled numerous local startups in the early years following his departure and more recently has adopted an advocacy role, lobbying governments to create the proper regulatory environment so Canadian companies can compete on the world stage. His feisty and frank approach will ensure that politicians stay on their toes.

Perhaps no one has done more to bolster the local tech economy than Mike Lazaridis. He would never admit so publicly or perhaps even to himself, but the amount of energy, money, drive and leadership he has poured into transforming Waterloo into "Quantum Valley" has all the earmarks of a redemption story.

Debate still rages about the lone inventor theory. Killer apps are usually the result of years of innovation by earlier inventors and the collective efforts of product teams inside every successful startup. The lone inventor theory is a myth perpetrated by Hollywood and pulp-fiction writers, goes the argument. Yet someone must have the vision and the drive to lead a team forward to create something truly remarkable. And Lazaridis was that person. As the technological genius behind the game-changing BlackBerry and the boss who ultimately called the shots on product development at RIM, much of the blame for the company's shocking decline must fall in his lap. RIM got complacent, took its eye off the ball, failed to anticipate where the market was going and responded too slowly when it was clear that the iPhone was the future. Yet larger forces were at work as well. Over the years when asked about threats to the BlackBerry, Lazaridis offered a stock answer: There will always be competition. It was too facile a response. There are degrees of competition and the smartphone market in the first decade of the twenty-first century was the most competitive market in the world, bar none. To expect Lazaridis to prevail in this cut-throat environment was perhaps expecting too much. He was not Superman. He accomplished great things with the BlackBerry, and he is trying for a repeat performance with quantum computing. Already there is fierce competition for the quantum gold. There will be more than one winner, and Lazaridis has laid the foundation to ensure Waterloo gets a piece of the prize.

All the same, not everything in the garden is rosy. In the past decade, some pillars of the Waterloo tech community have been sold to foreign investors. MKS, which made software management tools and was one of the area's oldest tech companies, was sold to a Boston-based software company in 2011. PTC, the new owner, pledged to keep all of the company's nearly 200 employees in Waterloo and even grow the business. Five years later, it quietly closed up shop in Waterloo. Watcom, Dalsa, Com Dev and Sandvine also fell into foreign hands and while their operations in Waterloo Region remain substantial, the loss of local ownership is troubling. Many of the newest generation of tech startups, firms such as Vidyard, North, Clearpath Robotics, Auvik Networks, Axonify, which makes employee-training software, and cybersecurity firm eSentire have raised venture capital south of the border. The cash was needed so they could expand into global markets. One can only hope they endure and grow into substantial enterprises without selling out to foreign interests. The future of the Waterloo tech community depends on them.

At the same time, no tech superstar on the order of RIM has emerged. Iain Klugman, CEO of Communitech, may prefer a forest of small to medium-sized trees to one Douglas Fir towering over the rest, but as the 2018 CBRE study notes it never hurts to have one or two outstanding companies to attract entrepreneurs and investment to the area. And yet opportunities like the one RIM capitalized on to build a global business only seem to come along once in a generation. Apart from taxi-hailing and tourist-accommodation apps, Silicon Valley has not produced anything significant since the Google search engine and the iPhone. The San Francisco area also benefits from attracting large tech companies built elsewhere such as Facebook, whereas Waterloo does not. Most of its successful companies were and are home-grown. Perhaps in the end, Waterloo and the Canadian tech industry are better off with firms like Open Text — steady, reliable, not-too-flashy, the anti-BlackBerry, but something built to last.

Acknowledgements

There are many people to thank for the completion of this book, starting with all those who agreed to be interviewed. Some sat down for several sessions over a number of years or pointed me to useful books or reference materials. I wasn't able to quote everyone but every insight proved useful, especially since Mike Lazaridis and Jim Balsillie declined or did not respond to several requests for interviews.

On the editing side, I am deeply grateful to friend Mike Langevin, who read my initial manuscript as it took shape and whose advice, sense of humour and encouragement cover the occasional pint of ale were crucial and therapeutic. Kristen Hahn also edited my first manuscript and offered key advice. Steve Izma acted as my quasi-agent and brought it to the attention of Lorimer. I owe much to Jim Lorimer who opened my eyes to the merits of writing about the Waterloo tech sector as well as Research In Motion.

This book would not have been possible without the mentorship of friend, author and former Record staffer Ian Darling who encouraged it from the start and bolstered my confidence along the way. His wife and fellow author Jane Ann McLachlan also deserves thanks for her advice to this first-time author.

Finally, many thanks go to my close friends and family, especially my three sisters and 92-year-old mom. Profound gratitude to my children Ryan and Brennan, their spouses and my four grandchildren who acted as my unofficial cheering section. My wife and my rock, Janet, deserves a special mention. This book took longer than expected and went through many twists and turns. She was there every step of the way.

Selected Bibliography

Alkema, Harold and McLaughlin, Kenneth. *A Chronology of Computing at the University of Waterloo*. School of Computer Science, University of Waterloo, 2007. (Available only in electronic format.)

Benay, Alex. *Canadian Failures: Stories of Building Toward Success*. Dundurn Press, Toronto, 2017.

Burton, Howard. *First Principles: The Crazy Business of Doing Serious Science*. Key Porter Books, Toronto, 2009.

Communitech. *We Built This, Volume 1: How Waterloo Region Ingenuity Is Shaping The Future*. Communitech, Kitchener, ON, 2016.

English, John and McLaughlin, Kenneth. *Kitchener: An Illustrated History*. Wilfrid Laurier University Press, Waterloo, ON, 1983.

Isaacson, Walter. *The Innovators: How a Group of Hackers, Geniuses and Geeks Created the Digital Revolution*. Simon & Schuster, New York, 2014.

Isaacson, Walter. *Steve Jobs*. Simon & Schuster, New York, 2011.

Merchant, Brian. *The One Device: The Secret History of the iPhone*. Little, Brown and Company, New York, 2017.

McLaughlin, Kenneth. *Waterloo: The Unconventional Founding of an Unconventional University*. University of Waterloo, Waterloo, ON, 1997.

McLaughlin, Kenneth. *Out of the Shadow of Orthodoxy: Waterloo @ 50*. Friesens Corp, Waterloo, ON. 2007.

McLaughlin, Kenneth and Jaeger, Sharon. *Waterloo: An Illustrated History, 1857-2007.* City of Waterloo, ON, 2007.

McNish, Jacquie and Silcoff, Sean. *Losing The Signal: The Spectacular Rise and Fall of BlackBerry.* HarperCollins Publishers Ltd., Toronto, 2015.

McQueen, Rod. *BlackBerry: The Inside Story of Research In Motion.* Key Porter Books, Toronto, 2010.

Open Text Corp. *Ten Years of Innovation: 1991-2001 and Beyond.* Open Text Corp., Waterloo, ON, 2001.

Ponzo, Peter J. *Computer Science at Waterloo: A History to Celebrate 25 Years, 1967-1992.* University of Waterloo, Waterloo, ON, 1992.

Scott, James. *Of Mud and Dreams: University of Waterloo 1957-1967.* The Ryerson Press, Toronto. 1967.

Sweeny, Alastair. *BlackBerry Planet: The Story of Research In Motion and the Little Device That Took the World By Storm.* John Wiley & Sons Canada Ltd., Mississauga, ON, 2009.

Tubbs, Graham and Gillett, Terry. *Harvesting The BlackBerry: An Insider's Perspective.* Wheatmark, Tucson, Arizona, 2011.

Vogelstein, Fred. *Dogfight: How Apple and Google Went to War and Started a Revolution.* Sarah Crichton Books; Farrar, Straus and Giroux, New York, 2013.

Notes

CHAPTER 1

1. Jacquie McNish and Sean Silcoff, *Losing the Signal: The Spectacular Rise and Fall of BlackBerry* (Toronto: HarperCollins, 2015) pp. 13–16.
2. The first commercial cellphones did not appear until 1983.
3. Mohamed Elmasry, interview, Jan. 28, 2015.
4. *Globe and Mail*, Aug. 20, 2010.
5. Savio Wong, email and interview, Feb. 26; Mar. 28, 2015.
6. Rod McQueen, *BlackBerry: The Inside Story of Research In Motion* (Toronto: Key Porter Books, 2010) p. 31.
7. McQueen, *BlackBerry*, p. 32.
8. Ibid., p. 34.
9. Ibid., p. 36.
10. Ibid., p. 41.

CHAPTER 2

1. Kenneth McLaughlin, *Waterloo: The Unconventional Founding of an Unconventional University* (Waterloo: University of Waterloo, 1997) p. 25.
2. McLaughlin, *Waterloo*, pp. 27–28.
3. It would later become George Brown College.
4. Wikipedia.
5. McLaughlin, *Waterloo*, pp. 52–54.
6. Ibid., p. 92.
7. Ibid., p. 97.
8. Porter would later go on to serve as UW's first chancellor. The university's main library is named after him.
9. McLaughlin, *Waterloo*, p. 64.
10. Ibid., pp. 170, 184.
11. Ibid., pp. 179, 203.
12. Ibid., p. 66.
13. Ibid., pp. 162–63.
14. Peter J. Ponzo, *Computer Science at Waterloo: A History to Celebrate 25 Years* (Waterloo Computer Science Department, 1992) p. 17.
15. McNish and Silcoff, *Losing the Signal*, p. 21.
16. Ponzo, *Computer Science at Waterloo*, p. 45.
17. Ibid., pp. 57–58.
18. Ibid., p. 57.
19. Ian McPhee interview, Feb. 3, 2015.
20. International Business Machines of Armonk, New York, which was the first company to build and sell computers on a broad scale.
21. Kenneth McLaughlin, *Out of the Shadow of Orthodoxy: Waterloo @ 50* (Friesens Corp., 2007) p. 193.
22. Wayne Bradley interview, Feb. 19, 2015.
23. McLaughlin, *Orthodoxy*, p. 187; Ponzo, *Computer Science at Waterloo*, p. 30.
24. McLaughlin, *Orthodoxy*, p. 184.
25. Ponzo, *Computer Science at Waterloo*, p. 89.
26. Email was invented in 1971 by a computer programmer from upstate New York named Ray Tomlinson. While working for BBN Technologies in Massachusetts, he created the

first email program to run on the ARPANET, the precursor to the Internet. Wikipedia.

27. Randall Howard, email, Dec. 1, 2018.
28. McPhee, Feb. 3, 2015.
29. Harold Alkema and Kenneth McLaughlin, *Chronology of Computing at the University of Waterloo*, 2007.
30. McPhee, Feb. 3, 2015
31. Waterloo Region *Record*, Oct. 6, 2005.
32. David Yach interview, Nov. 1, 2016.
33. *Record*, Nov. 17, 1994.
34. Sybase was acquired by German software giant SAP in 2010. SAP has kept the office in Waterloo. Its 2019 workforce stood at about 250 people.
35. McLaughlin, *Orthodoxy*, pp. 193–195.
36. *Record*, May 6, 2017.
37. Dan Younger, Biography of Professor Tutte, University of Waterloo website, Aug. 2002.
38. Dan Younger, interview, Oct. 17, 2018.
39. Yach, Nov. 1, 2016.
40. *Record*, Sep. 20, 2007.
41. Exchange Magazine, Kitchener, Jul.-Aug. 2009.
42. McLaughlin, *Waterloo*, p. 221.

CHAPTER 3

1. Dale Brubacher-Cressman interviews, April 24 and 29, 2014.
2. McQueen, *BlackBerry*, pp. 42-43.
3. Ibid., p. 43.
4. Ibid., p. 49.
5. Ibid., p. 53.
6. Michael Barnstijn, interview, Apr. 22, 2015.
7. Brubacher-Cressman, Apr. 14, 2014.
8. *Record*, Aug. 27, 2011. Years later, the RIM boss paid tribute to Davison by erecting a plaque not far from Lazaridis's office at RIM headquarters in 2011. The plaque officially renamed the space the Davison Memorial Room after the visionary government consultant, who had died the previous year at eighty-two.
9. McQueen, *BlackBerry*, pp. 56–57.
10. McNish and Silcoff, *Losing the Signal*, p. 10.
11. Ibid, p. 12.
12. McQueen, *BlackBerry*, p. 68.
13. McNish and Silcoff, *Losing the Signal*, p. 37.
14. Brubacher-Cressman, Apr. 24, 2014.
15. Alastair Sweeny, *BlackBerry Planet: The Story of Research In Motion and the Little Device That Took the World by Storm*, (Toronto: Wiley, 2009)3 p. 41.
16. McQueen, p. 61.
17. Ibid., p. 59.
18. Sweeny, *BlackBerry Planet*, p. 41; McQueen, *BlackBerry*, pp. 62–64.
19. *Record*, Apr. 23, 1993.
20. *Record*, Apr. 2, 1992.
21. Apple was widely ridiculed for the Newton, which ultimately led to the departure of CEO John Sculley and the return of co-founder Steve Jobs. Jobs never liked the idea of a stylus to write messages. "God gave us 10 styluses," he said, referring to his fingers. Walter Isaacson, *Steve Jobs* (New York: Simon & Schuster, 2011) p. 309.
22. McQueen, *BlackBerry*, p. 86.

CHAPTER 4

1. Pete Edmonson email, Mar. 26, 2015; interview, Nov. 5, 2018.
2. Graham Tubbs interview, Apr. 10, 2015.
3. Graham Tubbs and Terry Gillett, *Harvesting the BlackBerry* (Tucson: Wheatmark Inc., 2011) p. 26.
4. Terry Gillett interview, Apr. 10, 2015.
5. McQueen, *BlackBerry*, p. 98.
6. Brubacher-Cressman interview, Apr. 24, 2014.
7. McQueen, *BlackBerry*, p. 100.
8. Sweeny, pp. 61–62.
9. Tubbs and Gillett, *Harvesting*, pp. 50–52; Tubbs, interview.
10. Gillett interview, Apr. 10, 2015.
11. Tubbs and Gillett, *Harvesting*, p. 42; Gillett interview, Apr. 10, 2015.
12. Tubbs and Gillett, *Harvesting*, p. 44.
13. Brubacher-Cressman interview, Apr. 24, 2014.
14. McQueen, *BlackBerry*, p. 104.
15. Ibid., pp. 116–19.
16. Ibid., pp. 119–21; McNish and Silcoff, *Losing the Signal*, pp. 51–52.
17. McNish and Silcoff, *Losing the Signal*, pp. 57–58.
18. Ibid., p. 59.
19. *Record*, July 15, 1998.

CHAPTER 5

1. *Record*, Sep. 24, 2013.
2. *Record*, Feb. 8, 2000.
3. McNish and Silcoff, *Losing the Signal*, p. 78; *Record*, Jan. 14, 2000.
4. Rob Caldwell interview, Sep. 25, 2018.
5. Carl Zehr interview, Jan. 2, 2019.
6. Ken Seiling interview, Nov. 9, 2018.
7. *Record*, Aug. 6, 1997.
8. *Record*, Sep. 19, 1997.
9. *Globe and Mail*, Sep. 24, 1996.
10. *Globe and Mail*, Oct. 22, 1997.
11. *Record*, Dec. 13, 2000.
12. *Record*, Dec. 18, 2000.
13. Pete Gould interviews, Dec. 4 and21, 2018.
14. Wikipedia.
15. *Record*, Sep. 26, 2003.
16. Lindsay Gibson interview, Oct. 9, 2018.
17. Paul Lucier interview, Oct. 26, 2018; email, Jan. 11, 2019.
18. Pete Edmonson interview, Nov. 12, 2018; email, Mar. 24, 2015.

CHAPTER 6

1. McQueen, *BlackBerry*, p. 43.
2. *Record*, Apr. 25, 2000.
3. Manfred Conrad interview, Nov. 5, 2018.
4. *Record*, Apr. 19, 2001.
5. John Whitney interview, Sep. 13, 2018.
6. John Lind interview, Jan. 23, 2019.
7. *Record*, Apr. 19, 2000.
8. *Record*, Oct. 26, 2000.
9. Bruce Nicholson interview, Oct. 15, 2018.
10. Jim McIntyre interview, Oct. 23, 2018.
11. *Record*, Oct. 23, 2000.
12. Paul Lucier interview, Oct. 26, 2018.
13. Pete Gould interview, Dec. 21, 2018.
14. Rob Elder interview, Oct. 24, 2018.
15. Dale Brubacher-Cressman interview, Oct. 30, 2018.
16. David Yach interview, Sep. 28, 2018
17. Lindsay Gibson interview, Oct. 9, 2018.
18. Pete Edmonson interview, Nov. 12, 2018.
19. Internal review of RIM stock option grants, published in RIM news release, Mar. 5, 2007.
20. *Globe and Mail*, Mar. 6, 2007.
21. RIM news release, Mar. 5, 2007.
22. *Globe and Mail*, Feb. 6, 2009.
23. *Record*, Oct. 10, 2009, April 13, 2010.

CHAPTER 7

1. Gary Will interview, Sep. 26, 2018.
2. Will interview, Sep. 26, 2018.
3. Alex Benay, *Canadian Failures*, (Toronto: Dundurn Press, 2017) p. 7.
4. *Ten Years of Innovation: 1991–2001 and Beyond* (Waterloo: Open Text Corp., 2001) p. 31.
5. Benay, *Canadian Failures*, p. 8.
6. Sam Ogilvie interview, Nov. 21, 2018.
7. *Ten Years of Innovation*, pp. 3–4.
8. Ibid., pp. 8–9; Bray left Open Text in 1996. He went on to work at Sun Microsystems, Google and Amazon Web Services.
9. Ibid., p. 22.
10. Ibid., pp. 33–35.
11. Tom Jenkins interview, Oct. 15, 2018.
12. Ibid., Oct. 15, 2018.
13. *Ten Years of Innovation*, p. 47.
14. Benay, *Canadian Failures*, p. 11.
15. HP Computer Museum.
16. *National Post*, Feb. 29, 2000.
17. *Record*, May 5, 1999.
18. *Record*, Aug. 31, 2000.
19. *Canadian Business*, May 28, 2001.
20. Ibid.

21. The name itself has an interesting back story. Pixstream's original name was Pixel Scientific, named after the smallest unit used to measure a digital image. But the company was threatened with a lawsuit by a trademark troll company and changed it to Pixstream. Anxious to avoid a similar problem with Sandvine, employees were asked to submit names that were trademark-free, catchy and not obscene. Sand and vine emerged separately during the process and were then combined. Thereafter, employees were allowed to make up whatever story they wanted on the origin of the name. A popular one was drinking wine on a sandy beach.

22. *Record*, Sep. 8, 2017.

23. Brad Siim interview, Nov. 29, 2018.

24. Dave Caputo interview, Nov. 6, 2018; Speech to Sheridan College Convocation, fall of 2018.

25. Will interview, Sep. 26, 2018.

26. Bob Crow interview, Nov. 27, 2018.

27. *Exchange Magazine*, Jun. 2007.

28. *Record*, Oct. 4, 2007.

29. *Exchange Magazine*, Jun. 2007.

30. *Record*, Jun. 3, 2017.

31. *Record*, Nov. 7, 2009.

32. *Record*, Oct. 8, 2010.

33. Iain Klugman interview, Oct. 31, 2018.

34. Communitech website.

35. Randall Howard interview, Oct. 4, 2018.

CHAPTER 8

1. Wikipedia.

2. Michael Duschenes interview, Dec. 10, 2018.

3. Howard Burton, *First Principles: The Crazy Business of Doing Serious Science* (Toronto: Key Porter Books, 2009) p. 43.

4. Ibid., p. 92.

5. Ibid., p. 82.

6. Ibid., pp. 128–131.

7. *Record*, Oct. 24, 2000.

8. Burton, *First Principles*, p. 253.

9. Ibid., pp. 72–74.

10. McQueen, *BlackBerry*, p. 213.

11. Canada News Wire, May 22, 2007.

12. Burton, *First Principles*, pp. 268–69.

13. *Toronto Star*, Apr. 12, 2009.

14. *Record*, May 23, 2007.

15. Burton, *First Principles*, pp. 271–72.

16. Duschenes interview, Dec. 10, 2018.

17. Rohinton Medhora, "Wonk Friendly: What to Expect from Our Think Tanks," *Literary Review of Canada*, Jan. 2017.

18. Geoff Burt, "Is It Time to Rethink Think Tanks?" Waterloo Region *Record*, Sep. 16, 2011.

19. Medhora, "Wonk Friendly."

20. Rohinton Medhora interview, Nov. 13, 2018

21. Ibid.

22. Ibid.

23. McQueen, *BlackBerry*, pp. 214–15.
24. *Record*, Jun. 11, 2002.
25. *Record*, Sep. 25, 2002.
26. *Record*, Aug. 24, 2007.
27. *Record*, Oct. 30, 2010.
28. *Toronto Star*, Feb. 23, 2012
29. *Record*, May 1, 2012.

CHAPTER 9

1.   Rob Elder interviews, Jul. 8, 2014 and Oct. 24, 2018.
2.   *Toronto Star*, Sep. 9, 2008.
3.   Edmonson interview, Nov. 12, 2018.
4.   Brubacher-Cressman interview, Oct. 30, 2018.
5.   Paul Lucier interview, Oct. 26, 2018.
6.   Yach interview, Sept. 28, 2018
7.   *Record*, May 10, 2005.
8.   *Record*, Jul. 19, 2005.
9.   Aeryon was acquired in January 2019 by Flir Systems, an Oregon-based maker of infrared cameras, for $200 million US. Aeryon and its 220 employees will remain in Waterloo. *Record*, Jan. 29, 2019.
10. Dietmar Wennemer interview, Nov. 23, 2018.
11. Mark Pecen interview, Dec. 4, 2018.

CHAPTER 10

1.   *Record*, May 13, 1993.
2.   *Record*, May 22, 1999.
3.   *Record*, Oct. 24, 2002.
4.   Terry Pender interviews, Nov. 27, 2013 and Jan. 19, 2017; *Record*, Mar. 5, 2002.
5.   *Globe and Mail*, Dec. 16, 2002.
6.   *Record*, Dec. 17, 2002.
7.   *Ryerson Review of Journalism*, Apr. 16, 2014.
8.   Kevin Crowley interview, Oct. 14, 2016.
9.   Walcoff memorial service program, Oct. 7, 2012.
10. *Record*, Nov. 18, 2005. The fan sites would later multiply to include such names as CrackBerry, N4BB, BBOS.com and Berry Review. Other mobile devices such as the iPhone and the Android phones would spawn a multitude of fan sites as well.
11. Alastair Sweeny, *BlackBerry Planet* (Toronto: John Wiley and Sons, 2009) p. 94.
12. *Record*, Nov. 22, 2001.
13. *Record*, May 31, 2003; *Globe and Mail*, May 28, 2003.
14. McNish and Silcoff, *Losing the Signal*, pp. 125–26.
15. *Record*, Feb. 24, 2006.
16. *Record*, Feb. 25, 2006.
17. *Record*, Mar. 4, 2006.
18. *Record*, Jun. 17, 2006; Jul. 8, 2006.
19. *Record*, Sep. 16, 2006.
20. Crowley interview, Oct. 14, 2016.
21. *Record*, Sep. 19, 2006.
22. *Record*, Sep. 29, 2006.
23. *Record*, Oct. 6, 2006.

24. *Record*, Dec. 8, 2006.
25. *Globe and Mail*, Dec. 1, 2006.
26. *Record*, Dec. 19, 2006.
27. Brian Merchant, *The One Device: The Secret History of the iPhone* (New York: Little, Brown and Company, 2017).
28. Fred Vogelstein, *Dogfight: How Apple and Google Went to War and Started a Revolution* (New York: Farrar, Straus and Giroux, 2013) pp. 23–34.
29. McNish and Silcoff, *Losing the Signal*, p. 133.
30. Vogelstein, *Dogfight*, p. 32.
31. *Record*, Jan. 11, 2007.
32. Ron DeRuyter interview, May 25, 2016.
33. McNish and Silcoff, *Losing the Signal*, p. 100.
34. DeRuyter interview, May 25, 2016.
35. *Ryerson Review of Journalism*, Apr. 6, 2014; DeRuyter interview, Oct. 13, 2016.
36. Walcoff memorial service program, Oct. 7, 2012.
37. Ibid.

CHAPTER 11

1.   *Record*, Sep. 8, 2004.
2.   *Record*, Oct. 2, 2004.
3.   *Record*, Oct. 21, 2004.
4.   Lindsay Gibson email, Jan. 9, 2019.
5.   Vogelstein, *Dogfight*, pp. 52–53, 62–63.
6.   Rubin's image would later take a hit when he resigned in 2014 amid allegations of sexual misconduct at Google.
7.   Vogelstein, *Dogfight*, pp. 46, 53.
8.   Ibid., p. 49.
9.   RIM earnings call transcript, Jun. 18, 2007.
10. *Record*, Oct. 16, 2007; *Globe and Mail*, Oct. 16, 2007.
11. Gizmodo, Oct. 8, 2008.
12. Engadget, Oct. 8, 2008.
13. Gibson email, Jan. 9, 2019.
14. *New York Times*, Nov. 27, 2008.
15. RIM earnings transcript, Dec. 18, 2008.
16. Gibson interview, Oct. 9, 2018.
17. *New York Times*, Oct. 29, 2009.
18. McNish and Silcoff, *Losing the Signal*, pp. 165–168.
19. *Record*, Jun. 29, 1991.
20. *Record*, Apr. 17, 2004.
21. Savvas Chamberlain interview, Jul. 14, 2015.
22. *Record*, Feb. 11, 2011.
23. *Record*, Oct. 6, 2005.
24. Yach interviews, Nov. 21, 2013 and Nov. 1, 2016.
25. Vogelstein, *Dogfight*, pp. 101–2, p. 123.
26. McNish and Silcoff, p. 175.
27. Paul Lucier interview, *Losing the Signal*, Oct. 26, 2018

CHAPTER 12

1. Crowley interview, Oct. 14, 2016.
2. McNish and Silcoff, *Losing the Signal*, pp. 35–37.
3. McQueen, *BlackBerry*, pp. 120–22.
4. McNish and Silcoff, *Losing the Signal*, p. 18.
5. *Record*, Jan. 23, 2009.
6. *Globe and Mail*, Jan. 23, 2009.
7. *Record* Technology Spotlight, Oct. 31, 2011.
8. Randall Howard blog, August 3, 2010.
9. Randall Howard interview, Jan. 13, 2014; Howard email, Apr. 28, 2016.
10. After eleven years as UW president, Johnston was appointed governor-general of Canada in 2010 and remained in that post until 2017.
11. McNish and Silcoff, *Losing the Signal*, p. 178.
12. An operating system is a software program that serves as the foundation for all other programs. It determines where data is stored, how memory and processing resources are allocated and how application software interacts with hardware; Walter Isaacson, *The Innovators: How a Group of Hackers Geniuses and Geeks Created the Digital Revolution* (New York: Simon and Schuster, 2014) p. 357.
13. *Record*, Sep. 29, 2012. Dodge retired from BlackBerry in 2015 and was hired by Apple in 2016 to work with its automotive team; *Ottawa Sun*, Jul. 29, 2016.
14. *Globe and Mail*, Apr. 16, 2011.
15. Boy Genius Report, Jun. 30, 2011.
16. *Record*, Jul. 26, 2011.
17. Communitech, Jun. 28, 2011.
18. Mike Abramsky, RBC research note, Sep. 20, 2011.
19. *Globe and Mail*, Dec. 3, 2011.
20. RIM quarterly earnings report, Dec. 15, 2011.
21. *Globe and Mail*, Jan. 23, 2012.
22. *New York Times*, Jan. 22, 2012.
23. *Record*, Jan. 24, 2012.
24. *Record*, Jan. 28, 2012.
25. *Record*, Jan. 24, 2012; Jun. 29, 2012.
26. *Record* Technology Spotlight, 2012.
27. *Record*, Sep. 20, 2007.
28. Steve Woods and Verna Friesen, "Google Waterloo and 28 Years of UW Community," YouTube, Nov. 1, 2017.
29. *Record*, Oct. 10, 2008.
30. Woods and Friesen, Nov. 1, 2017.
31. *Record*, Feb. 25, 2012.
32. *Record*, Jan. 16, 2016.
33. Woods and Friesen, Nov. 1, 2017.

CHAPTER 13

1. *New York Times,* Jan. 30, 2013.
2. *Record*, Nov. 5, 2013.
3. John Chen, Greater Kitchener-Waterloo Chamber of Commerce, May 5, 2015.
4. *Record*, Dec. 21, 2013.
5. *Record*, Sep. 29, 2016.
6. BlackBerry annual report, 2018.

7. *Record*, Jan. 5, 2016.
8. *Globe and Mail*, Nov. 17, 2018.
9. *Globe and Mail*, Feb. 16, 2019.
10. Iain Klugman interview, Oct. 31, 2018.
11. Anthony Reinhart interview, Oct. 11, 2018.
12. David Yach interview, Sep. 28, 2018.
13. *Record*, May 6, 2014.
14. *Globe and Mail*, Jun. 12, 2018.
15. *Record*, Apr. 17, 2014.
16. *Record*, Oct. 11, 2014.
17. *Record*, Oct. 6, 2017.
18. "RIM's Mike Lazaridis Takes a Quantum Leap of Faith in Waterloo," *Fast Company*, Jan. 15, 2013; *Record*, Jun. 23, 2007; "Dream Machine," *The New Yorker*, May 2, 2011; Quantum exhibit, The Museum, Kitchener, Dec. 2016; Lazaridis speech to Waterloo Innovation Summit, Sep. 14, 2017.
19. Jim Balsillie speech to CanTech Investment Conference, Toronto, Feb. 1. 2019.
20. *Record*, Oct. 7, 2014; The second ship was found in 2016 using the same vessel financed by Balsillie; *Record* news services, Sep. 13, 2016.

CHAPTER 14
1. *Record*, May 15, 2010.
2. *Record*, March 8, 2015.
3. Matt Rendall interview, Dec. 17, 2018.
4. *Record*, May 4, 2013.
5. *Record*, Sep. 19, 2016; Oct. 15, 2016.
6. *Record*, Oct. 24, 2018.
7. *Globe and Mail*, Feb. 23, 2019.
8. *Record*, Oct. 29, 2012.
9. *Record*, Oct. 1, 2016.
10. *Globe and Mail*, Mar. 28, 2018.
11. Michael Litt interview, Dec. 18, 2018.
12. *Record*, Apr. 25, 2014.
13. *Record*, Jun. 5, 2018.
14. *Record*, Nov. 26, 2016.
15. Kurtis McBride interview, Nov. 30, 2018.
16. Gary Will interview, Sep. 26, 2018.
17. *National Post*, Dec. 1, 2007.
18. *Globe and Mail*, Feb. 13, 2017.
19. *Globe and Mail*, Jun. 27, 2017.
20. Tom Jenkins interview, Oct. 15, 2018.
21. CBRE Research, 2018 Scoring Canadian Tech Talent Report, Nov. 22, 2018.
22. Nick Waddell, email interview, Mar. 26, 2019.
23. *Record*, Apr. 7, 2018.
24. McKinsey and Co., Tech North: Building Canada's First Technology Supercluster, Dec. 4, 2016.
25. "Waterloo Talent a Magnet for Shopify Founder, Tobias Lutke," UW website, Oct. 5, 2015.
26. *Record*, Oct. 2, 2015.
27. Anthony Reinhart interview, Oct. 11, 2018.

Index